EMPOWERING MINISTRY

Ways to Grow in Effectiveness

DONALD P. SMITH

WESTMINSTER JOHN KNOX PRESS
Louisville, Kentucky

© 1996 Donald P. Smith

All rights reserved. No part of this book may be reproduced or transmitted in any form or by any means, electronic or mechanical, including photocopying, recording, or by any information storage or retrieval system, without permission in writing from the publisher. For information, address Westminster John Knox Press, 100 Witherspoon Street, Louisville, Kentucky 40202-1396.

Scripture quotations, except where otherwise noted, are from the New Revised Standard Version of the Bible, copyright © 1989 by the Division of Christian Education of the National Council of the Churches of Christ in the U.S.A. and are used by permission. Scripture quotations noted TM are from Eugene H. Peterson, *The Message: The New Testament in Contemporary English,* copyright © 1993 by NavPress, Colorado Springs, and are used by permission.

Excerpts from *How to Raise Your Self-Esteem* by Nathaniel Branden are copyright © 1987 by Nathaniel Branden and used by permission of Bantam Books, a division of Bantam Doubleday Dell Publishing Group, Inc.

Selected excerpts from pages 2, 158, 252, 260 from *A Generation of Seekers,* by Wade Clark Roof, are reprinted by permission of HarperCollins Publishers, Inc. Copyright © 1993 by Wade Clark Roof.

Excerpts from *The Seven Habits of Highly Effective People* by Stephen R. Covey are reprinted with the permission of Simon & Schuster Inc. Copyright © 1989 by Stephen R. Covey.

A complete list of acknowledgments appears on page 219.

Book design by Publishers WorkGroup
Cover design by Vickie Arrowood

First edition

Published by Westminster John Knox Press
Louisville, Kentucky

This book is printed on acid-free paper that meets the American National Standards Institute Z39.48 standard.

PRINTED IN THE UNITED STATES OF AMERICA

96 97 98 99 00 01 02 03 04 05 — 10 9 8 7 6 5 4 3 2 1

Library of Congress Cataloging-in-Publication Data

Smith, Donald P., 1922–
    Empowering ministry : ways to grow in effectiveness / Donald P. Smith. — 1st ed.
      p.   cm.
    Includes bibliographical references and index.
    ISBN 0-664-25479-9 (alk. paper)
    1. Pastoral theology.   2. Christian leadership.   I. Title.
BV4011.S574   1996
253—dc20   95-46245

EMPOWERING

Empowering is the ability to establish a climate in which people feel free to grow, learn, explore, and use their gifts in Christian ministry without fear of retribution.

A focus on empowering transforms ministry. It shines a spotlight on ways God is moving in the needy lives of ordinary people. Pastors concentrate less on achieving competence in their many roles and more on mediating power to others. Their preaching, teaching, pastoral care, and living seek to connect the daily lives of their parishoners to God's rich resources. They strive to free them from bondage to meaninglessness, to give them hope, and to challenge them to reach out to others in a suffering world.

We can grow in our effectiveness as pastors when we are empowered by the Spirit, love our realistic selves, and are purposefully learning how to empower others.

CONTENTS

PREFACE

What a daunting task! How audacious of me to think that I might add anything to the volumes already written on effective pastoral ministry.

When the editors of Westminster John Knox Press asked me to write on ways to grow as an effective pastor, I hesitated. Before long, however, I realized that I could not refuse. The assignment was attractive because the book was to be based on what I could learn from effective pastors themselves.

Ten years ago I spent several memorable days with about fifty effective pastors whose congregations were the subject of my book *Congregations Alive*. Their lives inspired me and led to some conclusions never put in print. I developed important hypotheses I was eager to test. Subsequently, I learned much from pastors whose churches informed my book *How to Attract and Keep Active Church Members*.

In writing these two books I concentrated on finding effective pastors from whom I could learn as much as possible. I avoided studying problem churches. Since then, I have discovered a parallel in sports. My tennis pro steadfastly refuses to tell me what I am doing wrong. Instead, he concentrates on showing me how to do it right. To focus on avoiding bad habits only reinforces them and deflects limited energies from improving my game.

Many contributors to a ministers' magazine I read spend most of their effort arguing over what's wrong with the church. To dwell on the negative only accelerates a downward spiral of defeat and despair. It offers too many excuses to avoid the tough tasks of discovering ways to release the tremendous potential for new life and power that often lies dormant in the church.

For more than twenty years I have felt that many authors concentrate on analyzing what is wrong with the church, as though such analysis will somehow produce solutions. They move from a picture of the negative to their perception of a plausible positive alternative. I have been convinced that here and there across the land there is an abundance of creativity in congregations and their pastors. It is just waiting to be shared with the whole church. So one of my passions has been to discover and disseminate that creativity. I have longed to see pastors and congregations share in the exciting possibilities that have already proven themselves. My now-familiar method of learning from creative congregations and pastors gave me confidence to try this new assignment.

Confirmation of my calling to this major project followed quickly. John Coffin, then director of the Stewardship and Communication Development Ministry Unit of the Presbyterian Church (U.S.A.), offered the partnership of the Office of Research Services. Without its expertise and its data processing capabilities, the task would have been impossible. Mary V. Atkinson secured the endorsement of the Church Vocations Ministry Unit.

Nearly three years ago, without a source of funding other than my author's advance, I began to work with the Office of Research. John Stewart, of Princeton Theological Seminary, brought the project to the attention of President Thomas W. Gillespie, who offered funding for data gathering. I am grateful for their faith in the possibilities of this research.

The task has been an arduous one involving the collection, analysis, interpretation, and reinterpretation of an enormous volume of data. Out of this came the completely unanticipated and exhilarating discovery that has shaped this book. Pastors who focus on empowering others are effective in nearly all areas of their ministry. That is what this book is all about. Interviews in person and on the phone have brought my conclusions to life in exciting ways. Pastors whose transformed lives are transforming the lives of others always inspire me.

I am deeply indebted to the competent staff of the Office of Research Services of the Presbyterian Church (U.S.A.), who managed data collection and analysis. Special thanks go to its director, Keith Wulff, for his valuable insights and direction of the process; to Barbara O'Hare, who helped in refining the questionnaires; and to Ida Smith-Williams, for her skilled and tireless programming. Her cheerful patience and perseverance in responding to my many requests for further examination of the data made that phase of the project a joy.

As conclusions were being formulated, I had the privilege of testing some of my interpretations and approaches in several lectures, seminars, and workshops at Princeton Theological Seminary, at presbytery-sponsored events, at the Early Ministry Institute of the Synod of the Northeast, and at the national Annual New Church Development Pastor/Spouse Retreat. For these opportunities I am grateful to John Stewart, Abigail Rian Evans, and Geddes W. Hanson of Princeton Seminary; to John B. Evans and his colleagues in South Carolina; to Virginia Robertson and L. John Gable in Iowa; to William Chapman of Palisades Presbytery; and to H. Stanley Wood of the national staff in Louisville.

Sharon Kroll, Anthony Lipnicki, Allen Nauss, Joan DeJean, and Ed Watts all provided useful material. William Chapman and Howard McCuen have been helpful as consultants. Several participants in Presbynet, the electronic network of our denomination, have shared their insights and directed me to resources of which I would otherwise not be aware.

A special word of thanks belongs to all the pastors who graciously responded to lengthy questionnaires and to those who shared in hours of interviews. The cooperation of their lay leaders helped give a balance to the responses of their pastors. It is my hope that readers will discover significant opportunities for growth through the insights and the exciting vigor that these busy folk shared with me.

In conclusion, I salute my loving wife and partner, Verna. She has shared her interviewing skills and has served as a valuable consultant. Beyond that, however, she has cheerfully endured the unusual amount of time I have spent away from mutual retirement pleasures. Her willing sacrifice and deep dedication have helped me endure the rigors of data analysis and long hours at the computer.

INTRODUCTION

This book is for you if you are an established pastor who wants to increase your effectiveness in ministry. It is for you if you are on the threshold of a pastorate and aim for faithfulness and excellence in ministry. It is for you as a seminary student preparing for ministry and exploring your pastoral potential. It should also be valuable to personnel committees and officers of congregations who are working as close partners with their pastors in a quest for maximum pastoral effectiveness. This book distills the best that several hundred highly effective "mentors" offer you out of many lifetimes of pastoral experience. Like any work of this kind, it is limited by the author's ability to hear what these pastors say. It depends upon his interpretation of voluminous data, collected and analyzed over several years.

The secret of excellence in pastoral ministry that unfolds on these pages comes from the discovery that "Empowering Pastors," those who concentrate their attention on empowering others, are more effective than other pastors in almost every aspect of ministry. This is demonstrated both in pastors' self-ratings and in ratings by lay leaders who work closely with them.

The model of "empowering ministry" described here is a composite picture of pastoral excellence. No single pastor in this study would be described this way, and no one could possibly measure up to this ideal of ministry. We are all human. Each of us has strengths on which we can capitalize and limitations with which we must deal. If you fail to fit this picture of pastoral perfection, do not be discouraged. Instead, accept this invitation to take a fresh look at yourself in the light of proven ministry possibilities. Mark those that challenge the unique you. Ask the Holy Spirit to help you discover the best you can be. Trust the gracious God who has called you. Set your sights on areas in which you plan to grow in faithfulness and excellence. Then move in directions that match your readiness.

The emphasis here is less on growing in one's understanding of alternative theories or specific techniques of leadership and management and more on growth as person and pastor. We are more concerned with being than with doing. What a pastor does is important. And Empowering Pastors—those who focus on empowering others—demonstrate a pattern of effective practice that I describe and advocate. But in the final analysis, who a pastor is makes a greater impact on the congregation than what a pastor does. Pastors are themselves their most important tools for ministry. Who they are makes possible what they do.

Others have summarized the findings of leadership theory and research. Many have carefully described what pastors can do to carry out their work more effectively. This study has found that a pastor's skills really are important. It deals with them. But it is more concerned with interpersonal and leadership perspectives. It concentrates attention on self-understanding and on the concepts of ministry, values, and priorities that effective pastors bring to their practice of ministry.

The serious reader is entitled to know something of the way in which this study was conducted and how its conclusions were reached. My goal was to gain a deeper understanding of what constitutes effective pastoral ministry and to learn from competent pastors ways they have been able to grow in their effectiveness. I sought to understand the more important conclusions reached by others, to test the validity of their findings, and to explore the potential of some of my own hypotheses. The skill of empowering others was but one of many dimensions of ministry that I had identified. Its primacy emerged during the course of the study and was not a preconceived focal point.

My first task was to prepare a one-page definition of an effective pastor, based upon relevant literature and my own previous research. Through Presbynet, an electronic network, I shared this with a number of pastors and judicatory executives. Their helpful comments led to a revision that became the basis for questions asked in this study. This "Preliminary Definition of An Effective Pastor" (Fig. 12.1) is included in chapter 12 because most of my hypotheses proved to be true.

The Office of Research Services helped select a multifaceted sample of "effective pastors" and compared it with a sample of average pastors, selected at random from across the denomination. We received 461 nine-page questionnaires from pastors who rated themselves on their effectiveness and told of their formative experiences. This was an amazing 74-percent response rate.

Three lay leaders, selected at random from each pastor's congregation, returned 833 shorter questionnaires in which they rated their pastor's effectiveness. This was a 60-percent response rate.

We studied the responses by extensive computer analysis. The results are shared in two forms. On responses with statistically significant differences at the 5 percent level or better I have often given percentage figures to show the extent of the differences. At a number of points I have included tabulations to help readers get a better overall view of the results.

In order to make the book reader-friendly, I have kept statistical references to a minimum. Therefore, many statistically significant comparisons between two groups are simply described by a general statement such as "Small-church pastors rate themselves higher than large-church pastors on . . ."

We used a five-point scale on most questions. On skill ratings, for example, the choices were 1 = No skill, 2 = Very little skill, 3 = Moderately skillful,

4 = Skillful, and 5 = Very skillful. Unless otherwise stated, comparisons are based on the combined total of the two highest ratings on each scale. For example, if we say that small-church pastors rated themselves as more skillful than large-church pastors, we are saying that a higher percentage of small-church pastors than large-church pastors rated themselves as "very skillful" or "skillful."

After studying the statistical results, I interviewed a number of selected Empowering Pastors in person and by telephone. My wife helped with some of these interviews. The extensive quotations from pastors throughout the book are from our interviews or from written comments in the questionnaires. They have sometimes been edited slightly for felicity of expression. I have sometimes combined and edited quotations from several pastors as though they were the response of one pastor. In every case, I have endeavored to protect confidentiality by eliminating names of individuals and congregations and references to specific situations or locations. Where a quotation gives no source, it is from one or more pastors who participated in our study. Except in quotations from books or other documents, names of pastors or churches are fictitious.

Because I have had ready access to Presbyterian sources of data, and to facilities for its analysis, this study draws upon responses from pastors and congregations of that denomination. As with previous research, which resulted in *Congregations Alive*[1] and *How to Attract and Keep Active Church Members*,[2] I concluded that gathering data from different denominations would require contacts and financial resources I do not have. However, in reference material, other than that which requires original data, I have sought to draw on a wide range of sources beyond the Presbyterian Church.

Fortunately, there are broad areas of similarity among mainline denominations. There are two major areas of difference. One is in polity. My interpretation of the data seeks to minimize that difference. The second is in the theologies of ordination and the sacraments. These are not central to this work. Theological differences on other matters covered here usually cross denominational lines. What has been learned clearly applies to most pastors and congregations. My previous books have proved to be widely useful to pastors and congregations of other denominations. I am confident that this book will be equally useful to all.

In quotations, when pastors use Presbyterian terminology, I have retained it. Otherwise I use generic terminology so that readers of every denomination will feel at home in our discussions. Thus "elder" is translated "lay leader," "session" becomes "board," and "judicatory" replaces "presbytery." Where Presbyterian terminology remains in the text, readers of other traditions may simply substitute comparable terminology from their denominations. What effective pastors are teaching us should then be useful to them.

PASTORAL EFFECTIVENESS

To grow in pastoral effectiveness one must know what pastoral effectiveness is. Several approaches to this question are possible.

Some might measure effectiveness by the degree to which a minister performs with distinction the activities expected of a pastor. This might include preaching, leading in worship, teaching, leading in Christian education, crisis pastoral calling, pastoral counseling, pastoral visitation, leadership, and administration. Senior pastors or heads of staff might be expected to focus major attention on certain of these functions, leaving others to members of their staffs. Associate pastors might be expected to be proficient in those functions directly related to their responsibilities, but not necessarily in others. Solo pastors would need to perform many of these functions themselves and to discover others they would share with leaders of their congregations.

One might measure perceptions regarding pastoral style by rating a pastor on such descriptions as "Makes creative use of diversity"; "Approaches change and conflict positively"; or "Is willing to take risks, even if failure might result." Ratings of leadership skills or styles of ministry are also possible measures of effectiveness. Examples of such skills and styles are found in the various exercises in chapter 12.

Some might measure effectiveness by results in the life of the congregation. Involvement of members in ministry to one another and in service to the community was the criteria we used in selecting churches described in *Congregations Alive*. Pastors of those churches have been included in this study. Other criteria that are somewhat more subjective might include the pastor's spiritual authenticity, the vitality of congregational life, or members' involvement in evangelism or social action. Some studies have been based on descriptions of desired pastoral behaviors most frequently selected by church members and pastors. Many have described effectiveness using some theoretical construct based upon a study of biblical passages.

One might measure perceptions of such results as "Inspires members to reach out beyond the congregation in service to others"; "Relates the gospel to issues people face in their personal lives and in society"; or "Helps people find meaning for living through worship, preaching, teaching, and so forth."

OBJECTIVE MEASURES

In an effort to find an objective assessment of effectiveness, measurable results are sometimes used. A low rate of membership loss over a five-year period was the criterion used in studies of congregations leading to *How to Attract and Keep Active Church Members*. Because I found significant leadership styles in pastors serving those churches, I included those "bonding pastors" in this study as well.

In the current study we selected two hundred congregations from across the entire Presbyterian Church that over a five-year period had the highest percentage increase in total membership. We chose another two hundred churches with the highest five-year percentage increase in reception of members by confession of faith. We then asked judicatory executives to judge which of their pastors had a significant influence on those results. These we included in this study. A similar effort to select pastors who had influenced increases in per-member giving was clouded by sampling difficulties.

NOMINATION

Because effectiveness involves a complex constellation of interacting factors, an alternative to "objective" measures presents itself. One can use ratings by persons who have an intimate knowledge of what is involved in pastoral ministry and who know the pastors in a given area. Their ratings can take into account the many interrelated dimensions of pastoral effectiveness. In this study we asked judicatory executives to nominate effective pastors either in their own or in some other presbytery. To encourage consistency in their nomination criteria, we sent each executive the one-page definition of an effective pastor that I had derived from previous studies of pastoral effectiveness. We also encouraged them to use their own criteria and asked them to tell us the criteria they had used.

FIT WITH THE CONGREGATION

A pastor who is effective in one congregation may not be effective in another congregation that requires different pastoral characteristics. For example, the demands upon pastors of very large or very small congregations can be quite different. Isolated rural churches, suburban churches, and inner-city congregations may need pastors with different gifts. I have attempted to deal with that reality as well.

PROBLEMS IN MEASURING
PASTORAL EFFECTIVENESS

There are problems with any method of measuring pastoral effectiveness. Objective measures do not necessarily reflect a pastor's effectiveness. Strong external demographic or sociological factors can influence measurable results such as gains or losses in membership. Internal dynamics of a congregation beyond the control of a pastor may have been involved. Effective lay leadership may have made the most important contribution. Pastors may have had little if any effect on the results.

Nominations of effective pastors and descriptions of competent pastoral behaviors can be quite subjective and depend greatly upon the perspectives and biases of those who rate them. Descriptors that seem to be objectively based in scripture are subject to considerable variation in interpretation.

In short, it is extremely difficult to decide exactly what constitutes effectiveness. No one approach alone seems adequate. To deal with this complexity we chose in this study to use a combination of the methods I have just described.

Finally, as a further attempt to determine which pastors are effective, we chose to examine our data from many perspectives. We used answers to the questionnaires themselves as alternative criteria of effectiveness. Whenever we discovered clues to possible criteria we pursued them.

EMPOWERING, A KEY FOR EFFECTIVENESS

Out of all our analysis it became clear that the one focus of ministry that relates most clearly to all other possible measures of effectiveness is a focus on empowering others. That discovery led to the title of this book and to its focus. We divided the pastors from all our samples into two groups. "Empowering Pastors," as I shall call them, rate themselves as skillful or very skillful in empowering others. "Other Pastors" is my name for the group who rated themselves as less than skillful or very skillful in empowering others. To our amazement Empowering Pastors rate themselves higher than Other Pastors in almost every measure of pastoral effectiveness. And this is not because these pastors have an inflated ego. Lay leaders rate Empowering Pastors higher than lay leaders rate Other Pastors in most of these dimensions. Empowering Pastors are more effective than Other Pastors in their preaching and other pastoral skills, in their leadership styles, and in the impact they make on the life of the congregation. The heroes of this book are pastors who have been empowered by God to help others find God's power. Throughout the book when we say that pastors empower others, it is with the clear understanding that they are but instruments of divine power and are not giving others power in their own strength.

How pastors empower others is described in the first four chapters. Chapter 1 tells why empowering is a key to pastoral effectiveness and describes its relationship to other dimensions of ministry. Chapter 2 shows how ministry empowers people when it answers their search for meaning with a gospel that speaks clearly to the issues they confront in their daily lives. Chapter 3 enumerates ways Empowering Pastors create a climate in which people feel free to grow, learn, explore, and use their gifts in Christian ministry without fear of retribution. Chapter 4 defines and illustrates the strong servant leadership style that empowers congregations.

Empowering Pastors are able to empower others because they themselves have been and are being empowered. Chapter 5 shows how personal and spiritual authenticity contributes to a pastor's empowerment. In it Empowering Pastors share their sources of maturity and self-esteem. Chapter 6 recounts the formation experiences of Empowering Pastors from childhood through seminary. It celebrates their commitment to intentional continuing education. It portrays ways that Empowering Pastors contribute to their own continued growth by their proactive search for excellence.

Chapters 7 through 9 analyze the constellation of skills that enable Empowering Pastors to empower others. They share ways they have developed those skills. Chapters 10 and 11 examine resources for living in the ministerial pressure cooker. Chapter 10 describes seven major sources of stress that pastors face and shares ways they cope with stress and recover from burnout. Chapter 11 then focuses attention on three major sources of sustaining power in pastors' lives: their assurance of God's call, the cultivation of their spiritual resources, and support they receive from others.

Finally, chapter 12 invites the reader to begin a growth pilgrimage and offers help for the journey. It turns from a description of Empowering Pastors to an application of their insights to a specific growth process. It tells how to plan for one's empowerment in partnership with the Spirit of God and outlines specific steps the reader may take to grow in effectiveness as a pastor.

All this comes to you with a prayer that it may inspire you to continue your growth in areas that are important to your particular ministry.

1

EMPOWERING TRANSFORMS MINISTRY

You will receive power when the Holy Spirit has come upon you.

—Acts 1:8

The gospel . . . is the power of God for salvation to everyone who has faith.

—Romans 1:16

Empowering God's people, as individuals and as a community, is the foundation of fruitful ministry. Pastors who themselves have been empowered, and who focus on empowering others, are much more likely to be effective. That is the one overarching conclusion from our study of over 460 pastors.

Come then and listen to the story of 340 Empowering Pastors (those who rated high in empowering others). Come to discover what empowering means to their ministries. See what has shaped their lives and how they grow. Join their growth pilgrimage. You too can grow in your effectiveness by expanding your capacity to release the Spirit's power in the lives of others.

EMPOWERING RELATED TO EFFECTIVENESS

Nearly three-fourths of all pastors in our study rate themselves as very skillful or skillful in empowering. These Empowering Pastors differ dramatically from Other Pastors, who rate themselves lower on empowerment. Compared to Other Pastors, the Empowering Pastors rate themselves as more effective in thirteen out of fifteen pastoral activities.

Are these high self-ratings by Empowering Pastors simply a function of unrealistically high levels of self-esteem? Clearly not. Eighty-six percent of lay leaders who serve with these pastors rate them high in the skill of empowering. Those Empowering Lay Leaders also are more likely than Other Lay Leaders to rate their pastors as very effective or effective in preaching, leading worship, teaching, counseling, calling, communication, resolving conflict, and in seven other leadership skills.

The validity of high self-ratings by Empowering Pastors is further under-scored by other research that has found that lay leaders' ratings tend to be higher than pastors' self-ratings. For example, a Lutheran study concludes that pastors rate themselves lower because they "can see the amount and quality of work they might have done or should have done and compare it with what they actually did accomplish."[1]

Empowering Pastors rate themselves significantly higher than do Other Pastors in thirteen out of fifteen descriptions of the ways pastors carry out their ministries. They are much more likely to inspire the congregation to grow into a caring community and to reach out beyond the congregation in sharing the good news and in serving others. A governing body executive who nominated one of the Empowering Pastors described him this way:

> He is consistently a good preacher and helps people understand biblical truths in today's context and how that might affect living out their faith. He approaches people and committees by helping them recognize their strengths and then challenges them to maximize those strengths. This has built strong lay leadership, sensitive to each other.
>
> Though many are retirees, they are one of our strongest mission/social action congregations. The outside community has recognized the uniqueness of this church and they have come, wanting to be a part of it. Young families new to the community see this older congregation as exciting and good role models for their family. This has activated new programming for the church.

WHY EMPOWERING ENHANCES EFFECTIVENESS

Why is a focus on empowering so important? Because it is the essence of the gospel. To empower someone is to release power in their lives. There are at least three meanings of power. It can mean authority. You give someone a power of attorney. They are authorized to act on your behalf. "But to all who received him, who believed in his name, he gave power to become children of God" (John 1:12). In Jesus Christ, God gives us authority to become adopted heirs, entitled to all God's resources.

The Greek *exousia*, which is used eighty-six times in the New Testament, can mean authority, jurisdiction, competency, right, and delegated influence. But it can also refer to capacity, freedom, or power. So power can mean competency or capability. After the disciples received the power of the Holy Spirit, they were able to do what they could not do before. The crucifixion left them defeated and depressed. They were hopeless and helpless. After the resurrection and Pentecost they were dynamic. They were empowered to turn the world upside down.

Dunamis is used most frequently to portray miraculous power, wonderful works that are signs of God's mighty presence. It conveys the sense of forcefulness and strength to accomplish wonders. So beyond capability, power can mean energy. We have power stations that generate energy. Without power a machine is worthless. It sits idle until we plug it in and turn on the power.

The gospel is the power of God to transform life. It connects us to God's dynamo and makes us whole. It empowers us, giving us the dynamic to live our lives as God intends them to be lived. Thus, a ministry that focuses on empowering connects people to God's resources for living and frees them from bondage to meaninglessness that weighs them down with apathy. An empowering ministry helps people find God's miraculous power.

When you think of empowering in those terms, it is no wonder that a focus on empowering leads to effectiveness in ministry. I was telling a friend about our discovery that pastors who rate high in empowering rate high in most other tasks of ministry. He replied, "When you think about it, that makes a lot of sense." Of course it does!

A New Focus for Ministry

Why is a focus on empowering so important? Perhaps it is because the spotlight of a pastor's ministry shifts to ways in which God's power is moving in the lives of people. It channels energy beyond coping with the heavy demands of ministry. Pastors concentrate less on achieving competence in their many roles and more on mediating the powerful resources of God to the needy lives of ordinary people. This gives a new dynamic to ministry. Is this not what our Lord meant when he said, "The Sabbath was made to serve us; we weren't made to serve the Sabbath" (Mark 2:27, TM)?

People are not made for the church, but the church for people. People are not made for preaching, but preaching for people. A finely crafted sermon that does not move people to respond to God's grace does not fulfill God's purpose for preaching. Preaching that does not give meaning, hope, and energy for living does not empower. People are not made to enjoy our beautiful worship services. Worship is given so God and worshiper can commune more deeply with each other. It is to open channels of power into lives that are powerless. Congregations are not made to fulfill our dreams for successful programs. Programs are valid only when they fulfill God's dream for the full potential of the people they serve. People are not made for theology, but theology exists to help ordinary folk understand and respond to God's story. As central to our faith as the Bible is, people are not made for the Bible, but the Bible for people.

So when our ministry concentrates on empowerment, our service to God inspires wholeness in lives of God's suffering people, whom we also serve. We are empowered by God to empower those whose lives we touch. When that transforms our calling, we see Bible, theology, preaching, worship, and program with new eyes. No longer are they skill-filled tasks of ministry. They become channels by which the power of the Holy Spirit touches the human condition of particular people who have particular needs.

It may also be that a focus on empowering gives the pastor what sociologist Samuel Blizzard calls an *integrating role*, defined as a minister's "goal orientation, or frame of reference to his work. . . . It is the end toward which he is working in his professional relationship with parishioners, church associations, community groups, and the general public. It is what he is trying to accomplish with people."[2] It ties together in one bundle all the tasks of ministry.

In other words, the integrating role is to the pastor what a mission statement is to a congregation. All pastors have to deal with an overwhelming variety of conflicting expectations from officers of the congregation, church members, the general public, and themselves. This can lead to conflict and confusion in sorting out priorities for their limited time and strength. An integrating role helps to give pastors a focus in their work and to provide a clear basis for interpreting to the congregation the priorities they select. A pastor whose integrating role is to help channel God's power into the lives of others is energized with a dynamic motivation for ministry.

Empowering Contrasts with Enabling

Empowering is clearly different from, and much more than, "enabling." Several dictionaries include *enable* in the definition of *empower*. This seems to equate the two words. But the word *enable* has come to portray weakness rather than strength. In relation to alcoholics, it means to reinforce the alcoholic's weakness and thus the drinking problem. The cliché of an "enabling ministry" has led some pastors to move in the direction of a laissez-faire approach to their members. This leads only to weakness, not to power. Thus, for example, Lyle Schaller contrasts initiating leadership with enabling. His clear implication is that enablers do not initiate.[3]

Leadership may contrast with "enabling," as it has come to be perceived. But it certainly is not antithetical to empowering. True leadership does not reinforce weakness and dependency. It empowers. To empower individuals or institutions is to enhance their power. It is to inspire, nurture, and serve them in such a way that they grow in their power to be and to do. In the context of the church, this means to communicate the gospel in such a way that people receive the wholeness of redemption and the power of the Holy Spirit. That gives them the resources and the freedom to become all God intends them to be. That challenges them to move out into the world in witness and service. In the church as an organization, to empower is to release all the potential that God has placed within the church to become Christ's body in the world. This requires initiative from highly skilled and dedicated leadership.

Empowering Fulfills Gospel Faithfulness

Empowering responds to the deep needs of people with God's resources. Contrary to what some might claim, a focus on meeting people's needs does not conflict with our faithfulness to the gospel or our responsiveness to the Holy Spirit. Rather, our calling is to root our lives in God's presence and power, as we strive to understand the conscious needs and the hidden longings of God's people. Then we seek to empower them by discovering channels that link the power of salvation to people's need for wholeness, hope, and meaning for living. And we do this in concrete ways.

After all, is this not what Jesus himself did in his ministry? Without doubt he was more sensitive to people's needs than any other person in all history. He mediated the healing power of God to the powerless. In compassion he brought that power to bear on physical, spiritual, and emotional needs of the powerless. As he said, "The Spirit of the Lord is upon me, because he has anointed me to bring good news to the poor. He has sent me to proclaim release to the captives and recovery of sight to the blind, to let the oppressed go free, to proclaim the year of the Lord's favor" (Luke 4:18–19).

2

MEANING EMPOWERS

If you continue in my word, you are truly my disciples; and you
will know the truth, and the truth will make you free.
—John 8:31–32

I am the way, and the truth, and the life.
—John 14:6

Without meaning, people perish. Finding meaning for living empowers people because it enables them to integrate their lives around a single goal—
a reason for being. Our study of three hundred congregations that have been particularly effective in retaining their members learned that an important bonding
agent is their members' discovery of meaning for living. That is a centripetal
force that draws people into the center of a congregation's life. Members who feel
they are being fed spiritually are more likely to be deeply committed to their
churches. They are more likely to say that their pastors articulate the meaning of
the Christian faith for life. They feel that their pastors help them deal with life's
problems from a Christian perspective. We found that members of congregations
with an average attendance of more than 50 percent of their membership are
more likely than members of low-attendance churches to say that they discover
in their congregational experiences deep meaning for their daily lives.[1]

A search for meaning is a crucial motivation for a broad cross section of wor-
shipers. It grows out of the deep void that makes many turn to Eastern religions
and to other hoped-for panaceas for meaninglessness and despair. Finding
meaning is important to the baby boom generation, which constitutes roughly
one-third of the U.S. population.[2] In his study of those born between 1946 and
1964, Wade Clark Roof reports that those who are returning to religion do so for
three reasons: (1) for family and children, (2) for meaning, and (3) for community. About their search for meaning, Roof says:

> A second set of reasons for returning has to do with a personal quest for mean-
> ing—for something to believe in, for answers to questions about life. Feelings
> of emptiness and loneliness, whether or not they are articulated in this way,
> lead people in such pursuits. Even among those who return supposedly for the
> children, as one astute pastor remarked to us, often "the children become a safe

vehicle for them [the parents] to come without ever admitting that there is something in it for them."[3]

MEANING THROUGH PREACHING, WORSHIP, AND TEACHING

In our current study, we found that out of fifteen dimensions that describe a pastor's approach to ministry, Empowering Pastors rate themselves highest on helping people find meaning for living through worship, preaching, teaching, and so forth. Ninety-five percent of Empowering Pastors, compared with 78 percent of Other Pastors, say that to a very great extent or to a great extent this accurately describes how they carry out their ministries. On a similar question, 90 percent of them compared with 77 percent of Other Pastors say that they "relate the gospel to issues people face in their personal lives and in society." Clearly, the communication of meaning for living is an important dimension for effective ministry. And one of the primary avenues for communicating meaning is through preaching, worship, and teaching.

Peter is pastor of a five-thousand-member congregation. He unabashedly advocates meeting people's needs in worship:

> Preach to needs . . . sermons that build up rather than beat up. Everyone markets, either poorly or well. We need to meet people's needs. This church would have died without it. When people complain that worship is a performance, I point out that we are offering either a good performance or a poor one. Wineskins are changing all the time. Our Sunday worship is the most loving, grace-filled, exciting hour of the week. It is attractive, relevant. It's just what wineskin you put it in.

The pastor of a four-hundred-member church says, "Power comes through preaching the word of God with connected applicability to our world. To communicate the truths of scripture to everyday life in applicable ways is the goal of my preaching."

Building Bridges of Meaning

How can pastors grow in their ability to help people discover meaning for living through worship and preaching? Donald McCullough, former pastor of the 2,000-member Solana Beach Presbyterian Church, is superbly skilled in doing this. After hearing one of his sermons, my wife turned to me and said, "He meets us in our world and lifts us out of it." That is preaching! That is empowering!

McCullough describes his approach to preaching by using the metaphor of bridge building developed by John Stott.

> If we are to build bridges into the real world, and seek to relate the Word of God to the major themes of life and the major issues of the day, then we have to take seriously both the biblical text and the contemporary scene. We cannot afford to remain on either side of the cultural divide . . . it is our responsibility

to explore the territories on both sides of the ravine until we become thoroughly familiar with them.[4]

McCullough starts on God's side of the ravine by sinking one pylon of the bridge into the bedrock of God's Word. First of all, he steeps himself in the scriptures, reading four chapters in the Bible each day and spending two to four hours in theological reading not connected with sermon preparation. Then, in sermon preparation he digs deeply into the study of the particulars of scripture. "I dissect the text, sentence by sentence, word by word, asking a thousand questions and trying to answer them myself before reading the commentaries."

He completes the bridge building by sinking the other pylon "deeply into the soil of humanity, the world."

> Exegeting scripture isn't enough: I must also exegete human life. Often the people who drain my emotions and distract my thinking are important resources for study. I want to know those with whom I minister, not in the way a salesman knows a client well enough to make a sale but rather in a way a husband knows his wife, with a participatory knowledge that transforms him as much as it transforms her. I don't want my knowledge to be simply utilitarian, for that leads to manipulation; it must be incarnational, for that leads to transformation. I've found the best way to know people is to listen to them.[5]

Reading widely helps in understanding the human side of the great ravine over which the bridge must be built. When he served as an Empowering Pastor of a 2,000-member church, McCullough aimed to read one book a week. At any one time he was working on four books: one on theology, one a novel, one a biography, and another on various subjects such as psychology, social or political commentaries, and other religious works. Through reviews and recommendations of people he trusts, he discovers good books that in turn lead him to other good books. In order to keep in tune with his people he watches some television, listens to rock music, and attends cultural events.

Empowering Pastors in churches of every size testify to the importance of building bridges of meaning. One pastor who serves a mid-sized church in the west gives himself the highest ratings on helping people find meaning for living and on relating the gospel to issues people face. His nominator agrees, describing him as "a very skilled pastor in helping people find meaning through worship, preaching, and teaching. His sermons are biblically centered and apply to peoples lives." How does this pastor bridge that cultural chasm? He advises, "Exegesis, exegesis, exegesis! Keep studying and restudying the scriptures until they start to change the way you think." Yet he maintains an intimate identification with the culture of his people: "I am myself a product of the Western region, which has its own characteristics and way of dealing with issues. I understand where people are 'coming from' and know how far and when to press sensitive issues. I also know some issues are so emotionally laden that it is pointless to try to 'solve' them or bring them into the arena of public conflict."

Knowing Your People

On the cultural side of the ravine, an Empowering Pastor of a small church gives this advice: "Get in touch with the people. Find out what's happening in their lives; their hopes, dreams, hurts. Be present with them when a pastor is needed." Another says: "Know your people. Call, call, call on homes. Be interested in their lives. Share their happiness and grief . Love the people you serve or move on. Preach the gospel, challenge them to service."

In a very large congregation the pastor cannot hope to pastor the whole congregation. One pastor, like many others who serve such churches, has found that his intimate congregation consists of the leadership of the church. From them and from others of the congregation who seek him out, he continually sharpens his knowledge of his people. "I am a student of people and relate scripture to their needs. I am a good listener and observer. I keep very close to our twenty-four elders, to our one hundred deacons and sixty-eight staff. I stay close to those people. They are my congregation. I have lunch with somebody four times a week. They might be anyone who wants to see me."

The pastor of a twelve-hundred-member congregation puts it this way:

> The congregation helps me preach better. Each year I spend one week of my study leave mapping out my sermons for the year. Before I leave for that week I write one hundred people asking them what topics they would cover if they were preaching. I also ask if they have read anything that would be helpful to me. I get a good response and this also leads to suggestions from the congregation all the time.
>
> My preaching gets better the longer I am with a congregation. That is because I am more invested, know more about the particular needs of the congregation and the community. I also know more how national or state agendas relate to people's struggles. Whenever I am writing, I think about the group I am talking to. I keep informed of people's needs by sitting down and listening to them. I do not do long-term counseling but I do hospital visitation, crisis counseling, and grief counseling.

When asked what advice he would give to a pastor who wanted to grow in effectiveness, another pastor said:

> Learn from your own experience, beginning with listening carefully to the members of your congregation. Think of yourself as entering a foreign country: you need to learn who these people are, what their culture is, in order to effectively minister to them. What's the bad news in their lives that awaits the good news of God's love and grace? Without knowing that, you're preaching to the wind! Tillich's method of correlation is a good method for ministry as well as theology: start by listening to the people because you begin with God's love for them in their concrete daily reality.

God's Story Meets Our Stories

The strengths of Empowering Pastors lie in knowing God, scripture, themselves, the people they serve, and the contexts in which they minister. They are gifted in blending these ingredients with the power of God's grace in their own lives. They know the written word and are in constant communion with the Living Word. They are in tune with and continually growing in their understanding and commitment to "The Story" of God's grace as it unfolded in the past and as it is unfolding in the present. They live out the relationship of God's Story to their own story. As one pastor put it, "In preaching there is a fine line between my story and *The* Story. I keep The Story before the congregation intermixed with my story."

By the power of love, Empowering Pastors sense the relevance of The Story to the life stories of their congregations. They move with freedom from Christ to context and from context to Christ and the community of faith. Thus, they empower individuals by communicating the gospel in ways that feed the hidden hungers of people and relate to their life situations.

They help people discover grace as a way of life by accepting people where they are in life's journey and helping them catch a vision of all that God's forgiving and sustaining grace challenges and empowers them to be. In short, they are more skillful in relating the gospel to issues people face in their personal lives and in society. They help people find meaning for living through worship, preaching, and teaching. All their contacts are avenues of grace.

THE IMPORTANCE OF CONTEMPORARY
IDEAS AND TRENDS

The importance of the cultural side of the ravine is emphasized by a difference in perspectives among participants in our study. Sixty-four percent of Empowering Pastors compared with 45 percent of Other Pastors describe their congregations as influenced more by contemporary ideas and trends than by history and tradition, or by an equal mix of contemporary ideas with history and tradition. Fifty-five percent of the Other Pastors feel that their congregations are influenced more by history and tradition.[6] Approximately half of the lay leaders in both groups concur with their pastor's perceptions of what influences their congregations. In contrast with these perceptions, both Empowering Pastors and Other Pastors say that their preference is to serve congregations that are influenced more by contemporary ideas and trends or by a balance with history and tradition. Only 13 percent of both groups of pastors would prefer to serve a congregation that is influenced more by history and tradition.

Why do pastors feel that way? Perhaps it is because congregations that are influenced too much by history and tradition are more likely to be inflexible and brittle in accepting anything new that comes to them. They might be called "closed" congregations. If they are located in communities that also are steeped in history and tradition, they will fit well into their communities. But both community and congregation will be like old wineskins that resist the new wine of the gospel. They will be open only to their past understanding of the faith and unable to translate that faith into meaning for a changing culture. Their danger is in being threatened by change and walling themselves off from the larger society. They can then become irrelevant to issues that are shaping their lives and the world as a whole. Or members can "lose their faith" because, in its frozen form, it no longer is relevant to the world in which they must live. Many pastors serve faithfully in such closed congregations, in spite of the difference they feel between their ideal and the realities they face. For them, as we shall see, an emphasis on empowering may provide a new source of hope.

In contrast with closed congregations, those that are influenced more by contemporary ideas and trends are more likely to be open to the new. We might call them "open" congregations. They are more likely to be in tune with the dynamic changes of culture and less likely to value the heritage of the past. Their danger is in being too open. They may drift away from their Christian heritage. A container that is open both at top and at bottom can hold nothing. To use other figures of speech, they can be blown about by every wind of change without foundations solid enough to sustain them. On the positive side, they are more likely to be able to come alive with the new wine of the gospel when it comes to them in meaningful terms. Pastors who are gifted in establishing creative connections between the gospel and the world will find them more responsive. They can help members discover a balance between the heritage of the gospel and the lives they must live in a changing world.

Congregations with a significant mixture of folk who are influenced by contemporary ideas and those who rely on tradition can be responsive to wise leadership that helps them relate the new wine of the gospel to the society within which they live. Their danger is that factions can develop between those who favor tradition and those who respond to the contemporary. Skilled bridge builders can avoid that pitfall.

Why Empowering Congregations Are More Open

Why do a higher proportion of Empowering Pastors than Other Pastors serve "open" congregations? There are at least two possible explanations for this. First, it may be because those empowering congregations are located in communities that are more open to the contemporary. In contrast, a higher proportion of Other Pastors may serve in more "closed" communities who cling to history and tradition.

There is some evidence for this. A higher proportion of Empowering Pastors serve suburban or small-city congregations. A larger percentage of Other Pastors serve rural, small-town, or large-city congregations. Rural and small-town churches are likely to be more conservative than those in suburbia. Many aging congregations in large cities cling to traditions in their efforts to survive. Also a larger percentage of Empowering Pastors than Other Pastors are heads of staff. Churches with multiple staffs are more likely to be open to contemporary ideas and trends than are churches with solo pastors.[7]

Skill in Bridge Building

Here we sound a hopeful note for pastors in tradition-oriented congregations. As we have said, solo pastors tend to serve such churches. However, our data suggests that solo pastors who focus on empowering others may be less likely than Other Solo Pastors to feel that their congregations are influenced by history and tradition. A higher proportion of Empowering Solo Pastors in our study feel no difference between their ideal and the realities in their churches.[8] It may be that the ability of Empowering Solo Pastors to communicate a relevant gospel has enabled members of otherwise closed churches to grow in their openness to the new. As people discover how the dynamic power of the gospel helps them cope with contemporary issues, they can afford to be more open. The changing culture need no longer threaten their heritage of faith.

Conversely, because many Other Pastors perceive their congregations to be closed to the new, they may be hesitant to grapple with the ways in which the gospel relates to changing culture. They may fear a backlash from "closed" members. Consequently their preaching simply reinforces the existing tendencies to emphasize history and tradition. Many of those pastors may also be less skillful in communicating meaningful relationships between biblical tradition and current culture. They may not know how to help members relate their faith to contemporary realities. These hypotheses need to be tested by further study.

Whatever the explanation, we conclude that pastors who wish to grow in their effectiveness should seek to increase their skill in building bridges from biblical tradition to contemporary ideas and trends. They will want to stretch the minds of their people to discover the sovereignty of God over all life. This task will be especially difficult for pastors who serve closed congregations in closed communities. They will need even greater skill as they seek to help their members find meaning for living in today's world. However, as pastors grow in this capacity, their people will also grow in their discovery of deeper meaning for their lives.

MEANING THROUGH EVERY PASTORAL CONTACT

Opportunities to build bridges of meaning are not limited to preaching. Breakthroughs to meaning can come whenever a pastor is with others. Moments of crisis in members' lives present particularly pregnant possibilities for them to grow in relevant sustaining faith. In a church of more than six hundred members, an Empowering Pastor affirms that a crucial dimension of his calling is "to be with people in times of crisis, mediating the strength, comfort, and hope of Christ; bringing the biblical message to bear on the contemporary." Moments of great joy or pain in people's lives can become lasting links to spiritual meaning. One pastor in a growing community has discovered marriage counseling as one such opportunity.

People are coming home to the church. Baby boomers, a huge element of society, are coming home especially when they get married. They want to get married in our church. Premarital counseling is a very important facet of our ministry here. We don't require couples to be members of the church in order to be married here. But we do require four hours of personal counseling. This is one of our great areas of evangelism. We ask why they want to get married in the church. Why a minister? We ask them to tell us their story. They reply that they do really believe in God, but they haven't been practicing as church members. We relate to them with grace and love just as if they were members of the church, except that nonmembers do pay a small rental fee for using the sanctuary. Others come to us when children come into their lives. We have programs for families, a nursery school, kids club, a couples fellowship, and seven classes for adults. This is one of the advantages of a large church. With a large staff we are able to provide a broad range of programs.

In ordinary contacts that a pastor has with people in the congregation or in the community, the pastor inevitably has the opportunity to build bridges of meaning. One pastor likes to think of himself as a "parish educator" who teaches and directs an education system. As a "symbolic person," he is "mentor for a religious community."

The pastor is a symbolic person. Everything about the person of the pastor is a statement that forms a kind of impromptu curriculum. It is imposed without an announcement or deliberation. Word gets out, after a while, that the pastor expects a certain demeanor at worship, tolerates certain kinds of conversation and not others, tends to spend her or his most intense efforts in one or another area of the congregation's life, giving it a higher priority than others. It is the pastor who indicates to the congregation the existence of a framework of values, instinctive responses, nonverbal approvals or rejections—indications to the congregation of a whole cosmos of instructions about the pastor's understanding of what ought to be.

Some will protest that this places too great a burden on a pastor. But it is the burden of being a living link with spiritual resources. Empowering Lay Leaders are more likely than Other Lay Leaders to say that their pastor spontaneously models acts of caring love. Empowering Pastors are more likely to make the same judgment.

Pastors Themselves as Bridges

There is a sense in which Empowering Pastors themselves become the living bridge between God's side of the ravine and the human side. In other words, they are called to live in two worlds at the same time. They immerse themselves in God's Story while they sharpen their awareness of their own stories and stay tuned to people's stories. They listen honestly to their own struggles. They listen deeply between the lines to words and feelings and body language of others in order to sense who people are and what they are about. They listen to what God may be saying and to what people are feeling. They keep conversant with the context within which they and their people live and with the issues of society that they face. Living in both worlds, they blend the two with the dynamic of love. When that happens, people are empowered for living.

Because these pastors are called to incarnate the inner world of the Spirit and the outer world of contemporary life, their readiness to share their own humanity becomes crucial in the communication of the gospel. One pastor who has been through great suffering in his own life describes what it is like for him to share his very human struggles. "I allow people to know me and my weaknesses in preaching and wherever I am. I very seldom preach something I haven't lived. My personal struggle with issues people are facing always comes through. I tell people that getting ordained doesn't shield ministers from the struggle that others face. I don't hide anything anymore."

Another pastor puts it this way: "Pastors need an openness to humanity, to their own and to others'. They need to be open to what is going on in the world—to do an exegesis of life. There is electricity in my life that comes from the dialogue of my humanity with the word of God. Because of that, I can listen to my people, to God, and to myself."

MEANING THROUGH COMMUNITY

In my two previous studies I found that a warm, caring community is a central ingredient in the lives of vital congregations that attract and keep active members and that reach out to others in service. Again, in this study of effective pastors that theme recurs. Eighty-eight percent of Empowering Pastors, compared with 65 percent of Other Pastors, rated themselves high on inspiring the congregation to grow into a caring community. Empowering Lay Leaders were also more likely than Other Lay Leaders to rate their pastors high in this skill.

The longing for communities of meaning is characteristic of our time. Indeed, the search for meaning is closely related to a longing for community. It is in intimate personal relationships that meaning often emerges. Roof describes that relationship in his analysis of the baby boom generation:

> For whatever reasons, they often turn to small groups and lifestyle enclaves in search of a quality of belonging and attention to specific issues they fail to find elsewhere. This quest for community takes many forms. . . .
> Community, of course, is an elusive term and can mean different things to different people; but in practical terms it refers to a group of people who share their lives and communicate honestly with one another, "whose relationships go deeper than the masks of composure and who have developed some significant commitment to 'rejoice together, mourn together, and to delight in each other,' " as M. Scott Peck puts it.
> It is these qualities that boomers look for—sharing, caring, accepting, belonging. The qualities themselves often are more important than the places where they find them.
> Community varies in its forms, but the qualities that make for its appeal are much the same. In all of this, what is most important is that people forge a link between their own experiences and religious and spiritual teachings. The yearning is about finding a connection between life and meaning, and about finding your own voice and expressing it.[9]

As boomers age we can expect increased attention to creating new forms of community. A more settled life, the end of child-bearing, and greater concerns about health and well-being should all create conditions for more community.[10]

Here then is a challenge to the church and to pastors who give it leadership. Peter Hobbie, in reviewing Roof's work, concludes, "Because the boomers like to search on their own terms, the church should allow boomer communities to form within a more flexible church structure. Through these communities, churches might both attract the boomers and avoid the divisions that boomers might bring."[11]

Small Groups of Connecting Christians

Roof's work underscores the value of Christian connecting with Christian in small communities of meaning. In such groups people study together, apply what they are studying to their lives, share their faith journeys, pray together, and support one another in dealing with life crises. They challenge one another to carry out their ministries. "Covenant communities" can commit themselves to spend regular time together in such sharing and mutual support. Or members can commit themselves to a common mission within the congregation or in the community as they also share their faith journeys. Such encounters may take place in Bible classes or other groups within a congregation.

Small group possibilities are nearly endless. Roy Oswald, senior consultant for Alban Institute, suggests opportunities for women's networking, men's awareness and meditation, or support groups for those who have lost a spouse through death or divorce or for those who suffer from cancer, are overweight, addicted, or unemployed.[12] One important way in which many Empowering Pastors help people discover meaning for living is in organizing or encouraging the formation of such groups. An Empowering Pastor who serves a congregation of nearly three thousand members has for many years given a high priority to the organizing and nurturing of "koinonia groups." He spends time in training their lay leadership and in providing them with materials. Over sixty such groups engage six to seven hundred members in journeys of faith discovery. The pastor believes that such encounters are central to helping people find relevant faith. He says:

> These groups enable members to share faith and open themselves to the whole dimension of being cared for in Christian community. In the koinonia groups we get heightened consciousness of what it might mean to be God's person in the world today.
>
> Groups will vary in effectiveness. Where they are effective, they are tremendous. I have less counseling here . . . than I did in a former congregation that had six hundred members. This is because people are ministering to each other. I see it particularly if someone loses a spouse or a relative. The koinonia groups gather around in caring and in following up.

Each koinonia group is led by a lay coordinator who has received extensive training and who was selected for the gift of caring. Coordinators must draw people out, listen to them, and keep in touch with them. Coordinators meet monthly with one of the pastors. At that time they go over the syllabus for the month, which has been prepared by the pastor.

In one series, for example, all koinonia groups were studying what it means for every Christian to be a minister. This was coordinated with a series of sermons on the same subject. As the pastor says in describing the program, "The stress in the koinonia groups, in the nurturing groups, in all of our Christian education, is to equip people for their ministry of reaching out, caring, and recruiting. We feel that we are not just nurturing people for their own benefit. It is in order to impact family life, community life, work life, life in the nation."[13]

The Importance of Trained Facilitators

Oswald flatly maintains that leaderless groups don't work. Someone needs to take responsibility for guiding group process and insuring equal opportunity for participation. In addition, group members need to depend on someone else in the group who is caring and trustworthy. This allows them to be released from the burden of being self-sufficient for long enough to experience grace. That time of renewal then allows them to go back into the world as a self-contained and self-reliant individual.[14]

Oswald believes that lay group facilitators may best be trained by participating in a support group led by a skilled facilitator. He suggests that pastors may start lay groups by first identifying those in the congregation who are called to a ministry of group facilitating and have the potential gifts for such a ministry. The pastor would then gather them into a small support group that would meet for six to twelve months with the pastor as group facilitator. From participants in that group the pastor could then invite individuals to facilitate other groups.[15]

Small Congregations Need Small Groups

The larger the congregation, the more critical it is to stimulate small groups. But it is a myth to assume that because members in small congregations know each other intimately they do not need small-group life. Small churches already have various small groups such as Bible classes, women's circles, and a choir. What is needed is to help such groups use those opportunities to develop the kind of trust relations that will enable them to share their faith journeys, discover meaning for their lives, and support one another along the way. In three years, a congregation that was located near a booming new housing development grew from 66 to 160 members. One of their strategies was to involve as many members as possible in some small-group activity.

> Members participate in one of two adult fellowship groups, one for those under forty and one for older folk. There is an adult church school class and a women's group. The choir has become a support group. Members have become involved in each others' lives. A koinonia group of up to sixteen members

meets weekly in one of the member's homes. After refreshments and a chance to "check in with one another," they study a book as stimulus for discussion and faith sharing.[16]

The pastor of a 285-member congregation has also found such groups to be an avenue for empowering new leadership.

> We gather people into small groups and get them to listen to each other. We have moved more and more into a small-group ministry. I wrote a curriculum on prayer and another on the Holy Spirit. One in three members of the church has participated in these groups. We asked people to give us the best time for them to meet. Then we took that information and gathered them into cross-generation groups of six to twelve people each. I trained six couples to lead these groups. That training is another way to empower our members. A woman who was trained in that program is now training three younger women to lead groups of six to eight women in our women's program. To take a leadership role in the congregation, she had to have the people's trust. Working with me built the trust and respect she needed.

MEANING THROUGH LIFE COMMITMENT

Finding ultimate meaning in life comes when one responds to God's call by committing one's life to Jesus Christ. As we shall see in chapter 6, a majority of pastors made such commitments early in life. Chapter 11 shows that a sense of their call to ministry is a strong sustaining force throughout their ministry.

Because their own commitment means so much to them, Empowering Pastors seek commitment from others. They are more likely than Other Pastors to have engaged in extensive or very extensive formal continuing education in evangelism. They are more likely to inspire members to reach out beyond the congregation in sharing the good news and in service to others. Sixty-five percent of Empowering Pastors compared with 40 percent of Other Pastors say they are eager to preach on financial stewardship, tithing, or proportional giving. Evangelism calls for a life response to the love of God. Service to others is a natural expression of that response. And the stewardship of our possessions is an important, tangible way we show our gratitude for that love. All are ways in which people express their life commitment to our Lord.

This suggests that Empowering Pastors place high priority on seeking life commitment from those whose lives touch theirs. Through that commitment they help people discover meaning in their lives. By challenging others to commitment they help empower them.

Meaning motivates people to discover life's possibilities and to grow as persons. Empowering Pastors build bridges of meaning for them to cross. The living Truth still sets people free. In the church, those who respond to that Truth are further empowered when they discover a climate in which they feel free to grow, learn, explore, and use their gifts in Christian ministry without fear of retribution. As we shall see in the next chapter, Empowering Pastors take the lead in establishing such a climate.

3

FREE TO GROW

If the Son makes you free, you shall be free indeed.
　　　　　　　　　　　　　　　　　—John 8:36, NKJ

Christ has set us free to live a free life. So take your stand! Never again let anyone put a harness of slavery on you.
　　　　　　　　　　　　　　　　　—Galations 5:1, TM

In nature we recognize the importance of climate. We do not expect tropical foliage in Alaska or a polar bear in the Amazon. Parched ground does not sustain tender seedlings. Oppressive heat and high humidity sap the energy of most people. Crisp fall days are invigorating. Climate makes a difference. People too thrive and grow in a healthy climate. They wither and die or resist and rebel under oppressive climates.

The climate in a congregation makes a difference in the lives of those who are a part of it. In some congregations people are alive and growing. The Spirit of God is moving in their lives. In others growth seems to be stifled and the climate is heavy.

How does anyone create a climate of freedom to grow? In one sense no one can. As Paul said, "Neither the one who plants nor the one who waters is anything, but only God who gives the growth" (1 Cor. 3:7). But in another sense there is much that we can do. We can cultivate the soil. We can plant and we can water. Empowered by the Spirit, we can set people free to be all that God intends them to be. We can be agents of God's empowering love. In our study, we defined empowering as "the ability to establish a climate in which people feel free to grow, learn, explore, and use their gifts in Christian ministry without fear of retribution." Interviews with Empowering Pastors added breadth and depth to our original definition.

CULTIVATING A HEALTHY CLIMATE

Pastors play a central role in establishing the climate in congregations they serve. Each congregation has a unique personality and an existing climate when a new pastor arrives. There are key figures in congregations who have an important influence on climate. The climate in some congregations may seem almost immutable. In some the climate is so oppressive that nothing can change it short of some divine miracle. But, allowing for those realities, it is pastors who make the greatest impact on climate. They are most visible to parishioners and communicate climate by everything they are and say and do. They can stifle vitality and creativity or stimulate it. This process begins at the very beginning of their ministries, or even when they are interviewed by a search committee. It broadens and deepens as tenure extends. The longer they serve the greater their impact.

How then do Empowering Pastors cultivate a climate in which people feel free to grow, learn, and explore? What can we learn from them? How can other pastors cultivate such a climate?

Loving People and Valuing Their Contribution

Empowering Pastors love the people to whom they minister. They believe in them and trust them. They highly prize what individuals have to offer to the life of the congregation. Over and over we hear the same refrain. It comes from pastors serving small rural congregations and large suburban churches. They say such things as

Love your people, enjoy them, brag on them. Show them you love them before you lead them. Earn a good hearing (the right to have your suggestions taken seriously) by caring greatly for those whom you serve and by doing your best to practice what you preach.

Let the congregation know you love and trust them. When you do, there's nothing they won't do to respond to your ministry. They need to feel loved in order to take risks and grow. Trust God at work in each person.

Do the people know you love them? For love covers a multitude of sins: personal, programmatic, administrative.

You really have to love the people. That can be hard sometimes. In a pastor-centered church, if the pastor is unhappy, nothing really happens. Unfortunately, in rural ministry we have many pastors who want to move beyond where they are. Once you go to a church, don't professionalize your calling by asking, Where is this leading me? One has to be responsive to the people in their needs, and not to one's own agenda. Love empowers. If you don't love the people, your ministry will suffer.

The longer a pastor serves a church, the more the capacity to empower increases. So I believe that the future of the church is in long-term pastorates. You get to know people and they get to know you. You become part of their lives and of the community. The key ingredient is to be their pastor, to care about them, take an interest in them, and share with them day to day. Then a relationship is built and a trust level acquired.

Respect your congregation's potential as theologians and trust their ability to deal with truth; love even the stinkers in your congregation!

Theologically we all affirm our love for people. God created them and called them good. Jesus Christ redeemed them and the Holy Spirit sustains them. We all are called to love one another and to serve others. That's why we are in ministry! No problem! We affirm it all with our minds. But sometimes our hearts don't respond. Then our actions are far behind. To live love in every circumstance, that's the rub!

Perhaps you remember the story of a noted child psychologist. On his day off, he installed a new cement sidewalk in front of his house. The forms were in place. The mixing truck dumped its load, and he labored long and hard to smooth it to perfection. After his nice warm shower, he looked out the window to admire his handiwork. There to his consternation he discovered children playing in his new cement. His tirade was loud and uncontrollable. A neighbor remonstrated with him, saying, "I thought, as a child psychologist, that you loved children." "I do," he replied, "in the abstract but not in the concrete."

Practicing Unconditional Acceptance

Agape love is unconditional. It flows from grace. Redemptive love accepts me as I am and transforms my weakness into strength. Grace from God becomes a way of life when we pass it along through tangible expressions of unconditional love.

Most people have never experienced unconditional acceptance. They have known only conditional love. Any love and affirmation in their lives has come when they have done what someone else wanted them to do. Families are the cradles of whatever love most people ever know. Even those children fortunate enough to live with caring adults may receive praise mostly for a good report card or for athletic achievement. All too often, rewards go to those children who live out thwarted parental dreams lost in mists of memory. Punishment falls on those who unwittingly step on some booby trap of parental frustration or failure. Love is expressed to those children who fulfill expectations of significant others. Children who fail to conform to adults' desires or ideals are depreciated or punished. At best (or at worst?) children are quietly ignored. Whereupon they try harder to earn the love they crave. At school, competition is the watchword: for grades, for sports, for other achievement, or even for citizenship. Our competitive culture trains us well. Apples of outstanding performance bring the teacher's praise. Peers accept us when we conform. Then the cutthroat marketplace seals our conviction that rewards come by works and not by unconditional acceptance. Is it any wonder that our minds inextricably link love and acceptance with our efforts to please others? To be loved we must perform satisfactorily. Can we be surprised that it is so difficult for most church members to comprehend the meaning of grace? The competitive mind is convinced that even our salvation must be earned.

Our definition of empowering closes with the jarring phrase, "without fear of retribution." This reminds us that many have had their shortcomings rewarded with reproof, rebuke, reprimand, admonition, or punishment. Conditional love shrivels the soul. One dares not risk for fear of losing love. An encounter with unconditional love unlocks the deepest wellsprings of our beings. It frees the soul to grow, learn, explore, and use our gifts in ministry.

Unconditional acceptance has a powerful transforming impact. Grace empowers. And, as we shall see, grace in one way or another is central to the experience of Empowering Pastors. Early in life, most have experienced unconditional love in a Christian home or in the warmth of a nurturing congregation. If not, they have discovered grace from those who ministered to them at some point when they suffered deep pain in their lives.

Because they have experienced unmerited love, Empowering Pastors have been freed to help others discover the power of grace. How do they communicate that grace? Of course they preach and teach grace. But beyond that, the way in which they relate to people communicates acceptance in very tangible ways.

Understanding People Empathetically

There is no better way to communicate unconditional acceptance than by demonstrating that one seeks to understand someone at a deep level without in any way conveying a judgmental response. In his *Seven Habits of Highly Effective People*, Stephen Covey gives the principle involved in empathetic communication. "If I were to summarize in one sentence the single most important principle I have learned in the field of interpersonal relations, it would be this: *Seek first to understand, then to be understood.* This principle is the key to effective interpersonal communication."[1] To this I would add, it is the first step in communicating unconditional acceptance. If people do not feel that you care enough to really understand them, they cannot be convinced that you accept or love them.

Eighty percent of Empowering Pastors, compared with 59 percent of Other Pastors, rate themselves as very skillful or skillful in listening. In like manner they are more skillful in empathizing. Said one pastor,

> People do not feel valued if you do not listen to them. Listen to everyone. Everybody has much to say. And the Holy Spirit speaks through some! Establish yourself as a compassionate listener. Competence in skills is very important, but compassion and empathy go a lot further in being a generally effective leader.

Listening to Understand

Covey defines *empathic listening* as listening with the intent to understand. He warns us that most of us listen with the intent to reply. For those of us in the pastoral ministry, this may be one of our greatest temptations. We are specially skilled in speaking. Few of us have been trained to really listen. We have so much to say, and the gospel is so important to us, that we tend to listen for opportunities to pass along our latest gem of wisdom. We are eager to share what we just know will be most helpful to the speaker. Sometimes we can hardly wait to respond to what is being said. Again Covey is helpful:

When another person speaks, we're usually "listening" at one of four levels. We may be *ignoring* another person, not really listening at all. We may practice *pretending*. "Yeah. Uh-huh. Right." We may practice *selective listening,* hearing only certain parts of the conversation. . . . Or we may even practice *attentive listening,* paying attention and focusing energy on the words that are being said. But very few of us practice the fifth level, the highest form of listening, *empathic listening* [with the intent to understand].[2]

Covey says that most people respond autobiographically. They evaluate by agreeing or disagreeing, probe with questions based on their own frame of reference, advise out of their experience, or interpret the motives or behavior based on their own motives and behavior.[3] Such responses are not helpful.

Reflecting on our temptation to bring our own agendas into every situation, the pastor of a large church says, "I seek to give people priority rather than program—to care what they think rather than to bring a single agenda of telling them what I think." Another pastor puts it this way, "An Empowering Pastor must have the capacity to listen between the lines and to hear people's stories. Empowering comes when a pastor stays tuned in to their stories, remembering that the person above all is most valuable to any process. I listen to people's stories but will not use them as illustrations in sermons since that violates confidentiality."

The pastor of the Foothill Church, which we studied in *Congregations Alive,* also took part in our current study. He is perceived as accepting, nonjudgmental, and helpful. He "deals with people wherever they happen to be." One member of that church reports,

> I think I know why I came to Foothill. It is because of the unusual nonverbal and persuasive ministry of our pastor. He reached out to me because I was lost. He was concerned about me, but willing to let me take my own time. He listened to me, but wouldn't give me answers. He gave me books to read. I realized that if I really wanted to learn, I would have to be a part of that church. The next thing I knew I was "hooked."[4]

Expressing Faith in People's Potential

The pastor of the Foothill Church knows how to listen empathetically. He discerned and cultivated this member's potential. He did not try to pour her into his mold but gave her permission to be and do what God had gifted her to be and do.

Believing in someone's potential has a powerful effect on how we treat that person. Our appraisal of their potential can become self-fulfilling. In a well-known experiment, teachers of an average class of students were told that their students were gifted. Students' performance in that class proved to be significantly above average because their teachers believed they could perform.

Research into the characteristics of effective schools has much to teach us in the church. It shows how school effectiveness is the product of the quality of leadership by the school principal and the quality of its teachers. We shall return to one such study at several points, because in many ways a school is one of the institutions in our society with the closest parallels to the church. School research has shown the crucial importance of expectations.

> Successful schools operated in a climate in which the professional staff believed their students could achieve and held high expectations for student accomplishments. There was a belief that their students could learn and a commitment to making sure that their students did learn. These positive staff attitudes were conveyed to the students. In contrast, staffs in low-achieving schools had a defeatist attitude. They tended to attribute the lack of student achievement to causes over which they had little control. . . . [They were] more pessimistic about their abilities to influence students and more often blamed their teaching problems on non-school factors, such as student abilities, student backgrounds, and lack of parental concern.[5]

Empowering Pastors give people a vision, individually and corporately, of God's potential in them. They communicate positive expectations. The pastor of a midsized congregation in a small town describes how this works for them. "We assume that people are here to be servants of Christ. We don't lavish praise when someone does something. We do say thanks but don't make a big deal of it. We assume they will be doing it and doing it well. People are grateful for each other in quiet, ordinary ways. We encourage people to support each other when a job is to be done."

Many mainline denominations are aging. Older adults are sometimes inclined to accept the status quo. They have already spent their energies on changing the world with little or no success. Some feel that further change is not worth the struggle. Now they are content to enjoy their remaining days. Older congregations in difficult situations often simply accept their inevitable decline and hang on to the friendships they enjoy among their dwindling numbers. Two pastors in our study report their most challenging experiences in the past five years:

> It has been to inspire, challenge, and involve an elderly congregation. I dealt with it by helping the elderly folk believe in themselves; that they were able and had the talent and resources to be the best and I kept before them the idea that if they didn't do ministry, nobody would in that faith community. It worked!

> My challenge has been continuing to meet the needs of the older members, while leading the younger people to become more active in the life of the church. I have often praised the older members for their wisdom and organized shepherd groups to reach out to younger families.

Validating and Developing the Ability to Choose

People are empowered when they feel they can make their own meaningful choices rather than simply respond to choices that have been made for them. Empowering Pastors encourage and reinforce people's ability to choose. They help them consider options, facilitate choices, and weigh potential directions. They give them time to own and accept new possibilities. The director of a counseling center who also pastors a small congregation feels that the making of choices is central to empowering.

> Empowerment underlies most of everything I do in the parish, with my clients and in my educational work with pastors. My goal is empowerment. But it is hard to define. I do this through a consistent pastoral presence, helping people consider options open to them, facilitate choices, and weigh the potential directions of those choices. I resist doing things for people. Rather I help them understand how to do things themselves. This requires a climate of a noncondemning spirit and a reverence and respect for their attempts and struggles and for the choices they make, even if they are poor choices. I seek to validate their ability to choose, not necessarily to validate the choices themselves.

Responding Positively to Aspirations and Initiatives

Responsiveness to the dreams and initiatives of members is an important key to empowering them. Empowering Pastors keep in touch with opportunities for service and with the concerns of their people. Initiatives of members are taken seriously, even if they cannot always be implemented. Whenever leaders catch a glimmer of concern on the part of some church member, or a hint that someone may be prepared to engage in some form of ministry, they are ready to help facilitate the development of such a ministry.

The pastor of a congregation with just over two hundred members has been highly successful in doing this, as his nominator points out.

> Jerry Johnson is serving a church that has been in a ten- to fifteen-year decline. He has been there almost a year and in that time the church's worship attendance has doubled, the church's enthusiasm for ministry has probably tripled. His ability to allow people to cite opportunities for ministry and then to go and work in those areas is extraordinary. If someone comes to Jerry with an idea for ministry he will support that idea. Consequently there is a great deal of enthusiasm in the church for new ideas for ministry, which tends to expand and expand in larger concentric circles.

The pastor of a somewhat larger congregation works hard to develop an atmosphere of responsiveness among the leadership of the church. He encourages members to dream of what their church might be doing. By modeling receptivity to their initiatives that grow out of those dreams, he is helping officers to be responsive too. He tells us how he does this.

> An atmosphere of receptivity has to be created. People are dreaming about what God might do here. Those dreams are risky to share. If they don't sense a receptivity to their dreams from the leadership, their dreams will be stifled. There needs to be openness, so people will dare to risk. I keep telling people there is no such thing as a bad question if it is an honest question. I work hard to apply it, and it has paid off. People are willing to ask questions and to risk. People take itty-bitty risk steps. They risk one inch, then two inches, and after a while they risk a yard or two. But they will test the ground first. As pastor I take the lead in this. But our officers are increasingly able to do it.

This pastor illustrates his approach by telling of the way in which a vital group of sixteen young couples began to meet in his church.

Most of them were non-Christians who came into contact with the church through marriages I had performed. An older woman began to pray for these couples. As she was developing this passion, I was praying for someone who would have a passion for them. Then one day, we met on the street. She shared her vision and I shared my prayer. So a team was established and she opened her home to that group. Now she has become the spiritual godmother of those sixteen young families, and out of that group have come one deacon and three elders. And her husband, who was not a professing Christian, has made his profession of faith.

FOCUSING YOUR MINISTRY ON GOD'S GIFTS

One of the most striking differences between Empowering Pastors and Other Pastors is in their ability to identify and assess their own talents and the talents of others. Sixty-five percent of Empowering Pastors compared with only 29 percent of Other Pastors rate themselves as very skillful or skillful in identifying gifts. This is the largest difference among all fifteen of the skill ratings in our study. Lay leaders are even more convinced of their pastors' skill in identifying gifts. They give their pastors higher ratings in this skill.

With a somewhat broader question, we asked the extent to which pastors and lay leaders agree that the pastor "helps people discover, develop, and channel their gifts into appropriate service." Empowering Pastors were much more likely than Other Pastors to get high ratings on this question. Out of fifteen items describing pastoral actions, this is one of four ratings with the greatest difference between the two groups.

Clearly we have here one of the most important avenues to empowerment. Pastors who empower others are skilled in identifying gifts and in helping people to develop and channel them into meaningful service. When we asked pastors to give illustrations of empowerment, a high proportion of them talked about identifying, developing, and channeling people's gifts.

Believing in Giftedness

Empowering Pastors have deep convictions about the centrality of giftedness in God's plan for the church. With the apostle Paul they are firmly convinced that God supplies the church with the gifts it needs for its mission in the world. As one pastor put it, "I believe the church is gifted. I have no patience with those who are talking about the church in terms of an economy of scarcity. Paul tells us that the church has been given every spiritual gift that it needs." And so he does:

Now God gives us many kinds of special abilities, but it is the same Holy Spirit who is the source of them all. There are different kinds of service to God, but it is the same Lord we are serving. There are many ways in which God works in our lives, but it is the same God who does the work in and through all of us who are his. The Holy Spirit displays God's power through each of us as a means of helping the entire church. (1 Cor. 12:4–11)

Empowering pastors believe that every person has gifts to be discovered and developed. They preach and teach this and make it a central reality of their approach to ministry. One Empowering Pastor after another affirmed this in our interviews:

Each person is a unique person and all people need to be listened to, affirmed, and encouraged to discover their uniqueness, where they fit into the body of Christ, and their role in the church. It is amazing the gifts that people have and a great mistake to think that we have all the gifts for ministry.

Empowerment is helping individuals, or the church as a whole, to discover their gifts and use them for furthering the kingdom. I truly believe that everyone has gifts for ministry. The challenge is to help folks discover them. We are always looking for ways to help people find out what their gifts are.

Central to my understanding of the pastor's role is to preach, teach, and enable lay people for ministry. Everything we do here is to empower people to discover their spiritual gifts and use them in ministry.

Helping People Identify Their Gifts

Empowering Pastors invite members' participation in the life of the church in such a way that they will discover their gifts. They give people permission to be and do what God has gifted them to do and be, rather than pressuring them into created positions.

I preach sermons geared to what they can do. I say to my congregation, "The same power that is at work in me is at work in you." When you start talking about their gifts, they are intrigued by the thought and don't run from it. Recently I preached a sermon on finding our gifts. "If you don't know what your gifts are," I said, "I have a test that you can take."

I do a lot of training, both for leaders and members, to help them discover and use their gifts. My advice to a minister who wants to grow in effectiveness is, "Encourage ministry to grow up from below, out of the congregation's gifts and concerns. Don't worry if you're not doing everything."

In orientation class I stress self-development and use a self-inventory in which people answer, What am I good at? What do I enjoy? What am I not good at? What do I not enjoy? Then we urge people to use the things that they are good at and work at the ones they would like to be good at.

Empowering Pastors help people discover their gifts by convincing them that they can do more than they realize. The pastor of a midsized congregation tells how he does this. "I encourage people to do more than they think they can do. I tell them that I believe they can do it. And I assure them that I will help them if they get over their head, and will get them in touch with resources. I believe in them, assess what skills they have, and encourage them only if I believe they can do it."

Another pastor describes how he helps people grow by taking small, achievable steps toward developing their gifts. "We try to involve those who are not confident about their ability. For example, we may ask someone who would be afraid to speak to stand up and say something at a fellowship dinner. Later that person may be ready to assist in worship."

Affirming People's Gifts

Pastors affirm the gifts that members demonstrate. Thus, they help people grow in the recognition and development of their gifts. Often people are unaware of the gifts they possess until someone tells them. "You have a gift of hospitality." Or "You have a gift of friendship that makes a big difference in our congregation." Or "You have a gift of discernment that keeps helping us know what issues we need to face." "Thank you for the gift of music that you so faithfully give to our congregation. You are a blessing to many of us." Such affirmations of gifts and of selfless service can open new vistas to members of a congregation and encourage them to use those gifts more freely. The pastor of a church with fewer than three hundred members shares his secret of encouraging growth.

Affirmation has a tremendous power. Many of our people have significant professional abilities. But I find when they walk into the church they have a real sense of inadequacy, not about their professional abilities, but concerning faith and scripture. So I do a lot of listening for anything I can honestly pass on to them as a stroke that affirms what God has done in their lives. I work hard at affirmation.

For example, we have a Logos program.[6] It has really flourished, and gives a wonderful place to involve adults in using their particular gifts. The teachers of our third- and fourth-grade groups had dropped out of the church in the early seventies. Two years ago they came back to the church on reaffirmation of their faith. They see themselves as baby Christians who don't know a lot. So every opportunity I get, I pass along to them the affirmation I have heard from parents of the children they teach. I not only tell them what the children have told their parents. I also say, "God is using you to impact the lives of these children."

Two other pastors make the same point:

My biggest challenge is remembering to express gratitude to people for all they do. We ministers are too prone to complain about what's wrong with the church. Yet the reality is that many, many people make great sacrifices for the sake of Christ's church. I'm becoming more intentional about writing thank-you notes, expressing appreciation from the pulpit, and so forth.

My top spiritual gift is encouragement and admonishment. I believe my strongest gift is encouraging people in their work and walk.

Channeling Gifts into Service

In spite of time limitations and preoccupation with other responsibilities, baby boomers, young people, and young adults are eager to be of service in ways that make a genuine difference to others. Empowering Pastors ensure that gifts of members are channeled into meaningful service. To be of service is an important need for many in our time.

Gifts that have been identified and encouraged will be developed in the life of the church only when members have opportunities to use them. Empowering Pastors find ways to channel members' gifts into meaningful service. Doing so takes different approaches in small and large congregations. In the former it can be done informally, provided the pastor or an assigned member consistently and persistently gives that linkage a high priority. In a large church some more formal mechanism needs to be put in place or members will be lost in the shuffle.

A pastor of a medium-sized church in a small university town sees the identifying of gifts as of prime importance. He says, "In a university community like this, folks are talented. We allow them to use their gifts in their field and don't have to educate them first. So identifying gifts is important. Folks know one another fairly well, so I have called on others to help identify those gifts. I consult with them when appointments are to be made or committees to be formed."

Another pastor who has served a series of small congregations in remote areas tells how he involves people in the use of their gifts.

My gift is probably to work with volunteers who know what they are doing, under the guidance of the Holy Spirit! We have served high-turnover congregations. We cannot wait for persons to volunteer. We have to urge them. We have been fortunate to have had seven major building projects in different congregations. These gave people a chance to put their physical as well as spiritual talents to work.

In the small churches where I have worked, volunteer labor has been the only labor available. Theologically, the church is the body of Christ, and practically, we put that into practice. I also work extra time with the members.

When you find someone with a talent, you keep it in the back of your mind. Sometime later, when you need something done, you call on the person with a needed talent to do it. One time a man asked me to call on him if we needed something built. I got back to him and he built panels that sit in front of the choir. We are blessed with people who know how to do things.

A third pastor of a small church, who also serves as consultant to a number of rural congregations, gives his advice:

In rural America or in small rural churches, "program" is a bad word. Instead, we work with "projects," which have a terminus. Empowerment in small churches and communities comes by identifying a project and finding people to do it. I may translate a program into fifteen projects, out of which only one would fly. When it does, I touch somebody's skill, need, or interest and get them involved in carrying it out. They are then tested in project after project, and are empowered. People who successfully complete several projects then are ready to serve in policy making and finally are ready for a position in the community.

Here is a good illustration of the principle of psychological success. As defined by psychologist Kurt Lewin, people will feel successful (1) when they choose their own goals, (2) when they feel their goals are challenging and meaningfully related both to their self-concept and to the goals of the organization, (3) when the means of reaching them have been self-determined, and (4) when they achieve the goals.[7] By taking small, achievable steps, members gain increasing confidence in their ability to take another step. This can be a powerful principle for empowering members when applied to everything they are asked to do in the life of the church.

Following Up

As we have suggested, matching gifts to opportunities for service requires someone's persistent attention. Without it nothing will happen. In small or medium-sized congregations pastors often play an important role in helping it to happen because they know both the members and the needs for service. The pastor of a small congregation in a large city describes how he identifies talent and channels it into the service of the church.

I observe people and get a sense of who they are, what they are about, what their skills may be, and what they care about. I try to enlarge the recruitment process that takes place in the church. I am constantly going through the directory with committees, asking them what about this person or that person. It may be a new member or someone who has been hiding in the corners. It is somewhat like scraping the bowl to get all the cookie batter into the oven. We look especially for people who are not in the stream of things. We explore the gifts they might contribute if they were asked. I use the membership list as a crutch, recognizing that I too am blind and make assumptions about who is available and who is not. I try to look at the directory with new eyes every time I do it.

Because of a sociological shift, volunteers have dried up. We must change our expectations regarding volunteers. People are more skeptical about taking an open-ended position. But people are always willing to do something specific. So we have developed an assignment sheet that is the essence of simplicity. We ask our committees to write up an assignment for everything they want done with specifics about what and when, and so forth. The wizardry is in the process, not in the form. Committees are very resistant to doing it, so I have developed a hand-drawn diagram of an hourglass. It charts the process of getting a job done. Dreams and goals and objectives are in the top of the glass. Results are in the bottom. The bottleneck is that the job needs to be stated very specifically. Until that is done, nothing is going to happen.

Another pastor describes his key role.

People need the pastor's endorsement, and it has to be public. Sometimes the pastor has to be an advocate for someone. In one church, we needed to do something about the money situation. I asked who in the congregation had the imagination to develop a feasible plan to deal with our need for money. They mentioned John. But they were not sure they wanted him to do the job. He had just been divorced and was involved in big business. When I talked to John he had a fantastic vision of what could be done. So I went to the natural leaders of the congregation and convinced them that they should let John do it. I plant a lot of seeds and cultivate them. Some of them take hold and grow.

In a slightly larger congregation the pastor has found a way to organize a recruitment process that matches the gifts of members with needs to be met.

We have a member who is a specialist in volunteer work. She has just gone off the session. She has helped us write job descriptions for every task in the church. This includes a very specific description of the task to be done, the amount of time expected, the beginning and ending dates, and the accountabilities of the assignment. So when people volunteer, we can give them a very specific assignment. We have just hired a part-time volunteer coordinator who is developing a support structure for our volunteers.

We have volunteers who clean the pews after church on Sunday so we won't have to hire someone to do that. Volunteers care for different parts of our garden so we don't have to hire a gardener. Volunteers come to the church between nine and ten every night to lock up the church. That way the church can be open during the day for people to meditate and use its facilities but is locked at night so the facilities will not be abused.

In my D.Min. I researched and wrote a curriculum for lay training. We get every person in leadership to take the course, which includes a theological base for lay ministry, use of the spiritual gifts inventory, and discussion of how people can use their gifts.

Large congregations may employ a part-time or full-time coordinator of volunteer ministries. Congregations with more limited financial resources have successfully used volunteers as "connectors" or coordinators. They arrange for new members to be interviewed regarding their gifts and preferences for service. A computer record of their responses can provide a ready access to information. Periodically each committee chair receives a printout with the names of people who have indicated an interest in serving in some way related to that committee's responsibility. In addition, whenever there is a task to be done, committee chairs can go to the data bank for names of persons to contact. The key is to find someone who is willing to spend the time to keep this process going.

Pastors who want to deal more responsibly with gifts of their members will find help in Marlene Wilson's *How to Mobilize Church Volunteers*. A word of warning! It is very important in setting up such a program to make certain there is adequate follow-up. If members volunteer to serve and are ignored, the process may do more harm than good. Instead of connecting volunteers with tasks, it will discourage future offers of service.

How does a pastor grow in effectiveness? By increasingly learning to accept people as they are and where they are in their spiritual journeys. By recognizing their potential and encouraging them to grow toward being all God wants them to be. By growing in the capacity to love and trust God's people: believing in them will bring out the best in them. By identifying gifts, developing them, and channeling them into meaningful service. All this takes strong, caring leadership.

4

LEADING POWERFULLY AS SERVANTS

Whoever wants to be first must be last of all and servant of all.
—Mark 9:35

You address me as "Teacher" and "Master," and rightly so. That is what I am. So if I, the Master and Teacher, washed your feet, you must now wash each other's feet. I've laid down a pattern for you.
—John 13:12–15, TM

We have already shown that pastors empower people. They help them find meaning for living and create a climate in which people feel free to grow. Now we see that Empowering Pastors also empower congregations. They do this by being strong servant leaders. This is another crucial key that unlocks the door to their effectiveness. They lead in order to serve the deep needs of their constituencies. They awaken members' understanding of what God intends the church to be and inspire them to join in mutual discovery of God's unique vision for their particular congregation. Then they involve them in full partnership to make those dreams come true. That kind of servant leadership empowers congregations.

Jim Jones has a deep personal faith commitment. He shares this with others on staff and in the congregation in such a vibrant way that many within the church are able to share their faith in dynamic service. His leadership in worship, preaching, teaching, and informal contacts helps many people find meaning for living. He clearly relates biblical truths to issues people face because he knows his people and cares so deeply. His thoughts are expressed in ways that are understandable for all individuals and groups. His personal life generates enthusiasm for the gospel. Officers study together. Jim plays an important role in providing educational opportunities for members and regular retreat experiences for families and others.

He inspires the congregation to grow into a caring community by his own deep and caring love. I know of people with cancer, job loss, and so forth, who have been helped through his personal care. They have continued to care for others out of the strength they have found in this fellowship. His own authenticity is contagious. Others are able to reach out beyond themselves and beyond the congregation in service.

Jim knows how to be a collaborator and leader. One of his strengths is his ability to share leadership. He recently supported the development of their staff with a co-pastor. Here is one church in which a co-pastorate strengthens the whole work of the local church as well as the presbytery. With the extended weekly staff meetings and small-group program that he developed, the church makes creative use of diversity and avoids unhealthy conflicts by facing conflicts and enabling people to serve God more effectively through their diversity.

This description was written by the nominator of an Empowering Pastor who serves a congregation of about three thousand members. But it is a beautiful description of other Empowering Pastors who give leadership to congregations both large and small.

OUR CALL TO SERVANT LEADERSHIP

Jesus made it very clear that all of us are called to servant ministry. He demonstrated this by taking basin and towel. Three of the four Gospels teach our servanthood. Mark tells us: "They came to Capernaum. When he was safe at home, he asked them, 'What were you discussing on the road?' The silence was deafening—they had been arguing with one another over who among them was greatest. He sat down and summoned the Twelve. 'So you want first place? Then take the last place. Be the servant of all' " (Mark 9:31–35, TM). But there are those who shy away from the concept of ministry as servanthood because it seems to imply exercising weak leadership or none at all. They see it as taking little or no initiative and meekly letting others shape the life of the church while they simply respond. But effective pastors are not doormats. They are vigorous servant leaders. They lead in order to empower people and the congregations they serve.

As Robert Greenleaf defines it in *Servant Leadership,* a servant leader is one who leads in order to serve, who serves the highest priority needs of others, and who prizes the contributions of each individual to the whole. He further develops his concept of servant leadership in his book by that title. Greenleaf was for many years director of management research for AT&T and held teaching positions at Dartmouth and Harvard universities. He was a consultant for Ohio University, M.I.T., Ford Foundation, Brookings Institution, and many others. His book, which grows out of many years of management consulting, was written for leaders in business, foundations, and community organizations, not especially for pastors and church members. But it speaks to us also.

Greenleaf says his idea of the servant as leader came from a book by Herman Hesse, *Journey to the East.* A band of men on a mythical journey are accompanied by a servant named Leo. Leo "does their menial chores, but . . . also sustains them with his spirit and his song. He is a person of extraordinary presence. All goes well until Leo disappears. Then the group falls into disarray and the journey is abandoned. They cannot make it without the servant Leo." Years later a member of the party becomes a member of the order that sponsored the journey. Only then does he discover that Leo, the servant, is in reality "the titular head of the order, its guiding spirit, a great and noble *leader*."[1] Says Greenleaf:

> The servant-leader is servant first—as Leo was portrayed. It begins with the natural feeling that one wants to serve, to serve *first*. Then conscious choice brings one to aspire to lead. That person is sharply different from one who is *leader* first, perhaps because of the need to assuage an unusual power drive or to acquire material possessions. For such it will be a later choice to serve—after leadership is established. The leader-first and the servant-first are two extreme types. Between them there are shadings and blends that are part of the infinite variety of human nature.
>
> The difference manifests itself in the care taken by the servant-first to make sure that other people's highest priority needs are being served. The best test, and difficult to administer, is: Do those served grow as persons? Do they, *while being served*, become healthier, wiser, freer, more autonomous, more likely themselves to become servants?[2]

In other words, servant pastors lead in such a way that members of their congregations and the churches themselves are healthier, wiser, freer, more autonomous and more likely themselves to become servants. One of the Empowering Pastors exemplifies servant leadership when he says,

> Like every pastor I have a certain amount of ego invested in my work, but I don't satisfy my ego needs by being possessive of the prerogatives of ministry. I am happy for others to do things and get the credit. When I left my last church the people there said, "We will miss you but we are not worried. We know how to be the church without you." They couldn't have built me a monument that was any more what I would have hoped and dreamed for!

THE PASTOR'S CRUCIAL ROLE

Although leadership in a congregation is exercised by many others besides the pastor, the style of a pastor's leadership is crucial. It either energizes or debilitates the congregation. It either inspires others to take leadership or it discourages them from doing so.

Looked at from a leadership perspective, perhaps the institution in society that most closely parallels the church is the school. In many ways the role of a pastor combines in one person the kinds of demands made upon both principal and teacher. The preaching and teaching responsibilities of pastors parallel those of teachers. A pastor's leadership demands are like those of a principal. Both must inspire and guide fellow professionals. And, like principals, pastors must be responsive to the constituencies they serve. Both must respond effectively to boards that have been chosen from those constituencies. Ultimately those boards and constituencies can exercise power over their employment. So we turn again to the major study of effective schools referred to in chapter 3. We see in the role of the principal a parallel with the kind of leadership a pastor needs to provide. "A school's effectiveness in the promotion of student learning was found to be the product of a building-wide, unified effort which depended upon the exercise of leadership. Most often research depicted the building principal as the key person providing leadership to the school."[3]

Pastors exercise strong servant leadership in the life of a congregation by inspiring commitment to a shared vision, marshaling the diverse resources of its membership in living out that vision, actively cultivating partnership with its leaders, and training them for their responsibilities. Our study finds that Empowering Pastors compared with Other Pastors are much more likely to:

1. See new possibilities for the future and effectively communicate that vision to others.
2. Make creative use of diversity.
3. Inspire congregations to grow as caring communities and in reaching out beyond themselves in service to the world.
4. Actively share power and accountability with church officers and staff.

Inspiring a Shared Vision

Most theories of leadership emphasize the importance of articulating a compelling vision to which followers can commit themselves. Greenleaf puts it this way:

> A mark of leaders . . . is that they are better than most at pointing the direction. As long as one is leading, one always has a goal. It may be a goal arrived at by group consensus, or the leader, acting on inspiration, may simply have said, "Let's go this way." But the leader always knows what it is and can articulate it for any who are unsure. By clearly stating and restating the goal the leader gives certainty and purpose to others who may have difficulty in achieving it for themselves.
>
> The word *goal* is used here in the special sense of the overarching purpose, the big dream, the visionary concept, the ultimate consummation which one approaches but never really achieves. . . . It is so stated that it excites the imagination and challenges people to work for something they do not yet know how to do, something they can be proud of as they move toward it.[4]

Without vision, congregations wither and members drift away. The remnant shifts into a survival mode and desperately clings to life. With a revived vision, congregations come to life again. Renewed vitality comes when disillusioned or jaded members rediscover what God means the church to be; when they become excited about new possibilities for their own congregation. Among Empowering Pastors we found innumerable illustrations of this. The pastor of a one-hundred-member congregation in a small city was nominated as an effective pastor with these words: "She involves the congregation in visioning what God can do through their ministry. She has helped them face their survival-mentality existence and choose to do more for Christ's sake. She has had the ability to analyze underlying issues, preach to challenge, affirm gifts of individuals and the congregation, and lovingly confront difficult people." Of her own ministry she reports: "I went into the situation believing God could transform not only individual lives but a whole congregation, to bring them from depression and paralysis to joy and life. I preached this expectation and acted on it and watched God at work through me."

The pastor of a 500-member congregation in a large city describes his biggest challenge in the past five years as

taking a dead, apathetic congregation with poor self-esteem and helping them to see that they were really a great group of people with unlimited potential to make a difference for Christ and themselves. I did this by helping them achieve little victories followed by more successes and new ministries such as Habitat, Adult International, Mission Outreach to Latvia, and so forth.

A congregation in a small city doubled from 150 members to 300 members. Under the pastor's leadership the church moved from a crowded downtown location to a new bulding about two miles away. "When I arrived here," the pastor says, "the congregation was extremely dispirited, losing members. I have been able to instill a certain amount of pride in the church, and have enabled the leaders to exercise their gifts in building up and strengthening the overall life of the congregation."

The pastor of a 70-member rural congregation in the Midwest has revitalized a dying congregation. It had experienced a series of pastoral changes over a period of years and could now afford only half-time pastoral service. Her nominator tells us,

Newly ordained, Jennifer Jones accepted this call and has done an exemplary job. The congregation has ceased its membership decline. New younger couples and children have been added. A church school has been started after many years of no church school. A music series is sponsored by the congregation for the entire community. A new elevator has been added to the building. The redevelopment that was aborted earlier seems now to be occurring with the stability of the pastoral world of Jennifer Jones.

Jones describes her ministry this way:

I have been able to help this small, rural congregation realize who they are now, and what ministries they have in a rural, declining area of our state. I have encouraged them, remained constant and helpful. I have been available to the community and active on the city council and the chamber of commerce. My biggest challenge over the past five years has been being female and all that means in this denomination. I am in a predominantly Roman Catholic town (85 percent). I have consciously been available; worked publicly in the town; lived an open, highly visible, high-profile life; visited a lot, calling on everyone regardless of denomination. I have been active in the county with Hospice and on economic development. I send letters to the editor of the small-town newspaper.

Visioning What the Church Is Called to Be and Do

There are two dimensions to dreams that awaken the response of officers and members alike. First is a vision of what the church of Jesus Christ is called to be and do. This grows out of a pastor's deep immersion in the scriptures. As with meaning-filled preaching, compelling visions come when pastors build bridges that apply biblical truths to the challenges that the church confronts today. People need to know what it means in our time to be the body of Christ and to be the people of God moving toward the promised land. We live in a world of alienation. Forces of contemporary life reinforce our human condition of estrangement from one another, from ourselves, and from God. People need to rediscover their calling to be ministers of reconciliation. Just as Israel was called to be the suffering servant of Jehovah, so is the church called to be the suffering servant in our world.

We live in a society that overemphasizes individualism and competition. People desperately need to discover communities of mutual support. Lives of countless people are gripped by hopeless ennui. Many feel their lives cannot really count for anything against the odds of powerful political, social, and economic systems. They need a sense of mission that challenges them to reach out to others and helps them discover how they can make a difference right where they are.

The pastor of a small congregation is known for a ministry that empowers lay leadership. He has led his congregation from dependence on denominational funding to full self-support. His leadership has resulted in high-caliber activities in the denomination's peacemaking program. This pastor explains how this has happened: "The church in mission, and the reasons for that mission approach have been carefully thought out by this congregation. For over ten years we have worked together to put this theology and philosophy to work."

The commitment of Empowering Pastors to partnership in ministry is deeply rooted in their theological convictions. Many of them would affirm the following composite statement:

> Both congregation and pastor here believe in the priesthood of all believers. They work at shared responsibility for ministry. Mutuality of ministry is important to me. Ministry is not something that I own, but something that I share with the whole people of God. It is given to the whole church.
>
> I believe the church is the body of Christ. Not everyone is a hand, or a foot, but each has a particular part to play in the body. I believe strongly in ordination to function. I am ordained to be a significant part of a team of people in a local community to do the work of the Lord. I am not above or better than others. They have gifts they are called to use. I also have particular gifts. My calling is to use them to lead a congregation in a full-time position. I have gifts of proclamation and counseling, and I see myself as pastoring and teaching. Those are significant parts of my work. This is blended with a general love for people.
>
> To me, Jesus' story of washing the disciples' feet is a guide to what the pastorate is all about. Equipping the saints for the work of ministry, helping people prepare for the work of ministry, is washing the disciples' feet.

Ministry is not confined to the church. It is not just for the sake of the institution. Ministry is within the fellowship but is also a function of the fellowship to the world. The church does not exist for itself, but for the community. We are to care about neighbors and about society, the small bits of society and the larger systems. Ministry is done in the world by members of the church in places where they work and play. I am a leader in helping them do that.

The Unique Calling of a Particular Congregation

The second essential dimension to awakening a common vision is to paint a compelling picture of the unique calling of a particular church. This clarion call helps a congregation to believe in themselves as God's people and to see what this means in specific terms within their own life and mission context. The pastor often takes the lead in helping a congregation to discover its unique mission. But wherever the initiative lies, this vision needs to be shared alike by pastor, key members, and officers of the congregation.

An Empowering Pastor of a large suburban congregation tells how he led them in an extended study of the book of Acts. They had one question before them: What does the early church tell us about our present calling to be the church? He recalls, "One thing that was very impressive to us was that what drew people to the New Testament church was not a lot of doctrine or doubt, but a desire to have a personal relationship with God. They had different ways of understanding it, and people were at different points with it. But what they had in common was that they wanted that relationship to grow."

Out of this study there emerged a strong cohesive sense of direction for the life of the congregation. Members committed themselves to study, share, and serve. Through study they continued to seek the relevance of the good news for their lives. Through sharing they sought to bear one another's burdens within the fellowship and to encourage every member to become a tither. Serving expressed itself in an enthusiastic reaching out in ministry to the world around them.[5]

Empowering Pastors compared with Other Pastors are more effective in assessing situations. Because they listen empathetically, they are able to sense the deep, hidden longings of their parishioners. In response to those longings they dare to dream. They discover what others are dreaming and dream with them. They are somehow able to communicate those dreams and to inspire people to dream with them. Out of fifteen skill ratings, the two top ratings lay leaders give to their Empowering Pastors are on "visioning" and communicating. The Empowering Pastors' self-ratings on these two dimensions are also significantly higher than ratings of Other Pastors.

Balancing Journeys Inward and Journeys Outward

Visions that empower combine some balance between the nurturing of the body of Christ and the outreach of that body. On the one hand, members are called to care deeply for one another and to learn how they can express that caring. On the other hand, they need to catch the vision of caring deeply for those who are not a part of the intimate koinonia of the church. A vision that emphasizes one to the exclusion of the other impairs the full health of the body. A body that gives without receiving loses its vitality. As in Death Valley, the water all runs out. What remains is arid desert. A body that receives without giving is like the Dead Sea. It can sustain no life within it.

Empowering Pastors challenge their members to support and nurture one another and to reach out to others. They are much more likely than Other Pastors to give high ratings to themselves on "inspires congregation to grow into a caring community" and on "inspires members to reach out beyond the congregation in service to others." Empowering Lay Leaders join in giving their pastors higher ratings on these two dimensions of ministry. Also, 68 percent of Empowering Pastors compared with 41 percent of Other Pastors give themselves a high rating on "inspires members to reach out beyond the congregation in sharing the good news."

Celebrating Diversity and Inspiring Unity

To serve the highest priority needs of others requires a creative use of diversity. Each member of a congregation is a unique individual with a distinctive background, set of interests, and reasons for being part of the church. Even in congregations that appear to be homogeneous, people differ in personality, age, marital status, and family composition. They vary in education, occupation, and lifestyle. Their perceived needs, commitments, and stages of faith development are different. Those needs can only be met by responsiveness to their differences, not only in personal contacts with the pastor but also in congregational activities and small-group experiences.

The Church Growth Movement pioneered by Donald McGavran tells us that churches grow when they seek "our kind of people." When there are different constituencies in a community, they advocate outreach that focuses on one of them, while remaining open to others that may come. This may be valid with some denominations, but mainline congregations tend to be more diverse than other voluntary organizations. To be healthy they must deal creatively with diversity. Pastors need to take the lead in helping them do so.

In our study of churches that attract and keep active church members—bonding churches—we found that in mainline congregations it is more important to emphasize diversity than homogeneity. Mainline churches that are growing seek in tangible ways to be responsive to diverse people. Jackson Carroll concludes from a review of research on mainline denominations that congregations that do not seek to meet the needs of their multiple constituencies "typically have lost members and have had declining participation."[6]

Our current study reinforces this finding. Sixty-six percent of Empowering Pastors compared with only 36 percent of Other Pastors rate themselves high on "makes creative use of diversity." In fact, self-ratings on this item by pastors in these two groups have a greater difference than ratings on any of the other fourteen statements describing the way pastors carry out their ministry. Lay leaders' ratings of their pastors on this item also have the greatest difference. Fifty-eight percent of Empowering Lay Leaders give high ratings to their pastors, compared with 44 percent of Other Lay Leaders.

Developing Tolerance for Theological Diversity

Empowering Pastors are more likely than Other Pastors to say that their ideal congregation would have a high tolerance for theological diversity. Both Empowering Pastors and Empowering Lay Leaders are more likely to say that their congregation does have such tolerance for theological diversity. However, to deal successfully with diversity a congregation needs an overarching sense of unity that bonds all the differences together in a common purpose. Without such unity, diversity can lead to disintegration of the fellowship or destructive conflict. When Paul uses the image of the body of Christ to describe the church, he does so to focus on the importance of unity in Christ. He assumes diversity and admonishes his readers to use that diversity in the service of the head of the body. Thus, theological diversity is not completely open-ended. Among Empowering Pastors it coalesces around a strong commitment to Jesus Christ as Savior and Lord and around a biblically based faith. We found this, for example, in a congregation that has grown from twelve hundred to two thousand members in nine years. The pastor says most of that growth has come from baby boomers.

> We are evangelical in spirit and our emphasis is on scripture. But our congregation is very diverse. Tolerance and diversity are very important to us here. Everyone, staff and members, believes that Jesus is Lord and Savior. Apart from that there is great diversity. There are families and a large number of singles and divorced people. We have closeted gays and lesbians, because they know that the pastors care for them deeply. There are members of Presbyterian Layman [a right-wing movement, socially, politically, and theologically] and people who subscribe to *Presbyterian Survey* [a mainstream publication]. And we celebrate that diversity.

Another congregation has grown from five hundred members to over fifteen hundred in ten years. Its pastor began his ministry there with a strong commitment to a breadth of ministry that would cover the diverse needs of all who might come. He has built the unity of the congregation upon biblical preaching and teaching and upon a Christ-centered ministry. Beyond that, however, the congregation welcomes many theological perspectives, with freedom for liberal and conservative points of view. There is a small group of charismatics in the church.

Uniting Diversity through Visioning

When asked what advice he would give to a pastor who wanted to grow in effectiveness, another pastor said, "Seek a vision for yourself and your congregation. Listen to others, learn their needs, their hopes, and their dreams. Be in prayer. Catch God's vision and stick to it." He shared his own experience.

This was a splintered congregation of very strong personalities that needed an individual who would restore community, provide vision, and build a team staff. It had many excellent but competing programs. For lack of a common vision they were working against and not with one another. I first earned their trust. I gave a common direction. I gave firm and persistent leadership, constructively challenging those who were destructive. I empowered people to do things by not controlling every detail, and by letting others creatively work as a part of the whole body, within the common vision.

This pastor, like others who empower congregations, was able to encourage and celebrate diversity and inspire commitment to a compelling unifying vision. Beyond that, he knew how to lead strong lay leaders into the development of shared leadership.

SHARING POWER WITH OTHERS

An important way in which effective pastors empower their congregations is by sharing power as partners. Ninety-four percent of Empowering Pastors compared with 79 percent of Other Pastors give themselves top ratings in sharing power and accountability with church officers and staff. This is a higher rating than on any other characteristic except "helps people find meaning for living."

In interviews, Empowering Pastors communicate a sense of liberation, purposefulness, and accomplishment because they are empowering others. They do not feel that they need to carry the load of ministry themselves but that ministry is carried on more effectively by others whom they have helped empower. The pastor of a small church says,

> I believe in the work of other people. I deliberately trust others with responsibility. Empowerment has something to do with the way I understand the church. I would not be content with a church where people just want to be there and sing hymns. Nor with a church that is only concerned with what it is accomplishing. What I want is to empower people for both being and doing. That takes some different skills than in a strictly task-oriented organization.
>
> In offering leadership to the session, I recognize that people in a leadership position as volunteers are there to express some sense of who they are, as well as to get things done. So it is important to give air time for people to vent their frustration with the way things are in the world, or to let them dream of things not attached to a task. Then when people decide to do something, I find practical ways to help them get it done. I don't have a heavy agenda for achievement in the church, so I am not driven.

Fashioning Triple Yokes

One of the greatest temptations of the pastoral ministry is to operate as a lone ranger. The responsibility we carry for interpreting the Word of God and for administering the sacraments exerts a subtle pressure on us to assume that we have the answers for every situation. We would never consciously affirm that, but we can easily fall into that trap without realizing what we are doing. Moses walked closely with God but he had to learn to share his ministry with others. We have no less a need for shared power than did Moses. When church officers and members share in the important planning and decision making of the church, they experience and exercise power in their lives. When they are partners in ministry, the congregation is empowered.

To use another figure of speech, we need to fashion triple yokes. Jesus said, "My yoke is easy and my burden is light." The image, of course, is of a pair of oxen bound together with a double yoke. Because the double yoke fits us perfectly, our yoke is easy to bear. And because our Lord is pulling the burden with us, our burden is light. Burnout is often the product of single-yoke ministries. Pastoral ministry can be a very heavy load indeed if we carry it alone. Our ministry is not ours, it is our Lord's ministry. God pulls the load with us. However, a pastor's partnership is not with God alone. Dual yokes will not do. We are partners in ministry with all God's people. So we need to consciously fashion triple yokes that bind us together in a joint ministry: Christ at the center, we on one side, and God's people on the other. Together with our Lord and with members of our congregations we exercise our ministries. Our triple yoke is easier than a double yoke and our burden is much lighter. We carry the load together.

There are of course different ways in which congregations can learn to share power. Some will be more appropriate in one situation than another. Most of the members in some congregations may be employed in positions where they are given little authority to make decisions. They expect to be told what to do. In their churches they may find it quite challenging to respond to the expectation that they will share ministry with the pastor. There are also congregations that have always lived under the rule of an authoritarian pastor. Those who remain may be content to passively expect to be told what to do. Or they may be eager to take more responsibility and need only to learn how. The transition to shared leadership in such congregations may prove difficult. It will take time, but the results will be rewarding. The pastor of a large congregation in a large city described how he worked at such a transition. "I followed the founding minister of the church, who served the congregation for over thirty years. He ran a one-person operation and the church had a very small staff. I welcomed him to assist in funerals and weddings and special events. I led the church through a two-year mission study, and worked patiently till they were ready to expand their view and add staff."

WAYS TO GROW TOWARD
GREATER COLLEGIALITY

"I do want to share power as a full partner with lay leaders and with staff," you say, "but how, specifically, do I do it?" Empowering Pastors from large and small churches have answers for you. As we reflect on what they say, we find at least nine ways to grow toward greater collegiality.

Keep Your Feelings Clearly Focused

Progress toward collegiality must begin with you. Your own attitudes will make a difference. Begin by committing yourself to a constant quest for ways to share power with your staff and lay leaders. Use whatever creativity and perseverance you can muster to build an active partnership.

Many pastors and church leaders hoard their power. Empowering Pastors have learned to share power. To rewrite scripture: One who protects power loses it. One who shares power finds it. Put that on your wall. Remind yourself of it.

It is not easy to share power with others. It takes a high level of personal security to let others share the limelight. Most of us tend to feel that if we want anything done right we had better do it ourselves. One must also be willing to risk failure if a colleague drops the ball. The pastors comment:

Be willing to "let go" so others can blossom.

I learned long ago there's no limit to the good that can be done if you don't care who gets the credit. I try to encourage and help and stay out of the way of good ideas.

Be able to admit you might be wrong!

One key is learning you don't have all the answers and that it's all right to acknowledge that to your church officers. For the most part they want to share ministry with you if they are helped to do so.

Call Capable Colleagues

An important mark of strong and capable leaders is the capacity to select outstanding colleagues who have strengths that complement their shortcomings. This applies to large churches with multiple staffs where pastors usually have a determinative voice in selecting professional colleagues. It applies to small churches without staff. In both cases pastors usually have an important role in recruiting lay leadership from the congregation. Yielding to the temptation to bypass strong leaders with great abilities because they threaten the pastor only weakens the congregation. A small church pastor tells us that "empowering is to approach people with respect, to recognize their gifts, and to value what they can offer. It involves selecting good leaders."

In multiple-staff situations senior pastors can fall into traps at two extremes of leadership. On the one hand, they can leave other staff members to their own devices without guidance or coordination. On the other, they can attempt to direct their every move. In between these poles is the ideal of coordinated interdependence. The Empowering Pastor of a very large church comments on this. "Our staff is not an extension of my ministry. Each is pursuing his or her specialty. I do not have my thumb in anyone's ministry. I don't know what's happening in the church. I bring self-starters here. They come here to practice their specialty, and the executive committee holds them responsible."

Prepare Colleagues

If we are serious about collegiality with church officers, teachers, and staff, we need to take time to explain their responsibilities and to prepare them for their tasks. Confidence and creativity come to those who know what to do and how to do it. Teach them, give them freedom, and watch them go!

The pastor of a very large suburban congregation believes in the important role that lay officers of the congregation play in sharing responsibility for ministry within the congregation. Because he believes that the minister is "part of a larger team of elders," he takes very seriously his obligation to prepare them for their responsibilities.

> I hold a high view of ordination. Elders are particularly called by God. They need to understand the positions to which they are called and to covenant to fulfill their responsibilities. Persons are gifted to do particular tasks. They are given responsibility after they are appropriately trained. Empowerment of elders comes when they are called, trained, and given responsibility. Education is an incredibly important part of our understanding of the church. When people are called to particular areas of service in our congregation, we spend time training them and working with them. Then they are given responsibility.
>
> We have five principal staffs. Our major job is to disciple persons so that they are able to fulfill their responsibilities. We have clear position descriptions for all our boards, committees, and subcommittees. We have annual retreats. These include spiritual times of worship, but their primary purpose is to say, "This is what we are called to do. Here is our structure. How does it need to be changed or modified in order to do what we are called to do? And so forth." So we add or consolidate or eliminate committees.

A pastoral counselor who also serves as part-time pastor is convinced that the key to empowerment is to train members of his very small congregation.

> I understand myself as the senior minister and my congregation as a congregation of ministers. My role is equipping them to do the functions of ministry that we are all a part of. I teach courses on how to minister in the context of grief, using Kubler-Ross's stages and beyond. I teach how to be a good listener using Carl Rogers's concepts of client-centered therapy. In addition they learn the common visitation skills for hospital and community visitation. I rely on the presbytery to teach skills related to the Book of Order, working with committees, and so forth.

Another pastor shares his approach to preparing his members for their tasks in the church.

> We don't do a lot of formal stuff. We do have officer training and encourage teachers. We use team teaching where people can learn from each other. We encourage members to take advantage of presbytery opportunities. I offer at least one disciplined in-depth Bible study a year. Others in the congregation are willing to share talents in areas of their education or experience and to help others use their talents. The principal of the high school, the superintendent of schools, and faculty in the college of education are members of the church. We use them in leadership education. We have a Lenten Soup-and-Study program in which lay people handle the program.

Structure Opportunities for Teamwork

Collegiality does not happen without communication. Structure your life as a board (in a small church) or as board and staff (in a large church) to make certain that there is a free flow of communication. Communicate! Communicate! Communicate! Plan together. Set goals together. Carefully and constantly coordinate your individual responsibilities. An Empowering Pastor of a large church involves leaders in a rigorous process of weekly communication.

> My job is to empower the staff and the elders. Every Tuesday morning at six-thirty the elders and staff meet together for one hour. In the first half hour, whoever is preaching the following week gives the sermon. Elders and staff critique the sermon. So the sermons are the collective mind of elders and staff. At first the elders were hesitant to do this, but when I started using what they gave me, they were more free to do so. When we disagree on something, we talk it through. They are very bright people. Many times they have saved my hide. Usually they are right.
>
> Following that meeting, the senior staff of fourteen people meet together to plan the week. Everyone participates in organizing what needs to be done and in delegating responsibility for doing it.

Call Clear Signals; Then Trust Colleagues

Anyone who watches football is well aware that a winning team depends upon clear signals. Each signal sets in motion a carefully orchestrated, complex series of moves by linemen and backs. When opponents carry the ball, home crowds sometimes raise the stadium noise level so signals will be drowned out. As in football, all players in our congregational teams need to know what to expect. Policies should be well defined and communicated clearly. Goals should be set. This is true for a church of any size, but the larger the church, the more important it is to organize the work of the congregation and to delegate responsibilities explicitly. Just as the quarterback is key, so also is the pastor. But quarterbacks do not always carry the ball. They give it to the particular player who is most apt to gain yardage, make the touchdown or the conversion. So Empowering Pastors allow other people to carry the ball and score touchdowns.

The principals of effective schools model many characteristics that contribute to effectiveness—in schools and elsewhere. They are assertive in their instructional role, goal and task oriented, action oriented, and well organized. They convey high expectations for students and staff, have policies that are well defined and communicated, give strong support to the teaching staff, and are adept at parent and community relations because they are gifted communicators.[7]

Know When to Let Go or Take Tough Action

There may be times when it is best to let go and fail. Timely benign neglect sometimes empowers a congregation. No one wants to see a program fall apart because some people do not follow through on their responsibilities. Pastors are particularly conscientious. So we are easily tempted to play the rescue game. When someone drops the ball, we pick it up and run with it. The play is saved, but the game is lost! Next time the pastor is expected to carry the ball.

The pastor in a small university town whose congregation has many talented professionals has designed his ministry to ensure that they take responsibility for the work that needs to be done. Early in his ministry he found that a little strategic benign neglect helped to turn a passive membership around.

I think that the personality of the pastor is important. I am not a type-A personality. For others empowerment is not developed easily. In this church I came to a situation in which two pastors had been type-A personalities who needed to be the center of attention. A new pastor needed to allow people to take responsibility. I moved in with that in mind. The presbytery asked me to come for six months and I have been here over thirty years. During the first year I allowed some programs to fail because people did not fulfill their responsibilities. From then on, they knew I was serious about letting them carry the burden.

During that first year I allowed the youth club to fail because no one had done any preparation for it. Before that the pastor had always stepped in to save it. From that point on, folks took their responsibility more seriously.

I have learned by experience working in the church not to be threatened by other people sharing power. I have seen things come and go. The world does not collapse if somebody fails, and if somebody succeeds I can allow them to do it. I don't feel it threatens my position.

One way to empower a congregation is to say no to myself. Lay people are too smart to do something in the church that the pastor is already doing. Leave the opportunity there for it to happen. For example, the surest way to kill the effort to get people to work with a senior-high program is for the pastor to jump into the breach. We need to leave the problem there for it to be solved by other people. I help to find a solution, but do not propose myself as the solution.

From the pastor of a small congregation: "Both my present congregation and the one I served before this have strong lay leadership and are accustomed to functioning very effectively without a great deal of pastoral input. My style emphasizes enabling the ministries of others and exercising a certain amount of benign neglect when laity are capable of carrying on without me. Lots of encouragement—minimum interference." From the pastor of a large church in a small town: "I have had to learn to let people fail without bailing them out. Also I have had to let people take credit when they succeed. This has been a challenging and an enriching experience."

Sometimes getting tough at a critical point empowers a congregation. The pastor of a medium-sized church reports on one such occasion. "I trust people to want to do their best. That does not always work out. For example a couple of folks have been trying to force their wills on a certain committee. They are not open to negotiation. So finally we had to dissolve that committee and organize another committee. We had to be tough. That was not easy, but it had to be done."

Another pastor inherited a congregation with a pathology of fighting in its history. When he began his ministry there, the congregation was dominated by leaders who loved control and power. They continually fought over gaining control. The clerk of session would not even let the pastor see the books.

My predecessor broke some of that control. But I ended up standing up to various folks who were in control. I put my ministry on the line several times in doing that. When I first met with the officers, two women got into a fight (physically). I went to them and said, "This needs to be resolved. We cannot tolerate this in church." One of them left the church.

Empowering means getting bad leadership out and getting good leadership in. We needed leaders who would seek the common good. I had to step into the nominating process and say, "I don't want this person as an elder." I had to make tough but necessary decisions that would enable others who are good leaders to take their place.

I look for people who can think in terms of the common good of the congregation. And that is a difficult thing to define. On the session now we have folks who think in those terms. They seek the will of God and the best for the congregation. I have been training those folks and reinforcing those ideas about leadership.

Give Colleagues Timely Support

Think of your primary task as making it possible for others (lay leaders and staff) to be effective in their ministries. Be their support system. As head of a large denominational agency I tried always to keep an open door. Much of my time, energy, and satisfaction came in serving as consultant to anyone on the staff who wanted to see me. I also took the initiative, dropping in on them to find out how things were going. We would talk about any problems or possibilities with which they were dealing. Be a mentor to all those with whom you work. The pastor of a large church does that. "We have turned the traditional staff pyramid upside down. I am holding them up. I am their mentor and support. My job is to empower them. I tell them, 'My greatest joy is to make you succeed.' I preach only half the time, and if one of the staff sells more tapes of their sermons, I rejoice in his or her effectiveness."

To empower others, do your own planning early enough to allow others time to relate effectively to what you are doing. Some pastors plan their sermon subjects a year in advance so that others can coordinate their responsibilities for worship. One pastor speaks for them: "I prepare a sermon list about six months in advance with scripture and hymns. That way the worship leaders know how to prepare and the choir director can choose subjects for the anthems that are compatible with the worship experience."

Let Program Bubble Up

Collegiality with the whole congregation will blossom when pastor and church officers are responsive to members' initiatives. When members express a concern about some issue or offer a program suggestion, one pastor has a ready response. "Why don't you do something about it?" he replies. Then he helps them find others who have a similar concern or are ready to respond to the dream. He guides them to resources and supports them in the effort. Another pastor of a medium-sized congregation says: "I have a philosophy that impacts empowering. I never begin a new program without a lay person who is passionately caring for that program. That way, if I grow weary, the program will continue. So we have several programs that are sustained by dedicated laypersons."

Listen for Corrective Opportunities

Effective pastors seek feedback on their ministry. They encourage church officers to evaluate programs of the church. Evaluation from others makes an important contribution to collegiality. We all need a constant flow of information from people with whom we work. Being receptive reveals many ways to learn how we are doing. The best way to shut down communication is to leave the impression that one is not really open to suggestions or to criticism. This can happen even if we are subtly unreceptive. Pastors who share power voluntarily submit themselves to mutual accountability with colleagues.

A major Lutheran study found that pastors who respond to feedback from parishioners enjoy a level of accountability to their congregations that makes them more effective. They feel they are being supervised. The study concludes:

Supervised pastors . . . are more satisfied, see themselves as more effective and value the importance of their work more than unsupervised pastors. Feedback is the key idea.

All pastors receive such feedback, but one-third of the sample who say they have no supervisor are apparently screening out this feedback. They do not see the feedback as supervisory in nature. They are accountable only to themselves. Role conflict must surely exist where a pastor thinks he is only accountable to himself, whereas lay leaders, peers and judicatory leaders think they perform a supervisory role. The unearthing of accountability as an issue is one of the major contributions of the Growth in Ministry study. Accountability or supervision seems to be a key to increasing both effectiveness and satisfaction.[8]

Those pastors who believe they are supervised also believe they receive more support from their local support group; they believe that the roles of priest and preacher, enabler, teacher-visitor, and personal and spiritual development are more important; they believe they have more work freedom; they believe their co-workers are more competent, friendly and helpful; they believe they are more effective as pastors. It is possible that, where role conflict is intense, the pastor does not accept the supervisory role of his official church council and unofficial supervisory feedback from his key leaders.[9]

One of the most helpful support systems for an effective pastor is a carefully chosen parish relations committee or personnel committee. A sixty-two-year-old Empowering Pastor of a small congregation enjoys a very supportive relationship with his personnel committee. He shows his confidence in them, along with a great deal of courage and self-assurance, when he says, "I have an agreement with the personnel committee. When they feel I am not working up to steam, they will let me know, and in two months I will resign or retire. I need them to help me. I can't tell when I am losing my effectiveness. I am too busy from early morning to late at night. "

Not many of us would dare take the kind of risk this pastor takes. However, as we shall see in the next chapter, such risk taking may not be as strange as one might think. Empowering Pastors enjoy a high level of self-esteem. Without it, sharing power with colleagues would be difficult, if not impossible.

5

EMPOWERED TO
BE REAL

We refuse to wear masks and play games. We don't maneuver and manipulate behind the scenes. And we don't twist God's Word to suit ourselves. Rather, we keep everything we do and say out in the open, the whole truth on display, so that those who want to can see and judge for themselves in the presence of God.

—2 Corinthians 4:2, TM

If a motto were inscribed on the hearts of empowered pastors, it would read, "Be real." Their lives resonate the truth in Paul's words to the Corinthians. Overwhelming evidence confirms that open integrity is always the core of effectiveness. Without it ministry falls dead. Repeatedly, Empowering Pastors emphasize the importance of authenticity.

I'm real. That's my greatest asset. A minister who was playing the role of the formal pastor would be dead in the water here. I am believable; we need credibility, the same inside and outside the pulpit.

Be who you are. Authenticity is absolutely critical. Quit playing pastor games. Be real no matter what. Be as transparent and direct with your values and feelings as possible, in sermons, performance reviews, and leadership. If you believe what you preach, people notice and respond.

My background has left me with a firm commitment to be real and with a high value on integrity. Be a person first and a minister second. I am John Jones who is a minister rather than a minister who is John Jones. My ministry is an extension of me as a person. I am fortunate not to have grown up in the church because I didn't know enough not to be me.

Whatever effectiveness I have, I look to God. To whatever degree I can, I seek to be responsive to God's Spirit. In my approach to life I must be myself. I do try to be diplomatic but never try to be what others expect. I cannot pretend.

Spiritual integrity is the foundation upon which effectiveness is built. A pastor must be the same person in the pulpit, in committees, in social activities, in homes, and in the community. This is true for both Empowering Pastors and Other Pastors in our study. There is no statistically significant difference between their self-ratings on "lives with consistency, integrity, and spiritual authenticity." More than 83 percent of both groups rate themselves high on this dimension. And more than 88 percent of their lay leaders concur.

It seems that even to survive in the pastorate requires authenticity. Stephen Covey's powerful portrait of the impact of authenticity on effective interaction with others underscores why this is so.

> The real key to your influence with me is your example, your actual conduct. Your example flows naturally out of your character, or the kind of person you truly are—not what others say you are or what you may want me to think you are. It is evident in how I actually experience you.
>
> Your character is constantly radiating, communicating. From it, in the long run, I come to instinctively trust or distrust you and your efforts with me.
>
> If your life runs hot and cold, if you're both caustic and kind, and, above all, if your private performance doesn't square with your public performance, it's very hard for me to open up with you. Then, as much as I may want and even need to receive your love and influence, I don't feel safe enough to expose my opinions and experiences and my tender feelings. Who knows what will happen?
>
> But unless I open up with you, unless you understand me and my unique situation and feelings, you won't know how to advise or counsel me. What you say is good and fine, but it doesn't quite pertain to me.[1]
>
> If I try to use human influence strategies and tactics of how to get other people to do what I want, to work better, to be more motivated, to like me and each other—while my character is fundamentally flawed, marked by duplicity and insincerity—then, in the long run, I cannot be successful. . . . Only basic goodness gives life to technique. . . . In the last analysis, what we are communicates far more eloquently than anything we say or do.[2]

Without personal and spiritual authenticity a pastor is doomed to frustration and failure, for integrity is the sterling quality most devoutly sought by God's people.

WHAT PEOPLE SEEK IN A PASTOR

The most comprehensive study ever conducted on ministry in America was a combined scholarly effort of twenty authors and involved participation of over twelve thousand people in the United States and Canada. About five thousand active ministers, laity, seminary professors, seminary seniors, and denominational officials, from forty-seven denominations, responded to 444 descriptions of ministry. After extensive statistical analysis of the data, the study found ten clusters representing the most important characteristics sought in young priests or ministers by those respondents. (See Fig. 5.1.) Four of the top five clusters describe characteristics of the minister as a person. Six of the top ten refer to a pastor's character. Of the remaining four, one deals with leadership, two with counseling, and one with the content of ministry.[3] Note that where skills are involved, they are used in performing roles of ministry that depend upon important personal characteristics.

Fig. 5.1. Characteristics Sought in Ministers and Priests

1. Accept their limitations and serve without concern for public recognition or acclaim
2. Carry out commitments, regardless of pressures to compromise
3. Serve as Christian examples the comunity can respect because their belief in the gospel expresses itself in generosity
4. Acknowledge mistakes and limitations, recognizing their need to learn and grow
5. Develop a sense of community within the congregation by getting to know members and developing trusting relations with them
6. Take responsibility in completing tasks, deal with differences of opinion, and recognize their need to grow in pastoral skills
7. Are perceptive counselors who reach out to people under stress with sensitivity and warmth that frees and supports them
8. Express a positive approach, remaining calm under pressure
9. Focus on God and God's Word as preachers, teachers, and leaders in worship
10. Enable counseling

Source: Adapted from David S. Schuller et al., *Ministry in America: A Report and Analysis* (San Francisco: Harper & Row, 1989), 19.

This monumental study highlights the fact that the person of the minister is the principal tool of pastoral ministry. It is the pastor's integrity, positive approach, and Christian example that are most important to parishioners and colleagues. What counts is a pastor's generosity, sensitivity, warmth, ability to establish trusting relations, dependability, capacity to acknowledge limitations and to admit mistakes, and willingness to learn.

It is not difficult to argue that ministry, whether by pastor, priest, or rabbi, is the one profession that most makes use of the person of the professional. An Empowering Pastor tells how he learned this:

My first church was the one I had served as a student minister. They always called me Bob. When I became their installed pastor, some of them asked, "What do we call you now? Pastor? Bob?" One of them said, "I'm going to call you 'parson.'" "Why call me parson?" I asked. "To remind you that you have to be a person first." He wanted to know my warts. He wanted to know me as a person. I understand now that I needed to be relational and not programmatic or administrative.

Being a Pastor While Being Yourself

It is not easy to live authentically as persons while fulfilling our responsibilities as pastors. To express all our feelings in a counseling situation can interfere with the counselee's progress in coping with her or his own feelings. Or to "tell all" our inmost thoughts from the pulpit can focus attention on ourselves rather than on the gospel. Yet not to share our own experience of sin and redemption and empowerment in very personal terms may fail to build those all-important bridges of meaning that are so crucial to effective ministry. It may help, then, to look at the relationship between ourselves as persons and ourselves as pastors. As Nathaniel Branden points out, authenticity does not require that we "tell all" in every situation.

> Living authentically does not mean compulsive truth-telling. It does not mean announcing every possible thought, feeling, or action, regardless of context, appropriateness, or relevance. It does not mean volunteering private truths indiscriminately or promiscuously. It does not mean offering unsolicited opinions about other people's appearance or offering exhaustive critiques—*necessarily*—even when solicited. It does not mean *volunteering* information about hidden jewels to a burglar.[4]

Sometimes in ministry, faithfully fulfilling one's pastoral role must take priority over sharing one's authentic self. Ben Patterson has described his own struggle to fulfill pastoral roles while sharing himself as a real person.[5] As pastors we are expected to listen empathetically, he says, and by expressing our thoughts or feelings when we should be listening, we may sidetrack an opportunity for ministry. The pastoral role can check our individualism, keep issues in focus, keep emotions under control, enable us to love when we don't feel like loving, and focus attention on Jesus Christ rather than on ourselves.

Yet while fulfilling our roles as pastors we need to be genuinely human, to share our struggles and reveal our shortcomings. Then we can openly celebrate the resources of God's grace that have enabled us to cope with our limitations. This is the story of God's people. Over and over, in the lives of faithful servants, good news takes flesh and dwells among the people. That too is our calling. Only then will people encounter a real gospel. Patterson says,

> People are much more interesting than any function they serve. I can play a role and even play a crowd, but I will not connect with people if I do. It's only when I reveal my humanity, confessing some of my faults and weaknesses publicly, that people relate to me.
> And then they can relate better to the gospel. When people see my humanity and the gospel as a vital part of their pastor's life, they're more likely to think Christ can be a vital part of their lives too.[6]

So being human while fulfilling a pastoral role is not only possible, it is essential. We do this by delicately balancing the expression of our authenticity as a person with the appropriate particular demands of our calling as pastors.

Patterson does this by publicly confessing his discouragement only in retrospect. He does not do so in the midst of his down times. He may express anger at something outside the congregation. But he never expresses anger at the congregation. He does talk about his own struggles with anger. He resists talking about "every little administrative blunder" but does admit his "big mistakes" when he makes them.

Each of us must work out our own balance between self-revelation and pastoral discretion as we seek to express our integrity as pastors and as persons.

Being an Empowering Pastor

All this makes quite clear that a pastor cannot be effective without being real. However, a pastor can be real without being effective. A person can be authentically authoritarian, immature, and insecure. Integrity and maturity usually complement one another, but they are not identical. Authenticity alone does not ensure effectiveness. More is needed.

What, then, in addition to spiritual integrity, are the characteristics of Empowering Pastors? What are their essential qualities as persons? What are their natural gifts ? What attitudes and beliefs lie behind their styles of ministry? What skills do they possess? And which of those skills do they consider most important? What formative experiences have shaped their spiritual and professional lives? What can growing pastors learn from them?

Our current study used a framework developed as a follow-up to the research behind *Congregations Alive*. It was obvious that pastors in that study were highly effective, especially in their ability to inspire and work with people. So we decided to learn more about them. We wanted to know how they differ from the average Presbyterian pastor.

We gathered approximately fifty of these pastors into three small consultations in different parts of the country. We asked them to share critical experiences in their professional development and to take the Myers-Briggs Type Indicator. Through group conversations and questionnaires we gathered information that we then compared with the opinions of lay leaders in their congregations. Later we gave these same questions to a random sample of Presbyterian pastors and lay leaders through the Presbyterian Panel.[7]

I asked an organizational development consultant to study *Congregations Alive* and list the skills he felt would be essential to carry out the style of leadership described there. Together we developed a list of twenty skills. The current study has reduced that list to fifteen skills, eliminating five that did not distinguish clearly between servant leaders and the average Presbyterian pastor. As we shall see in chapter 7, Empowering Pastors excel in all the remaining fifteen skills, in comparison with Other Pastors in the present study.

As we worked, the consultant and I were keenly aware of a significant dilemma. If one is to look at skills that pastors use in their ministries, it is extremely important to distinguish, where possible, between that which pastors bring to servant leadership by who they are (i.e., their personalities, beliefs, and values) and the particular skills they have been able to learn. Therefore, we developed three categories of inquiry: core essences, values and beliefs, and skills.

1. *Core essences* are those characteristics of a person that are at the very core of that person's being. These characteristics are extremely difficult, if not impossible, to change in any significant measure. They include a person's

temperament, personality, preferred style of approaching life, or psychological type, to use the terminology of the Myers-Briggs Type Indicator.

2. *Values and beliefs* are those characteristics of a person that can be learned, but that usually are so deeply ingrained that they are difficult to change. These include such things as a person's basic understanding of life and of human nature, self-concept, openness to change and to risk-taking, and so forth.

3. *Skills* include significant behaviors and styles of working with people and with the content of ministry that have been learned or can be learned either in formal educational settings, self-study, or in life experiences.

Using this framework we are now able to suggest the following characteristics of Empowering Pastors. Under *core essences:*

1. They trust themselves, trust others, and trust their environment.
2. They are centered and secure and willing to be vulnerable.
3. Their personal sense of security enables them to receive from others.
4. They naturally tend to empower others.
5. They are eager to grow and open to change.

Under the category of *values and beliefs* we suggest the following characteristics of Empowering Pastors:

1. They value interdependence in their relationships with others, because they have grown beyond dependence and independence.
2. They believe it is important to share their power and their profession as ministers of the Word.
3. They view change as an opportunity rather than a threat.
4. They are willing to take risks and encourage risk-taking by their congregations.
5. They value diversity when it is not inconsistent with their deep theological commitments.
6. They believe in the potential of people. Members do not need to be cajoled into undertaking their calling to ministry. Rather they will respond readily to a vision of their possibilities.
7. They are committed to the empowerment of others as one of the primary goals in their ministry.

PERSONAL CHARACTERISTICS OF EMPOWERING PASTORS

Against the backdrop of these descriptions we can now look at some of the more important personal characteristics of Empowering Pastors. In the following conclusions we see reflected many of the core essences and values and beliefs we have just summarized. We found that Empowering Pastors had in common these characteristics:

1. Empowering Pastors exhibit a strong sense of personal and professional power. They are more likely than Other Pastors to report that they never or rarely feel a sense of powerlessness in their work. They are also more likely to say that they rarely or never feel conflicting or ambiguous expectations for their work. In other words, they feel secure in meeting the demands of ministry and are on top of their responsibilities.

2. They value diversity. We have already seen that Empowering Pastors are more likely than Other Pastors to desire congregations with a high tolerance for theological diversity. Diversity for them is creatively challenging rather than threatening.

3. They welcome change. They are much more likely than Other Pastors to feel that they approach change and conflict positively. Seventy-four percent of Empowering Pastors compared with 47 percent of Other Pastors rate themselves high on this.[8] Their openness to change may also be inferred from the fact that they are more likely than Other Pastors to feel that their congregations are influenced more by contemporary ideas and trends than by history and tradition.

In three years, a very small congregation in a small town has grown from forty-one to sixty-nine members. When we contacted its pastor, they were engaged in a $50,000 project to make their building handicap-accessible. The pastor lists "experimentation" as the most important influence in his effectiveness. "Every church I have served has graciously granted me the freedom to experiment in all areas of ministry." His advice to pastors who want to grow in their effectiveness: "Love the Lord your God with all your heart, mind, and soul. And love all your neighbors as yourself. Be open to life experiences and open to experiment and change."

4. They are risk takers. Risk-taking relates closely to one's openness to change. Sixty-nine percent of Empowering Pastors compared with 45 percent of Other Pastors rate themselves high on being "willing to take risks, even if failure might result." The pastor of a one-hundred-member church in a small city says that her biggest challenge in the past five years has been inspiring and enabling a congregation to grow in their outreach. Her goal has been to help them be willing and able to take a faith risk, even when failure is a possibility. She did this, she says, by "equipping members with courage and skill, and by demonstrating my courage and my skill and confidence." Other pastors might join in the advice given by one of their colleagues. "Make a fundamental decision to be a risk taker, a pastor who is never just a caretaker, who knows how to empower lay leaders to do caretaking as well as outreach. Try new ways of doing things. For example, 'pushing' people to be open to new information, culture and language. It's scary to change, but it's important. Welcome diversity."

5. They are energized by crisis. Half of Empowering Pastors compared with 35 percent of Other Pastors say that their typical response to a crisis is to find that their energy increases and they become more effective. Only 5 percent compared with 12 percent of Other Pastors say that they find it difficult to act as quickly or as skillfully as they would like. The rest of the pastors in both groups affirm that they are able to keep calm and deal with a crisis as best they can.

6. They manage conflict skillfully. Fifty-seven percent of Empowering Pastors compared with only 26 percent of Other Pastors feel that they are very skillful or skillful in resolving conflict. Empowering Lay Leaders are also much more likely than Other Lay Leaders to give their pastors high ratings on this skill. In fact, the differences between the skill ratings of Empowering Pastors and Other Pastors are greater than on all but two of the fifteen skills in our study.

THE MATURITY OF EMPOWERING PASTORS

In all of this we have really been describing mature persons with high levels of personal security. Out of many years experience as a judicatory executive and consultant with the Alban Institute, Edward White concludes that pastors who are able to empower laity (1) are secure in their sense of self; (2) can clearly define themselves; (3) are grounded in the midst of ambiguity and anxiety; (4) are clear about their possibilities and limitations; (5) do not need win/lose solutions; and (6) have a sense of self-worth that is rooted in the gospel of grace rather than in success or self-fulfillment. An Empowering Pastor is "One who is not threatened by those who seem bigger or smarter or stronger."

To illustrate his point he reminds us of the character Anna in *The King and I.* When she learns that no one's head must be higher than the king's, she stoops before him. He then stoops, so she must go further. Finally they both are kneeling with heads on the floor. White then asks, "How many times do our clergy leaders do this to their followers? Staff and laity get the message and are constantly stooping to oblige."[9]

The marketing slogan of one poultry distributor is "It takes a tough man to make a tender chicken." To paraphrase that, "It takes a tough pastor to be a servant leader." It takes a very secure pastor to share power with others. Conversely, insecure pastors are threatened by the competence of others. They bolster their own self-doubts by maintaining control of every situation. They must always be right. So they are likely to be authoritarian in their approach to ministry.

Covey gives us a very helpful analysis of maturity. He describes a "maturity continuum" from dependence to independence to interdependence. As we read his words, it is not difficult to recognize that Empowering Pastors are able to be effective servant leaders because they have become interdependent people.

> On the maturity continuum, *dependence* is the paradigm of *you* — *you* take care of me; *you* come through for me; *you* didn't come through; I blame *you* for the results.
>
>   *Independence* is the paradigm of *I* — *I* can do it; *I* am responsible; *I* am self-reliant; *I* can choose.

Interdependence is the paradigm of *we*—*we* can do it; *we* can cooperate; *we* can combine our talents and abilities and create something greater together.
Dependent people need others to get what they want. Independent people can get what they want through their own effort. Interdependent people combine their own efforts with the efforts of others to achieve their greatest success.[10]

If I am emotionally interdependent, I derive a great sense of worth within myself, but I also recognize the need for love, for giving, and for receiving love from others. If I am intellectually interdependent, I realize that I need the best thinking of other people to join with my own.

As an interdependent person, I have the opportunity to share myself deeply, meaningfully, with others, and I have access to the vast resources and potential of other human beings.

Interdependence is a choice only independent people can make. Dependent people cannot choose to become interdependent. . . . they don't own enough of themselves.[11]

THE IMPORTANCE OF SELF-ESTEEM

Emotional interdependence is possible for those with healthy levels of self-esteem. To use Nathaniel Branden's imagery, this is because they are not at war either with themselves or with others. So self-esteem makes an essential contribution to the empowerment of others. Branden, who has been called "a pioneer in self-esteem development," goes on to say,

The higher our self-esteem, the better equipped we are to cope with life's adversities; the more resilient we are, . . . the more likely we are to be creative in our work, . . . the more ambitious we tend to be, . . . the more likely we are to form nourishing rather than destructive relationships, . . . the more inclined we are to treat others with respect, benevolence and good will since we do not perceive them as threats, . . . the more joy we experience in the sheer fact of being.[12]

Note that two of the characteristics identified in Figure 5.1 are direct indicators of healthy self-esteem. Accepting limitations without concern for public recognition or acclaim (number 1) reflects a capacity to derive a sense of self-worth from internal resources rather than from external plaudits. Acknowledging mistakes and limitations, recognizing their need to learn and grow (number 4) demonstrates an honesty with self that is essential to self-acceptance.

Indeed, a high level of self-esteem is essential for an empowering ministry. After rating herself on our questionnaire the pastor of a small church in the West said, "I see I've evaluated myself pretty highly. A little overconfident, perhaps? But I think it's essential to feel capable and skilled at the job you do. There are thousands of things I can't do, but they're not part of my job."

Another pastor of a small church in the South observes that when you have a healthy sense of your self-worth, "you can allow parishioners to be your teacher and can be their teacher. Without it, if parishioners start ministering to you, you are threatened and cannot learn from them." The pastor of a large congregation in a small city says, "The better you feel about yourself, the better you are going to be able to do what you do. Every minister feels a sense of inadequacy at some time. Receiving counseling is a sign of strength, not of weakness. All pastors have times when they get down. At those times one needs to try to understand what it is that is causing this feeling."

Healthy Levels of Self-Esteem

To enhance the self-esteem of others, Empowering Pastors must themselves have a high level of self-esteem. Without it we can be so eager to protect and develop our self-esteem that we are unable to free others to be all that they can be. Our study found that Empowering Pastors are more likely than Other Pastors to have very positive feelings about themselves and their ministries. They are more likely to agree or strongly agree with all the following statements:

I feel very good about myself and my ministry.
Leaders of the congregation where I serve are very responsive to my ideas.
I feel I am accomplishing more in my ministry than I did five or ten years ago.
My gifts and style of ministry meet the needs and expectations of my present
   congregation.

Enthusiastic affirmation of these statements suggests healthy levels of self-esteem. As we shall see in chapter 10, these responses may also mean that Empowering Pastors have a more positive feeling about the match of their gifts with opportunities for ministry in the congregations they serve. But of course such positive feelings also make a significant contribution to self-esteem.

Two definitions of self-esteem may be helpful at this point. In the introduction to his *Culture-Free Self-Esteem Inventories*, James Battle says, "Self-esteem refers to the perception the individual possesses of his or her own worth. . . . It is . . . a composite of an individual's feelings, hopes, fears, thoughts and views of who he is, what she is, what he has been, and what she might become."[13] Nathaniel Branden gives us a more extensive definition.

Self-esteem is the reputation we acquire with ourselves.[14]

[It is the experience that we are] appropriate to life [and to the requirements of life.] It has two components: a feeling of personal competence and a feeling of personal worth. In other words, self-esteem is the sum of self-confidence and self-respect.[15]

More specifically, Branden says, self-esteem is

1. Confidence in our ability to think and to cope with the basic challenges of life.
2. Confidence in our right to be happy, the feeling of being worthy, deserving, entitled to assert our needs and wants and to enjoy the fruits of our efforts.[16]

Self-esteem, on whatever level, is an intimate experience; it resides in the core of our being. It is what I think and feel about myself, not what someone else thinks or feels about me.

[It] is always a matter of degree. I have never known anyone who was entirely lacking in positive self-esteem, nor have I known anyone who was incapable of growing in self-esteem.[17]

Loving Your Realistic Self

I like to say that healthy self-esteem is "to love your realistic self." It is openly accepting and loving our very human fallible selves with all our warts and foibles. We can do this because God's love accepts us just as we are, and because fellow Christians accept, love, and support us, in spite of our shortcomings. Therefore we dare to face ourselves and to risk the openness of being who we are. We can be real! Paul reminds us that "we have this treasure in clay jars, so that it may be made clear that this extraordinary power belongs to God and does not come from us" (2 Cor. 4:7).

Our Lord's second great commandment is for us to love our neighbors as ourselves. We usually emphasize the first part of this verse: We must love our neighbor. But the second is the key to the first. We must first love ourselves. A healthy self-love is the foundation for love of others. If I don't love my realistic human self with all my shortcomings, I can't very well love my very human neighbor or my very human parishioner. So self-esteem underlies creative authenticity and maturity. And those qualities provide the essential personal foundation for servant ministry.

Of course we are not talking about narcissistic self-centeredness or arrogant self-indulgence. Only God is the center of our universe, and the first commandment calls us to love God with our whole being. If we do that, we cannot love ourselves as though we were the center of existence.

Jesus said that we are to take up our cross and follow him. Unfortunately the church has often interpreted this as a call to self-depreciation. Many members have heard such a strong emphasis on self-denigration that they feel guilty if they seek self-fulfillment. The assumption is that a Christian is called to wear a psychological hair shirt.

Fortunately there is a growing recognition that a healthy self-acceptance enhances our ability to take up our cross and follow Christ. Certainly there is no better-integrated personality in all history than our Lord himself. His high level of self-esteem enabled him to affirm his divine sonship. Knowing who he was, he was able to set his face toward Jerusalem, meet the betrayers, and take up his cross.

Raising Our Level of Self-Esteem

Is it possible to increase our self-esteem? Battle strongly implies that if it is not impossible, at least it is difficult. He concludes that "perception of self-worth, once established, tends to be fairly stable and resistant to change.[18]

An Empowering Pastor of a very small congregation, who also serves as the director of a pastoral counseling center, comments on what it takes to develop a healthy self-esteem.

In the development of personality every person has a self-identity, the core of which has developed by age nine or ten. After that it changes very little over the years. What can change is our understanding of that core and the behavior that flows from it. Our behavior is the garment that our core wears. Our salvation can come in understanding how that self-worth was determined in our formative years and how it affects our behavior.

I know why I am insecure. I was the youngest of five children of a poverty-stricken family. We lived in the poverty culture of a mill-hill community (a textile community). I am as insecure as I ever was. But I understand what it can do to me so it won't blindside me.

To build one's self-esteem takes a lot of self-reflection. Most of the time it takes a support group if not a therapeutic community. All of us are wounded, but we are wounded in different ways. Functional families can wound just as do dysfunctional families. We are all wounded, but not everyone realizes it. If we don't realize our woundedness we are *wounded wounders* rather than *wounded healers*. To build self-esteem we need to discover how we are wounded.

Branden in *How to Raise Your Self-Esteem* makes a strong case for growth in self-esteem. He asserts that we have a choice regarding how we perceive and accept ourselves. By choosing how we will deal with what life has dealt us, we can grow in self-esteem.

Self-esteem . . . is a function, not of what we are born with, but of how we use our consciousness—the choices we make concerning awareness, the honesty of our relationship to reality, and the level of our personal integrity. A person of high intelligence and high self-esteem does not feel more appropriate to life or more worthy of happiness than a person of high self-esteem and modest intelligence.[19]

He gives the reader of his book an extensive prescription for raising self-esteem:

1. Live consciously by respecting the facts of both your inner and your outer worlds.
2. Accept the reality of who you are and of your life experiences. This does not imply that you have to like what you accept, nor that it precludes a desire to change. In fact self-acceptance is the precondition of change.
3. Reject guilt based on the value preferences or standards of others.
4. Take steps to free yourself from legitimate guilt based on your own standards:
   accept responsibility for what you have done
   acknowledge what you have done to persons you have harmed
   make amends for what you have done
   make a firm commitment to behave differently in the future
   understand and forgive yourself
5. Forgive and embrace the child you once were.
6. Take full responsibility for your own actions and act accordingly.
7. Live authentically; act honestly with self and with others.[20]

As Branden develops each of these points in chapter after chapter, he prescribes sentence-completion exercises he has used successfully in helping counselees raise their levels of self-esteem. Readers who wish to raise their levels of self-esteem may find these exercises helpful.

God's Grace Builds Self-Esteem

It is interesting to note that Branden's prescription gives prominence to dealing with guilt, forgiveness, and acceptance. That is the essence of the gospel. In Jesus Christ, God forgives our guilt and accepts us as we are. When we respond to God's forgiving love and acceptance, God frees us to accept ourselves as we are.

For Empowering Pastors, self-esteem is deeply rooted in varied experiences of God's grace. For a majority, grace has been mediated by loving Christian families from birth, or before. Three-fourths of all pastors in our study say that their childhood home was either very happy or happy. Nearly half of Empowering Pastors say that faith discussion with a Christian parent was very important or important in the development of their effectiveness as a pastor.

For most pastors in our study, the community of faith has been the womb that has birthed and nurtured maturity in the Spirit. Without such early nurture it is doubtful that most of these pastors would be in the ministry today. Over 70 percent say that church experience as a child, as a young person, and as a young adult has been very important or important to the development of their effectiveness as pastors. Empowering Pastors are more likely than Other Pastors to feel that their church experience as a young adult has been very important to their formation. They are also more likely to say that participation in a high school youth group or college fellowship has made an important contribution to their pastoral effectiveness. We conclude that for most pastors, early life experiences have blessed them with a high level of self-esteem. Positive experiences of various kinds along the way have reinforced this in their lives and ministries. In humility they can give thanks to God for who they are. But even they have areas of vulnerability that can creep up on them in unexpected situations to threaten their self-esteem. They need to enhance their awareness of those booby traps so that they will not be blindsided by them. The pastor of a large church voices his experience, to which other Empowering Pastors would resonate.

I have a strong self-esteem that comes from the family in which I grew up. I have a secure marriage. My grandmother was a godly woman who made an impact on my life. Like Timothy, I grew up knowing I was a child of God. This was with me from my baptism and I have never doubted that God loved me. I was married at age twenty-one and have a wonderful, secure marriage with great feelings of being father and husband.

I struggle with how to minister to those who have not had that supportive background. It all goes back to grace. You are loved unconditionally in our congregation. You are not looked down upon just because you were divorced or abused. But persons who have come from areas of pain need to seek counseling and training in caregiving. And growth in self-esteem does not come overnight. It is incredible the number of hours it takes. To help members grow we have Theos and a couples fellowship. We are comforted that we may comfort others.

We all have security and insecurity, and we must deal with our areas of insecurity in order to grow in self-esteem. For me, empowerment has come as I have trusted that there are people who have better knowledge than I do. For example, I know that our minister of music has more knowledge of music and hymns than I do. She selects the hymns because she has the knowledge. If I feel that they do not fit, I go to her and we consult about it. Our worship committee makes many decisions about the worship services.

Self-Esteem against Overwhelming Odds

For some pastors, it seems, the cards were stacked against self-esteem. They have had to struggle to come to love their unlovely self-image. A remarkable number of the Empowering Pastors I interviewed have discovered God's grace through deep pain and suffering. Angels of mercy have ministered to them, and therapy has enabled them to put their lives together again. New resources of God's grace help them daily to maintain a healthy self-esteem. The pastor of a large church in a small town describes his pilgrimage of grace.

We surely have to get to a point of looking at empowerment from the perspective of conversion, a change of perspective on life. We are all impacted by where we are from. My parents were divorced early in my life. I lived in a very unstable environment. This made a tremendous impact on me. We were running all over the country, living in cars, and there was some abuse. When I was seven, I went to live with my grandparents and they raised me. I did not realize it at the time, but my grandparents did something wonderful for me. At an advanced age they raised a second family before they died. So I am very grateful for the nurturing I received from them. The church was key in my life because my grandparents saw that it was important.

Persons need to take whatever experience life has brought them and appropriate it for the life they must live. I have done business with what happened earlier. I have sought a relationship with both parents, even though I was not close to them. I have tried to understand that they were human. I have never felt the desire to be bitter. Now I can see them as real and not as some fantasy. So I have better understanding of them and of myself. I have had a lot of counseling and some therapy. Mentors in the church have helped me.

I am also one who, looking back, has the feeling that God's presence was with us whether or not we were aware of it. There is always more to the picture than we ever really see. We are living in an age when people are victims of their past. I have empathy with others who are going through that, because I have been through that experience myself.

In my interviews with Empowering Pastors I was deeply impressed with the amount of suffering through which many of them have passed. I had selected pastors to interview by reviewing the questionnaires of all those who had rated themselves as very skillful in empowering others. Out of those with this highest rating, I chose to interview a number who seemed to have an important perspective on their ministry or a meaningful story to tell. Over and over I discovered that through their own illness or through divorce or the illness and death of a spouse, they had, in the words of the prodigal son, "come to themselves." The tender, loving heavenly Father had run out to meet them in their distress, and members of their congregation, colleagues, and counselors had supported them as they rediscovered grace at ever-deeper levels.

An alcoholic and a cancer survivor tell their stories.

I am an alcoholic and have been a loser a good portion of my life. AA turned me around. I have learned a whole lot about myself and have undergone a lot of change. Several years ago I was in danger of losing everything. A member of my parish, an elder, was an alcoholic, so I turned to him and asked for help. He took me to AA and served as my sponsor. I might not have gone into the program if it were not for him. I had to trust him enough to ask for help. In fact if it were not for that elder I might be dead now. I came from an alcoholic family, and a good portion of my pain in life came from my alcoholism and the denial of an alcoholic family. My spiritual life was distorted by denial.

Undoing all that denial was a struggle. There is a sense of giving up in order to face it. Most of us give up only after having fought. At first it feels like a terrible defeat. Later we catch on that it is quite a gift.

Not all the turning points of my journey are visible to me. But I have discovered that my colleagues view me differently than they did two or three decades ago. I used to be judgmental. Now I seem to be viewed as humble. I remember that before the program I used to sit in presbytery, listening to my colleagues and thinking how phony they were. I was in a deep, dark mood about them, and about the church in general. Within two years after the program, I was different. In presbytery I was moved by the sincerity of those who were speaking. My whole perspective had changed.

This has greatly empowered me in that I really know and have experienced the closeness of God as a spiritual power doing for us what we can't do for ourselves. That takes away a lot of fear. The work is really not up to me. And if things don't come out right, maybe that is OK too. It has empowered my ministry because people would like to know that faith really matters in concrete terms, and I am able to testify to that.

Now I am more accepting of everyone's contribution in our congregation, whether or not I agree with them. I am able to respect the motivations and concerns of most of my conservative brothers and sisters because I know where they are coming from in their experience. Now I really am an empowering pastor. It makes an enormous difference.

A committee of officers and members in our congregation undertook a major study of church growth. Before my transformation I would not have been willing to trust people with research and development. Everything was all up to me. I had to do everything. You know how easy it is to get on a spiritual ego trip. Now I was able to empower them. In fact, I feel I had nothing to do with it.

I am a cancer survivor. I do especially well in ministering to those with life-threatening illnesses. Surviving cancer has drawn me closer to my Lord and has helped me be a more understanding pastor. I know how it feels to face the possibility of your death while still relatively young.

An effective Empowering Pastor of a large church left the pastoral ministry for a time because of his divorce. Through his suffering he discovered grace as a way of life.

After seminary, I was involved in youth ministry. That was a time of suffering in my life. My wife wanted a divorce and left me. The head of staff rejected me and I thought my ministry was over. I went through a program of individual and group therapy. I thought I would go into law, worked for an attorney, and took law courses at night in government. A young faculty member there befriended me and suggested that I not go to law school, but take an interdisciplinary course leading to a Ph.D. in government. A friend referred me to a pastor who had had an experience of divorce similar to mine. I started attending his church. He befriended me and later asked me to work part-time on staff while I studied at night. Later I became their first full-time associate pastor. I taught political science and struggled with whether to continue in teaching or in the pastorate. My desire to train people for their ministries led me to continue in the pastorate.

Two therapists have been there for me across the years. They have listened, affirmed, and inspired growth in me. My son's teenage drug use drove me to Al-Anon. This twelve-step spiritual recovery program is also central to my continuing growth. It has connected me to my brokenness and the brokenness of our world.

Another, who pastors a very large congregation, proclaims the recurring theme: Grace is the central reality in life and ministry for those who have experienced brokenness.

My divorce and therapy in my twenties, followed by brokenness, taught me grace and compassion that helps me give those same gifts to others. After therapy, I took a master's degree in counseling. It was very valuable in correlation with the gospel.

Not everyone has to go through the sewer pipe I have gone through. But if you aren't grace-filled and know brokenness you had better pray for that kind of deep experience of God's grace. We need to be fellow strugglers. Pastors should seek it desperately if they don't have it. Pray for that. Pray for a real heart to serve people. The church needs wounded healers for the next century.

I tell my elders that if I am going to err in my ministry, it will always be on the side of grace. Jesus can handle our brokenness. The only thing that can hurt us is if we hide our need for grace. I am very much into twelve-step programs of various kinds. Our church is a hospital for sinners, not a house for saints. Many of the staff I call have been divorced. They are very dependent on the Lord and on prayer. We are a motley crew and are always surprised by what God can do through us. The only magic we have is what God can do through brokenness. We are a medical clinic. Each of us has our own specialty.

GRACE AS A WAY OF LIFE

For all these pastors and for many more, the redemptive love of God has invaded their lives. Grace has become a way of life. Day by day the Holy Spirit empowers them to be real. Self-esteem is not a once-for-all-time accomplished reality in anyone's life. Renewal of God's grace renews self-esteem. One Empowering Pastor described it this way:

I need to keep up my self-esteem, which I define as "imputed worth." My up-bringing left me with a lot of guilt. I continually need to remind myself that my worth comes because God gave it to me, through God's acceptance of me. This is the startling reality of God's amazing grace. That gives the self-esteem. This is what Romans 7 and 8 is all about. Because of grace we start each day as if we are just born anew.

It is difficult for me to stand in the pulpit and look out at the people who need help I haven't given. I look out and see this person that I didn't get out to see. All around the congregation I see all my mistakes, things I did or failed to do. So before I preach I remember "in Jesus Christ you are forgiven." I remind myself that the past has no control over the future. Everything is fresh and new.

Another put it this way: "Self-Esteem is crucial to ministry. I get mine by be-ing loved and healed by Jesus Christ. It comes from understanding who we are at the foot of the cross." This love of the realistic self makes it possible to share one's vulnerability. As this pastor put it, "I allow people to know me and my weaknesses in preaching and wherever I am. I very seldom preach something I haven't lived. My personal struggle with issues people are facing always comes through. I tell people that getting ordained doesn't shield ministers from strug-gles that others face. I don't hide anything anymore."

These pastors know how right Paul was when he wrote to the Corinthians:

I was given the gift of a handicap to keep me in constant touch with my limi-tations. Satan's angel did his best to get me down; what he in fact did was push me to my knees. No danger then of walking around high and mighty! At first I didn't think of it as a gift, and begged God to remove it. Three times I did that, and then he told me,
"My grace is enough; it's all you need.
My strength comes into its own in your weakness."
Once I heard that, I was glad to let it happen. I quit focusing on the handicap and began appreciating the gift. It was a case of Christ's strength moving in on my weakness. Now I take limitations in stride, and with good cheer, these limi-tations that cut me down to size—abuse, accidents, opposition, bad breaks. I just let Christ take over! And so the weaker I get, the stronger I become." (2 Cor. 12:7–10, TM)

One cannot help but be inspired by the lives of Empowering Pastors. The way in which the power of God has led them through tragedy to triumphant living encourages us to remember that with God all things are possible.

6

THE POWER IN
BECOMING

Therefore prepare your minds for action; discipline yourselves; set
all your hope on the grace that Jesus Christ will bring you when he
is revealed.

—1 Peter 1:13

Pastors, prepare your minds for action. To empower others one must
first be empowered. If we are going to be able to establish a climate in which people feel free to grow, learn, explore, and use their gifts in Christian ministry, we
must ourselves live with such freedom. We must be growing, learning, and exploring throughout our ministries.

We have seen that Empowering Pastors experience such freedom because the
forgiving and renewing power of God has freed them to be themselves. By the
grace of God they have accepted their strengths and their shortcomings as persons and as pastors. This has strengthened their self-esteem and freed them to
grow purposefully. They have been freed to maximize their strengths and minimize their limitations.

Now we look at the lifelong process of personal, spiritual, and professional
formation that has shaped Empowering Pastors. We find little that distinguishes
their childhood experiences from those of Other Pastors in our study. It is not until their adolescent and young adult years that statistically significant differences
in their growth patterns are evident. Then as young adults we find them much
more likely than Other Pastors to demonstrate a continuing strong drive toward
growth. They never arrive. They are always pressing toward the mark for the
prize of the high calling in Christ Jesus.

EARLY FAITH FOUNDATIONS

An overwhelming majority of all pastors in our study draw on deep reservoirs
of power from firm faith foundations laid in their childhood and adolescent
years. Seven out of ten pastors in both groups began their formative faith experiences growing up in caring churches. Their experiences remind us vividly of
Paul's words to Timothy: "What a rich faith it is, handed down from your grand-

mother Lois to your mother Eunice, and now to you! And the special gift of ministry you received when I laid hands on you and prayed—keep that ablaze! God doesn't want us to be shy with his gifts, but bold and loving and sensible" (2 Tim. 1:5–7, TM).

While there are many individual differences in detail, the early church experiences of both Empowering Pastors and Other Pastors in our study are probably quite similar overall to those reported by the following two pastors.

Church was always exciting and joyous. It nurtured me from a Christian perspective in every facet of life, teaching me to live with hope and joy. The covenant community of those struggling to be faithful is the air I breathe, the water I drink. The church has defined me, sourced my identity, revealed Christ to me. Growing up in the church has enabled me to develop good "instincts" for ministry.

My church was the finest Christian example I know of what a true church is: large doses of love, the Westminster Shorter Catechism, a vibrant youth fellowship, sound preaching, community involvement. Our pastor was respected. Something very real happened to me. I have had a lifelong desire to have others experience what I experienced.

For both groups of pastors, positive family nurturing was important in their growing up. Three out of four recall a happy or very happy childhood and 45 percent say that discussions with a Christian parent have been important or very important in their later effectiveness as pastors. Fewer women than men pastors had happy childhoods. A little more than half the women say that their childhood was very happy or happy, compared with three out of four men. And one-fourth of the women pastors compared with 9 percent of men pastors say that their childhood was somewhat unhappy to very unhappy. Of course family circumstances varied. Here are three examples of the very different ways in which many pastors learned from their home experiences.

My Christian family made an important impact on me. My parents were models of what they believed. Matters of faith and church activities were an integral part of their lives. Their faith was the source of early commitment for me. Family involvement helped to shape my active participation as a young person. They always supported any efforts I made to be involved in the life of the church. I have been fortunate in that each of my several pastors has been a role model.

I was the oldest and only son. I was very close to my father, who was a Presbyterian elder with a high commitment to the church. We did many things together: backpacking, hiking, and so forth. He was a successful executive who worked hard, communicated, and was a peacemaker between union and management. When I read *Seven Habits of Highly Effective People*, I realized that I had already been doing most of those things. I had learned them from my father. Because of his work we moved nine times before eighth grade. As a result, meeting new people is an adventure for me rather than a threat. I get my professionalism from my dad and nurturing and caring from my mother. In our home the theme of affirmation was very strong. This has influenced my style as a pastor. I affirm my congregation and build on their strengths. I never challenge without offering hope.

My father was an alcoholic. My mother died at age forty-one, when I was twelve. But our congregation was a wonderful church family. The people of God are absolutely the greatest teachers I have had! An excellent, gifted, and caring pastor oversaw my Christian growth and faith development. We had very supportive and loving grandparents, aunts, uncles, and I had some of the finest grade and high school teachers. My mother and maternal grandparents openly and readily discussed all matters of life from a faith perspective, and all three had a personal, vital relationship to Jesus. My mother was a lifelong Presbyterian. She committed me to God before I was born and kept me involved in church. My great-grandfather was a commissioner to General Assembly one hundred years ago. My father was Catholic. We could talk about anything in our family having to do with belief. The mixed Catholic/Protestant marriage opened me to an ability to question and disagree and remain faithful to God. I was loved.

The Congregation as Family

Those pastors whose families were dysfunctional or whose parents were not involved in the church often found that a loving congregation became their family. For many, a wise and caring pastor or a committed layperson lightened their lives with love.

My childhood church provided acceptance and affirmation that I did not get at home. I felt acceptance, love, and belonging in ways I did not feel in my family. I felt awe and wonder in worship, even as a very small child. For me, as a young person seeking to find an identity, the church provided a safe and loving environment for exploration. The Director of Christian Education in my home church was very influential and supportive, and I continue a good relationship with my pastors.

Four out of ten pastors say that a conversion experience made an important contribution to their effectiveness as pastors. The rest have been nurtured into faith. For many of them the process was so gradual, so natural, and so permeating that they feel as though they have dedicated themselves to Christ all their lives.

I was brought up in the home of my maternal grandparents, good Dutch Reformed Calvinistic folk. So strong was my sense of God's claim, a conversion experience would be impossible. Growing up in the church allowed me to see the church as a very human institution replete with all the politics, foibles, and shortcomings of any other human group.

Even those who point back to a conversion experience often see it as a culmination of faithful nurturing that preceded it. For example, a pastor who grew up in the church says, "My public acceptance and commitment to Christ at a Billy Graham service made explicit what had been growing for years." Where a conversion experience is mentioned, Empowering Pastors are much more likely than Other Pastors to have had such an experience before age eighteen (80 percent compared with 66 percent).

Some, of course, had conversion experiences at later ages. "I experienced a personal crisis while participating in the antiwar movement during college years. This led to a much deeper, life-changing faith. Following this, I became involved in a local Presbyterian church and had a very positive experience. I was hired to work with the youth of that church. It was wonderful! I decided to become a minister at that time."

Role Models

It is difficult to overestimate the lasting impact on children and young people of dedicated and caring Christian laity and pastors. We see this quite clearly in the lives of both groups of pastors in our study. A majority say that an early faith relationship with a Christian layperson has been important or very important to their effectiveness as pastors. Two out of three feel that they were strongly influenced as children or young persons by pastors they now view as role models.

One particular Sunday school teacher took a personal interest in us as her students. She was also very knowledgeable of the Bible! Because of her example, I am a more effective pastor.

Our young pastor was a vivacious, loving person. He cared for youth and had a tremendous vitality. He made living a Christian life real to me.

A youth advisor couple greatly influenced me. My pastor served as a strong encourager and role model.

Many adults, besides our parents, took a keen interest in us and our spiritual development. I had the good fortune to have contact with many fine role models in the ministry as a child and youth. My pastor influenced dozens to enter the ministry or full-time Christian service. He combined solid theology with genuine humanity. As a young person I was exposed to many quality evangelical leaders who modeled their faith in a positive way.

I had good experiences as an older teen and young adult in church work and was influenced by older adults in those experiences. My pastor during my high school years took time to talk with me about faith, church, and ministry, and was a positive influence.

Dynamic and courageous acts by my childhood pastor helped form my vocational goals. He invited the children of our black custodian to Sunday school in segregated central Texas in the early 1950s.

As a young person I witnessed and experienced a strong, caring, transforming pastoral leadership. I worked at a church camp with many strong and caring pastors who challenged me to ministry.

Both of my parents were ministers, each with different gifts. They were strong role models for me. I learned not only expression of faith in words and actions but also the importance of a variety of gifts.

THE PIVOTAL HIGH SCHOOL
AND COLLEGE YEARS

Chronologically speaking, we first see a difference between Empowering Pastors and Other Pastors in their high school years. A majority of both groups feel that participation in a high school youth group or college fellowship was important or very important in the development of their effectiveness as pastors. However, Empowering Pastors are more likely to feel that this was important. Several of them tell of ways in which leadership in those groups and in the life of the congregation led to their commitment to the pastoral ministry.

Sunday school teachers took me seriously, as did our pastor. They called me by name and gave me leadership roles in class and in worship. Experiences in our high school youth group trained me to stand up before others, to read, pray, and give talks. I served as moderator of Presbytery Westminster Fellowship. High school and college leadership positions helped me discover that I could plan, organize, motivate, and accomplish things. I could be a leader. My church supported and encouraged me as a leader. I taught a church school class during college in a warm and supportive congregation. This plus my home church "called" me into the ministry.

My youth and young adult experience in the same small church were influential because I was entrusted with leadership responsibility. I served as chair of evangelism and as an elder. I even preached my first sermon when I was a senior in high school. Summer camp experience confirmed my call to the ministry. Confirmation of "the call" is a tremendous influence on one's effectiveness!

My high school youth group was crucial in my faith development and in my view of ministry. It was always an important support group in my formative years. It taught me honesty, openness, and faithfulness. Commitment of one's life to Christ was emphasized. I emphasize that commitment in my ministry. We were very involved in the church and it has affected my view of what makes for an effective church.

In my high school youth group, I experienced Christian community with soft boundaries, lots of acceptance, and encouragement from other youth and sponsors. A great place to grow in agape love. I wasn't a part of the "in" group at high school, but everyone was "in" at church. It was a great model to me of ideal youth ministry. It is there I was nurtured, challenged, and confirmed in my faith.

Westminster Fellowship in the fifties gave me a sense of connection with the church. There I had wonderful experiences of acceptance and challenges to faith and growth. Charismatic leaders, music, retreats, and study all made their impact on my formation.

Nearly half the Empowering Pastors say that their experience in a summer conference or work camp was important or very important in developing their effectiveness as pastors. For many, it was a time of decision to dedicate their lives to Christ. For others that decision solidified their faith experience and led to their feeling a call to pastoral ministry. For some, it provided an atmosphere where spiritual questioning could take place. Other writers have shown that it is very important to give young people opportunities for such questioning. One pastor's experience leads him to say, "It imprinted on me the need to make faith questioning OK for others as well."

THE URGE TO GROW

From the perspective of personal, professional, and spiritual development, perhaps the most important characteristic that differentiates Empowering Pastors from Other Pastors is their greater urge to grow, especially through continued study. The pastor of a large church puts it this way.

> If I am to be able to empower others, I have to find ways of empowerment for myself. The church here offered to support me in a D.Min. program in biblical studies and preaching (hermeneutics). I have worked hard to develop my skills in interpreting scripture to the modern world in relation to problems people are facing.
>
> It has become more and more important to develop my own spirituality. None of us has the human staying power over the years unless we discover a lifeline. For the past ten years or more I have really been diving into the fundamentals. I teach Bible classes during the week, and have found that to be one of the ways I nurture myself. I have been seeking to understand the scripture and to understand and nurture myself.
>
> For me, Eugene Peterson's book *Working the Angles* is a model for ministry. Praying the psalms has revolutionized my life spiritually. It has caused me to love the Word in a devotional way. I'd like to be a "man of God." If that's missing, we are simply not going to have the spiritual power we need.

There are at least three characteristics of Empowering Pastors that channel and liberate their urge to grow. First, they understand themselves well enough to know where and how they need to grow. Second, they are risk takers who dare face the potential pain of growth. Third, they are proactive people who plan and carry out their growth plans.

Self-knowledge

There can be little or no growth without knowledge of oneself. Without it we can delude ourselves into thinking we are growing, when we are really repeating old lyrics with new tunes. There is power in disciplining our minds and hearts to face who we really are, and in growing toward all that God calls us to be. Power multiplies in those who continually grow with such a focus. Pastors who live by grace discover power when they proactively pursue their personal, professional, and spiritual growth. They get to know themselves and discover their gifts and liabilities.

The Risk of Change

To grow, one must be open to change. There is no growth without change. And change can involve considerable risk. Empowering Pastors are growing because, as we have seen, they are much more likely than Other Pastors to be risk takers and to approach change and conflict positively. One seminary student, who was white, took a clinical pastoral internship in a county hospital with a confrontational black supervisor. He remembers both the pain and the value of that experience. "I connected with a new culture that at first terrified me. I hated my supervisor as well as the program itself. I hated it all until the last couple of months. Then the crisis broke."

Learning can involve considerable risk and great rewards. In his introduction to the Lutheran study *Growth in Ministry*, Thomas Kadel observes, "Growth is an expanding and a maturing; a process rather than an event. The old line is true—'When you stop growing, you start dying.' Sometimes growth is quite painful and other times it can be exhilarating. But almost always it involves some risk, some casting off of the old and familiar and rewrapping oneself in new garments."[1]

Proactivity

Empowering Pastors are *proactive* people. They are goal oriented and work at achieving their goals. They have actively shaped their own roles and pastoral styles. They are not passive dependents. Of course, they have been shaped by interaction with the congregations they have served, just as they have helped to shape those congregations. They have given high priority to their spiritual, personal, and professional development through self-study and through continuing education activities following their graduation from seminary. They illustrate Stephen Covey's first three habits of highly effective people. At the risk of oversimplification, I would summarize those three habits this way:

Habit 1: Be proactive, not reactive. Choose how you respond to life's circumstances.
Habit 2: Begin with the end in mind. Set your purpose on what you value most deeply.
Habit 3: Put first things first. Discipline your self to your purpose; live by your own deep values.

The pastor of a medium-sized congregation began his ministry with a pattern he has pursued since then.

When I went to my first pastorate I decided I would do three things: (1) I would write out every sermon in full, to force me to think clearly and to write clearly. But I would never read a sermon. (2) Any other talk I gave I would never write out. I would prepare notes and speak extemporaneously. (3) I would read good literature as a way of developing a style and a use of words that would say what

I wanted to say and would have some degree of elegance. This has served me very well over the years.

THE URGE TO GROW THROUGH EDUCATION

Empowering Pastors are much more likely than Other Pastors to say that their educational experiences beyond college have been important or very important to the development of their pastoral effectiveness. Growth in mind and spirit is one of their deep values. Among all the twenty-nine self-ratings on experiences that have contributed to pastoral effectiveness, the three greatest differences between the ratings by Empowering Pastors and Other Pastors are in the importance they ascribe to graduate work, seminary-related field education, and continuing education. (See Fig. 6.1.) This reflects an eagerness for scholarship related to their parish responsibilities.

Empowering Pastors are more likely than Other Pastors to feel that their seminary courses were important or very important to the development of their effectiveness as pastors. The pastor of a small congregation in a small town describes her urge to grow in seminary and the impact it has made on her ministry. "I took the toughest stuff I could: education, deep and sound biblical work, and preaching. This has given me confidence in the pulpit, helped me to be prophetic, keeps me renewed and fed so I can feed. I preach with authority because of education and that helps my congregation to heal and grow."

As is evident in their comments, seminary courses shaped Empowering Pastors in various ways and for different reasons. For most, the content of their courses developed a deeper understanding of their faith and laid a firm foundation for the intellectual and spiritual demands of their pastorates.

Seminary courses answered my primary questions—both intellectual existential and professional.

Seminary opened me up to a new world. It helped me think intellectually and get perspective on issues.

Fig. 6.1. Pastors for Whom Postcollege Education Has Been Important or Very Important

	Empowering Pastors (%)	Other Pastors (%)	Difference (%)
Seminary courses	68	63	5
Seminary-related field education	59	43	16
Graduate work	51	34	17
Continuing education	60	45	15

Strong seminary teaching in parish work gave me tools with which to think and feel.

I found a happy union of the spiritual and the intellectual, especially in studies at Edinburgh.

Contact with a community of seminary professors that believed in my potential gave me solid training to develop that potential.

For other Empowering Pastors, the seminary professors themselves as persons made a lasting impact.

There was a professor of New Testament who had great influence on my style of ministry—his personhood more than his scholarship.

There were probably a dozen or more seminary professors whose own faith and learning shaped my future.

My faith was initially intellectual. I credit seminary courses with showing me the inherent weakness of a purely intellectual faith. This was not always what the courses intended.

Two professors, in particular, showed me intellectual excellence, integrity, and faith that were complementary and congruent. I was hooked!

Field Education Experiences

Empowering Pastors are more likely than Other Pastors to feel that seminary-related field education has proved to be important or very important to the development of their effectiveness as pastors. A review of their experiences shows that the kinds of field education they accepted involved both risk and proactivity.

The pastor of a church in which I worked was a model of caring and creativity in the pulpit and parish. His sermons, hugs, and healing services are memorable. Working with a hospital chaplain gave me experiences of caring, comforting, and helping people face death. I led Bible study in a center for the mentally and physically impaired.

A junior high group I worked with helped me fall in love again with the church that had disappointed me as a high school and college student. It showed me how versatile the church is.

I spent a year as a chaplain at a nursing home. I wanted to understand how people were treated at nursing homes.

In seminary one summer, I did a church survey, door to door in a new area. A church came of it.

I was in a church with an excellent education program working with a pastor who knew how to work with people.

A great congregation put me in charge of a large and growing youth program, welcomed my preaching and teaching—offered friendship.

I worked with a wonderful pastor, my second year in seminary, who really helped me decide to continue toward ministry.

Fewer than half the pastors in our study had the opportunity for an intern year. However, of those who had internships, 73 percent of Empowering Pastors and 67 percent of Other Pastors feel that it has been important or very important to their effectiveness as pastors.

I took an intern year, back when that was rare. The minister had a heart attack ten days after I arrived, so I suddenly became responsible for a large church. It forced me to grow up. In that kind of situation you've got to do it, whether you know how or not. You just do it. From time to time the pastor would preach. One Sunday when he was scheduled to preach I was teaching the men's Bible class. Looking up, I saw one of the minister's daughters standing in the door-way. It was just thirty minutes before service and I knew I was going to have to preach that morning. I closed the class, went up, read over one of the ser-mons I had prepared in class, got up, and delivered it. I grew up in that church because I had no option but to perform.

This was learning by doing and learning with good counselors there to give guidance. It was ministry in a safe environment.

Under the encouragement of an affirming head of staff, I found that seminary took on new meaning after experiencing day-to-day ministry.

I was an intern for one year under a pastor who preaches excellent sermons and helped to write our denomination's new Book of Worship. It was a great learn-ing experience.

Graduate Work

Empowering Pastors are more likely than Other Pastors to feel that graduate work has been important or very important to the development of their effec-tiveness as pastors. More than two-thirds of them, compared with fewer than two-thirds of Other Pastors, say they have engaged in graduate work. Of those who have done graduate work, 74 percent of Empowering Pastors compared with 54 percent of Other Pastors feel that it has been important or very impor-tant for their effectiveness.

Graduate work gave me a fund of knowledge, helped me develop a disciplined approach to learning, and facilitated writing skills.

It was in graduate study that I had to rethink my theology. It was a hard time for me, but a life-changing time.

One pastor of a medium-sized congregation also serves as director of a pas-toral counseling center. In the description of his continuing-education experience we get a feeling for the breadth of learning possibilities that graduate study can provide.

My pattern of continuing education has changed over the years. In the early years I engaged in graduate work during the summer, working on my doctorate. I spent summers in two different seminaries.

When I became the director of a pastoral counseling center, I set up a program by which a certain percentage of income earned by each counselor was set aside in a fund for that counselor's continuing education. This amounted to several thousand dollars a year for each therapist. If they did not use it that year, they lost it. If I had three thousand dollars a year, I made sure I used it. I could get involved in month-long training programs. I wrote the guidelines broadly enough so colleagues could have different types of experiences. Out of that program, for the first time I had access to funds that allowed me to do a wide variety of things.

Since I have been at this church I have continued to study pastoral counseling, organizational development, and therapy. Indirectly this has done more for me than courses the seminaries put on. As a stimulus to me I have studied subjects that would add to my fund of knowledge and would expose me to ways of thinking that would not normally be a part of my thinking. I have also chosen specific areas to enhance my skills and expertise. I have had ongoing training during all of those years in such subjects as psychoanalysis, Transactional Analysis, Gestalt psychology, and marriage and family counseling.

Pastoral Care and Clinical Pastoral Education

Since their graduation from seminary, 26 percent of Empowering Pastors compared with 16 percent of Other Pastors have taken extensive or very extensive formal continuing education in pastoral care, clinical pastoral education, or counseling. Among their testimonies to the value of clinical pastoral education (C.P.E.) are the following:

My advice to pastors who want to grow in effectiveness is to get clinical pastoral training if they have not previously had it. The summer after seminary spent in C.P.E. training was of tremendous help for me and my wife. She took the training with me and has been my greatest inspiration and help in pastoral ministry. She is the prime reason for my effectiveness.

A pastor needs understanding of three documents: the biblical document, gained in seminary; the living human document, gained through study of psychology and sociology; and the self-document, gained in clinical education. C.P.E. should be required in the preparation of every minister. In our part of the country we do not require it, but there is an oral tradition that ministers need to have it. Most take at least a quarter.

A number of hospitals and mental health centers in our region are offering an extended C.P.E. program for pastors, one day a week for eight months. We have peer groups, didactics and seminars, visitation, and clinical work in churches under individual and group supervision. Participants get one unit (four hundred hours) of C.P.E. This is the equivalent of one-fourth year of full-time clinical pastoral education. It provides an excellent opportunity, especially for midlife clergy.

The Doctor of Ministry Degree

A little more than a third of all pastors in our study have worked on doctor of ministry (D.Min.) degrees. This was by far the largest concentration of students in any degree program. Its value is shown by the fact that it received one of the highest percentages of write-ins under the question, "How important have each of the following been to the development of your effectiveness as a pastor?" One pastor wrote, "My D.Min. program was revolutionary. It reconstructed my views of ministry and was the basis of my moving from a position as associate pastor to pastor." Another said, "The most valuable part of my D.Min. program was my experience of peer review in the group part of the program."

Empowering Pastors are more likely than Other Pastors to have taken their D.Min. in pastoral care or evangelism and less likely than Other Pastors to have taken their D.Min in biblical studies. This raises some interesting questions. We have already pointed out that Empowering Pastors are more likely than Other Pastors to build bridges of meaning from biblical material to the lives of their people. Why then have they been less likely to take their D.Min. degrees in biblical studies?

A clue to the answer emerges when we discover that Empowering Pastors are more likely than Other Pastors to say that their ongoing Bible study and exegesis is very valuable or valuable for their personal and professional development. Ninety-one percent of Empowering Pastors compared with 84 percent of Other Pastors say this. They also are more likely to feel that lectionary study with church members is valuable or very valuable for their personal and professional development, although the number of those who do this is small.

Could it be that their undergraduate seminary work has already equipped them with the tools of exegesis and hermeneutics? Day by day, they are using those tools. Already they are giving priority in their personal time to in-depth Bible study. They feel a need to grow in other areas. Therefore, they use their continuing education opportunities to broaden their competence in pastoral care/clinical pastoral education, evangelism, and other areas. We have already seen one possible confirmation of this theory in that Empowering Pastors are more likely than Other Pastors to say that their seminary courses have proved to be important or very important to their effectiveness as pastors.

It is also possible that Other Pastors concentrate so much energy and attention on biblical studies both at home and in continuing education that they neglect "the other side of the bridge."

MOTIVATION FOR CONTINUING EDUCATION

Apparently the choices for continued education indicated by Empowering Pastors in this study match those found in other studies. A 1982 continuing education study of nearly two thousand active ministers in twelve denominations found that "clergy do most of their theological studies while they are at home, and they go away to work mostly on skills for ministry." Study at home "focused on biblical/doctrinal/historical theology, followed by personal and spiritual growth, then by skills for ministry, and issues in church and society. When they went away for study, their primary focus was skills for ministry, followed by biblical/doctrinal/historical theology, and personal/spiritual growth."[2]

A November 1983 questionnaire given to the Presbyterian Panel gathered the responses of 828 pastors, 749 elders, and 1,551 members. Respondents felt that "improving practical skills such as preaching, counseling, administration, and so forth, is the most important reason for taking part in continuing education."[3]

The urge to grow and learn motivates pastors to continue their education in spite of obstacles. For example, a pastor who serves in a remote area of the country reveals his love of learning.

> Working in remote situations, I have had to build up my own library. I belong to four book clubs and buy carefully. I read fifty to eighty books a year and have about 120 reference books for Bible study and perhaps five hundred books on other subjects. I have used my reading to help understand the people in my congregation. For example, to understand a doctor in my congregation I read three or four novels about doctors. I read widely and make notes that I keep in a large card file of illustrations.
>
> For many years I had to pay for my own continuing education and received no time for it. I was on my own. The Board of National Missions didn't give any funding. In spite of that, I found the experiences refreshing!
>
> My call now provides five hundred dollars a year for continuing education. That is just wonderful!

Following a 1984 study, the Society for the Advancement of Continuing Education for Ministry concluded that four conditions favor participation in continuing education: (1) positive relationships within the parish and regional unit, (2) self-assessment by ministers of their needs, (3) self-formulated goals for learning, and (4) a judgment as to whether the learning project will contribute to competence in ministry.[4]

Empowering Pastors enjoy these conditions. They generally enjoy positive relationships with their congregations and boards. Most understand themselves well enough for their needs to be clear. And as proactive persons they set goals to increase their competence.

Empowering Pastors are more likely than Other Pastors to feel that continuing education has been important or very important in developing their effectiveness. Comments on their questionnaires and in interviews suggest an important reason. They are practitioners of intentional continuing education. They have clear reasons for the courses they take. This contributes greatly to their growth and is in contrast to patterns of many other pastors. A comment from the pastor of a medium-sized congregation illustrates this.

> From the beginning of my ministry, continuing education has played an important part in my development. When I accepted the call to my first solo pastorate, I asked for two weeks of study leave and expenses. This was before presbyteries included study leaves in their calls. I was the second minister in the

presbytery to do this. There were twenty or thirty Ph.D.s in our congregation of four hundred members. To them continuing education was natural, so they said "of course."

I realized from the first that seminary was only the beginning of my education. When I graduated from seminary I could have been sued for malpractice. I set myself the task of reading from thirty to fifty books a year. I kept a record of the books I read. They were of all kinds: novels, theology, and so forth.

I took the study leave time mostly with seminary-based programs—for example, a reading week at a seminary. Out of this a network developed.

My most memorable continuing education event was a national conference on Science for Clergy—two weeks at Oak Ridge with hands-on science experiences. In 1970 I enrolled in the S.T.D. program because I felt the need for focus and direction in my continuing education. I worked on that degree 15 years.

PLANNING FOR CONTINUING EDUCATION

Various studies underscore the importance of planning one's continuing education in relation to one's growth goals. The Growth in Ministry Project conducted in the late 1970s with four hundred congregations of the Lutheran Church in America and the Lutheran Church, Missouri Synod, concluded, "There is very little correlation between pastors' selection of continuing-education courses and those subjects which they consider important. There was just as little correlation with areas in which they felt effective or ineffective. In short, there seems to be no pattern."[5]

Mark Rouch, in his analysis of continuing-education patterns in many denominations, quotes Thomas Brown as saying that many of those who came through career-development centers had actively engaged in continuing education. "However, there appeared to be an appalling lack of positive correlation between their continuing education and the central problems, hopes, goals of their ministry."[6]

A recent study of continuing education also shows that most pastors do not make long-range plans for their continuing education: "Only about one-fourth of the pastors and specialized clergy said they have a long-term plan in place for continuing their education, and 58 percent of the pastors and 44 percent of the specialized clergy said they do not have a plan but simply respond to announcements and promotions. Continuing education that is participated in so haphazardly cannot be very effective."[7]

Obviously, those who engage in a D.Min. program are making long-range plans. But on the whole, other long-range disciplined study toward clearly defined goals tends to be crowded out by the pressures of the pastorate. Proactivity yields to reactivity.

Rouch advocates a pattern of planning that we shall explore in more detail in chapter 11. He says,

Planning begins with ministry, not education. . . . The right question [is:] what is it about my life and ministry that I want to change?

Two sets of variables affect how we answer that question: (1) satisfaction/dissatisfaction and (2) effectiveness/ineffectiveness. Among the various roles of ministry and the particular tasks within them are some which give us satisfaction while others do not—and in varying degrees. Some we carry out effectively, a few with great competence; some ineffectively, a few dreadfully so.

A simple analysis of ministry around these variables is one of the best ways to decide what you would like to change."[8]

This pattern of planning for growth is precisely what we find in the responses of many of the Empowering Pastors. It is but a part of their broader commitment to growth in pastoral effectiveness. Once pastors understand their strengths and limitations and those tasks of ministry which satisfy or dissatisfy them, they are in a position to decide what they want to change and how they want to change it. Changes may involve modifying one's approach to the tasks of ministry or modifying oneself through continuing education. There are, then, three steps: (1) Understand yourself and your ministry. Where are you most effective and where is a change needed? In consultation with church officers, examine the needs of the congregation and consider how your gifts meet or fail to meet those needs. (2) Decide on ways you can change your approach to ministry to make the best use of your strengths and minimize your liabilities. (3) Decide on ways you wish to grow through continuing education. Use your study time to maximize your strengths and/or minimize your weaknesses.

Knowing the Needs of One's Ministry

The place to begin is with a knowledge of oneself and of one's ministry. Ask, What are my strengths and limitations? What does this congregation need from me as its pastor? Working closely with a personnel committee or pastor-parish committee can be very helpful to anyone who is open to criticism and to suggestions. Involvement in career-center counseling can open new vistas of self-understanding when pastors are willing to risk honestly confronting themselves. Quite a number of Empowering Pastors mention the value of counseling or therapy in developing their self-knowledge. Others describe the values they have discovered in knowing their Myers-Briggs type. In chapter 12 we will deal further with ways to understand oneself.

Shaping Ministry to Maximize Srengths
and Minimize Weaknesses

Many Empowering Pastors emphasize the importance of capitalizing on one's strengths. As one of them puts it, "First decide where your own gifts lie. Then engage in ministry receptive to those gifts." Another says, "I wish I were better at the things I'm already good at. I like building on strength. How to get better? As the old saying goes, 'How do you get to Carnegie Hall? Practice, practice, practice.' "

The pastor of a large congregation advises taking a point of strength and letting it serve you well in an area of weakness. "Funerals have been difficult for me," he says. "We had twenty funerals here last year. I decided that I had to work harder on those funerals and determined to take one of my strengths, pastoral care, and let it work for me in that arena."

Others join him in suggesting maximizing strengths and/or minimizing weaknesses:

I have carefully selected my associates and key leaders in that (1) they are spiritually mature and (2) have a different gift mix than my own. I'm especially conscious of gathering those around me who are strong where I am weak.

I have done a good deal of self-study and know my gifts. I am low on organization, so I depend on others to organize and make things happen.

Form a high-powered committee to deal with one of your areas of weakness. Once members are involved, they will feel they are making a significant contribution.

I am capitalizing on my own tendency to be hurt by learning to be more sensitive to the hurts of others.

To correct for my tendency to withdraw into a dream world, I am applying dreams to my real situation.

I tend to be more program oriented than people oriented. I like to get the job done. I am learning to be less "up tight" about tasks and to show more interest in people. Security in my pastoral position has been the most significant factor in this growth process.

I am growing in my ability to collaborate by minimizing my personal tendency to dominate and by learning a style of ministry from a colleague who was head of staff in my first parish.

Planning in the Light of a Needs Assessment

A second way to maximize strengths and minimize shortcomings is to develop long-range plans for continuing education that will meet one's own needs and the needs of the congregation. One pastor advocates carefully coordinating one's home study with continuing education events. He says, "It is helpful to 'bundle' your continuing education, rather than selecting subjects at random. One can bundle reading with other continuing education. I wanted to work on preaching so I did a series of things on preaching. One could do a series of studies on small groups, for example." Another pastor developed his program out of a deep sense of need.

I have chosen my courses in the light of my sense of a need in my ministry. When I began the ministry I felt totally inadequate for the pastoral ministry. For me that was a motivator. When I was in seminary they had thrown out all the core courses, so we could choose whatever we wanted to take. I took a lot of biblical courses. But when I began my work as a pastor I didn't even know how to baptize a baby.

When I served as an intern, there was heavy drug use among the young people, and I wanted to reach out to those kids. I took training in counseling. My background with a solid training in counseling has been a real blessing. I took it in "Conjoint Family Therapy," a family systems approach. I also had some therapy in which I worked on some of my own issues. This has been very helpful in understanding myself and in working with people. Knowing myself has enabled me to work unselfishly with others.

One of the best ways to develop plans for continuing education is to discuss possibilities with one's pastor relations or personnel committee. This provides an opportunity for valuable indirect feedback on one's performance without the possible trauma of direct confrontation growing out of problem situations. It is a good way to educate key members to a pastor's dreams and needs. They can then serve as interpreters to boards and to the congregation as a whole. It can result in win/win study programs that meet a pastor's felt needs while responding to a board's sense of where pastors can more effectively lead at the growing edges of the congregation's life. As one pastor put it, "Each year I take one week on what I want to do, and one week on what the session and its personnel committee feels it would be helpful for me to study." Another pastor reports,

> I have my continuing-education plans approved by the personnel committee. The session may see a need and suggest that I study it. For example, they suggested that I study evangelism. I wrote up the experience and the session developed a five-year plan.
>
> I look for subject areas and take classes that I feel will help the congregation. When I return, I type up and distribute the notes for session and those who would like them. That way the church gets their money's worth from my education. Usually they don't pay attention to the notes right away. I took a workshop on baby boomers. The people had never heard of them and put my notes away. Later, when I was talking about baby boomers, an elder asked, "What do you mean, 'baby boomer'?" "Read the session paper," I replied.
>
> This year I felt the need for time to complete some of my writing. People have used some of my writing in Sunday school classes. I can test the audience there. I have been writing a book on premarital counseling for junior high young people. When one counsels with couples just before their marriage it is often too late. So my goal is to effect change in junior high young people, ten years before they need to change. I asked for one week to do writing and the personnel committee was very agreeable to that.

PATTERNS OF CONTINUING EDUCATION

Among Empowering Pastors, as with Other Pastors, there is no common pattern of continuing education. Pastors develop their own patterns to fit their personalities, their learning styles, and their situations. In the sections that follow, some patterns that we observed are illustrated by pastors' descriptions of their approaches.

Self-directed Reading

For some pastors, a self-directed program of reading on the job and on study leaves is the primary method of continuing education. This method may be more difficult for solo pastors than for senior pastors whose primary responsibilities involve preaching and who have staffs to cover some of their other pastoral responsibilities.

I learn as I go, am an avid reader, and read heavily for sermons and in management literature. I do a good deal of secular reading to keep up with the world. I am not doing any [outside] continuing education except for my own personal reading. I take sabbaticals as reading and rest time. They are renewal times for me. I am a good student and serve one of the most highly educated congregations. But they are interested in hearing the gospel related to their needs.

I take two months off every summer and take an additional month every other year. If you want to be effective, it is very important to get away without being obsessed about being productive. It makes me more productive when I get back. Ministry is not my whole life.

My study is self-directed. Selected reading in seminary or university library settings has been a major source of renewal, discovery, and stretching, both intellectual and spiritual, which for me converge at some point.

I visit seminaries, spend time in the library for self-study, and talk to professors who give me suggestions of books to read. I read a book a month, *Monday Morning, Presbyterian Outlook,* and *Christianity Today.*

Reading Combined with Study Leaves

Probably the most frequent pattern of continuing education is some form of regular reading and planned study leaves.

I do regular reading and plan time away for continuing education. In the late '70s I worked on a D.Min. for three years. Other than that I go to two different seminaries for conferences, picking out some area I want to concentrate on.

Aside from voluminous reading, most of my study has been in church history as I have been working on my Ph.D.

Graduate Theological Study, Workshops, and Seminars

Some pastors cite graduate-level courses in theology, followed by workshops and seminars.

The first three years after I was ordained in 1976 I spent getting my M.Th. in New Testament biblical studies. Following that, I worked on my D.Min. Since then I have attended the annual Large-Church Pastors Conference in February. It has three outstanding principal speakers, each of whom gives seven speeches. It is a high-content occasion and my contact with other large church pastors has become for me a support group.

Seminars and D.Min. Degree Courses

For some pastors years of seminar work is followed by work on a doctor of ministry degree.

I've attended twenty or more outstanding continuing-education events with many foci and a D.Min. program completed in the eleventh year of my ministry.

All my career I have valued continuing education highly. I have taken mostly seminars. About ten years out of seminary I started a D.Min. It took me twelve years. Doing a significant piece of continuing education gives one a new grip on things. One very helpful program was on power and conflict, a week-long residential lab, which I took in the mid-seventies. It was a transforming experience. Recently I took the Alban Institute seminar, "New Visions for a Long Pastorate." I have participated in the festival of homiletics.

Travel and Study

Combining study with travel can be a helpful pattern when it follows years of intensive continuing education in seminars or degree programs.

An important part of my present continuing education is related to travel mixed with study. I have traveled to England, Scotland, and Israel. This year I have been teaching a Monday morning class on the life of Paul in preparation for a trip we are taking to Greece in July.

Seminars for New Pastors

A number of Empowering Pastors mentioned Young Pastors' Seminars as having been invaluable to their development during the critical early years of their ministries. They participated in a nationally sponsored program for all pastors in their third, fourth, and fifth years of pastoral ministry. Each year for one week they met with colleagues from the same part of the country under the guidance of resource leaders of mature pastoral experience. A growing number of middle judicatory bodies now carry on similar special programs for new pastors.

I cannot say enough about the importance of the three weeks, over three years, of help I received at the Young Pastors' Seminars our church sponsored.

Young Pastors' Seminars helped me deal with a demonic senior pastor who had no self-esteem or self-worth. The great staff of the Young Pastors' Seminars were positive role models.

In the Young Pastors' Seminar I said, "My goal is to be a good pastor." I was really interested in pastoral counseling, so I took a D.Min. with a heavy component of counseling and therapy training.

My advice would be to take advantage of Young Pastors' Seminars, clergy study groups, retreats, and all opportunities to develop collegial support.

Team Involvement in Continuing Education

One pastor advocates participation of both pastor and spouse in continuing-education events. This, he suggests, helps develop mutual support and team work. Another pastor turns to colleagues for participation and support. Such team involvement in continuing education can enhance the quality of a learning experience and build support relationships at the same time.

One of the most helpful things I have discovered is to go together with a buddy to a continuing-education event. Doing it together is valuable in a lot of ways. Sometimes you can get it cheaper; you can share transportation and lodging. And the ride going and coming back is hard to put a price on. It builds a support relationship.

PATTERNS OF SPIRITUAL DEVELOPMENT

In most of our measures of spiritual life we found little difference between Empowering Pastors and Other Pastors. Eight out of ten pastors in both groups feel that prayer and meditation are very valuable or valuable to their personal and professional development. They are equally likely to spend time in retreats. The one measurable difference is in whether they feel they take time for prayer and meditation. Forty-eight percent of Empowering Pastors compared with 30 percent of Other Pastors say that they are very effective or effective in taking time for prayer or meditation. In fact, among sixteen activities on which pastors in our study rated themselves, this was one of four with the greatest difference between the two groups in their self-ratings.

It is difficult to determine what pastors understood by the words "take time for." From comments on the questionnaires and from our interviews, we believe it may have meant different things to different pastors. For some it meant setting aside a particular time each day for solitary prayer. For others it may have meant consciously pausing, though briefly, in the midst of activities to reach out to God.

Whatever it meant to our respondents, it is safe to assume that the range of interpretations are the same within both groups of pastors. Therefore, two things seem clear. (1) Different approaches to prayer and meditation seem to meet the spiritual needs of different personalities of the pastors in our study. (2) Empowering Pastors feel that they are actually giving higher priority to prayer and meditation than Other Pastors feel that they do.

Chester Michael and Marie Norrisey, in *Prayer and Temperament*,[9] have described different forms of prayer in relation to the four basic temperaments developed by David Keirsey and Marilyn Bates out of the Myers-Briggs Type Indicator. Roy Oswald and Otto Kroeger also describe the relationship of temperament to prayer and different forms of spirituality.[10] One value of that analysis is to legitimate for pastors their own unique approach to spiritual development and thus assuage any guilt they may feel for following a pattern different from those advocated by others. We find this in the comments of one of the Empowering Pastors.

> Myers-Briggs helps us understand that there are different preferences and different styles. You need to find out what your preference is and let it happen that way. An introvert who is restored and renewed by meditation should claim it and go and meditate. An extrovert, on the other hand, may get a support group. Don't worry about your not being fed by going into your closet to pray.
>
> I was tormented in my early ministry because everyone said that quiet devotional time before dawn is the way to save your soul. But sitting before God with a Bible on my lap just doesn't work for me. When I sit quietly I think about basketball and countless other things. People will tell me how much silent meditation in the communion service means to them. It doesn't do anything that moves my soul. But when the elders come up and eight different voices say "The body of Christ for you," I am communing with the Spirit in that communal act. That's the way it works for me. Pastors can move toward self-acceptance—finding out what is their style and blessing it. And not letting people with a different style put them in a box of inappropriate expectations. We have the tools to do it.

Those who wish to understand their preferences for prayer and meditation in relation to their own temperament may wish to study one or more of several sources listed in Resources for Further Reflection. In sections that follow, we simply give some illustrations of the differences we found, without trying to relate them either to Oswald and Kroeger's analysis or to that of Michael and Norrisey.

Daily Disciplined Time for Prayer and Meditation

The most prevalent pattern of spiritual development seems to be a daily time set aside for prayer and meditation. A pastor whose nominator says that he has especially deepened the spirituality of his medium-sized congregation gives this advice:

> Spend the first hour of every day in prayer with your God. Get a good spiritual director, find a good retreat center. Listen to God first, then do whatever he leads you to do. If you don't spend time in prayer every day, don't bother to pick up your paycheck. Pray for your congregation and love them. Let God use you, and watch out!

Many pastors find the daily discipline of prayer to be essential.

> I cultivate my own spiritual life with reading and with daily morning and evening prayer. My wife and I walk three miles every morning before I go to the office. That gives us time for reflection. I grow through participation in church activities such as the prayer groups.
>
> There is a direct relationship in the effectiveness and joy in my ministry and my pursuit of the face of God.

I engage in a lot of prayer, not on retreat. I take time for myself, down time when I can catch a vision, dream, think, imagine, and get in touch with God's Spirit. When I am under stress I use tools—spiritual guidebooks. One that I have found helpful is *Prayers and Guides for Ministers*. It is a collection of classics that follows the lectionary. I also go back to some of the piety of my childhood. I allow time for spiritual growth, and do not apologize to myself or to the congregation for taking it. I have participated in Cursillos and Emmaus Walk.

Solitude

Some pastors find it difficult to maintain a daily disciplined time for prayer and meditation. But they say quiet time is important as one of the ways in which they deal with stress and burnout.

My prayer life is not consistent. Every other day I have some form of solitude: prayer, thinking, meditation. Solitude is important for a sense of my own peace and comfort and for reevaluating things. Ministry is very consuming physically, mentally, emotionally, and spiritually. So I take a day off and find it very helpful. I also work very hard. A couple of interns with us didn't want to work hard. But you have to work hard in the ministry. I have learned to relax. For example, I used to return to my desk after a funeral. Now I may take a walk. Every now and then I take an extra day off and go skiing. The people encourage me to do that.

Ongoing Spiritual Dialogue

Two pastors share their experience of "praying without ceasing" as they go about their busy days.

For me, prayer is real and constant, not on a timetable of regularity. I sit at the piano with a hymnbook. Sometimes I sing, or just play. I kept a prayer diary for a number of years, but don't do that right now.

My primary spiritual growth comes through prayer and being open to the Holy Spirit. My entire day is an ongoing conversation with the Lord. Sometimes this leads me to journaling. Sometimes reading through the Bible in a year, or reflecting on other devotional material. The primary gist of what I do is ongoing dialogue and openness to the Lord. One of my prayers is, "Lord help me be open to the leading of the Spirit so that I might do what you would have me do; so that I might receive from others what you might have me receive." That is the keynote of my life.

This morning as I was driving to church I saw one of our inactive members. Suddenly I felt an inner urge to go back to have a cup of coffee with him. So I prayed, "Lord, do you want me to have coffee with Joe?" I went back and we started to chitchat. As the conversation progressed, he began to minister to me. I needed to have him minister to me.

So when I feel an inner urge I often take the risk. And when I do, 95 percent of the time the Lord confirms that was what he was leading me to do. So I have encouraged others to do it too. In one Bible class we talked for forty-five minutes about the inner nudges of the Spirit. One of the members told how she had learned to listen to these inner nudges and to take the risk of responding. "Wow!" she said. "This is for real! This was the voice of God."

Spiritual Development as an Intellectual Journey

A majority of our pastors list "prayer and meditation" first among their three most important spiritual disciplines. However, 38 percent say that either "preparation for preaching" or "Bible study and exegesis" comes first, followed by prayer and meditation. As one put it,

> I am not a person driven by emotional experience. My approach to the Christian faith is far more from the academic side than the experiential. Not surprising, therefore, to me at least, is that I have not experienced great spiritual highs and lows over the years. My living the Christian life has been level rather than up and down. Broad reading feeds my spiritual growth . . . novels, mysteries, and so forth.

Group Sharing and Prayer

Interaction with other Christians is an especially important source of spiritual renewal to extroverts. Several respondents testify to the importance of support groups and prayer cells.

> The biggest challenge I have found in my ministry has been setting time aside for my own emotional, spiritual, and mental health. I have actively sought a support group and have found church members and friends outside the church very helpful. Sorry to say, I have not found genuine support in the presbytery.

> I am not an inward person. I went to a retreat where there was extended silence. It was not helpful. My spirituality comes as I involve myself with others.

> I attend two small-group meetings a week for prayer, sharing, and study.

> My spiritual growth comes from participation in twelve-step programs.

Special Techniques

Respondents reported using various other unique techniques to enhance spiritual development:

> Before every worship service I spend time praying in the sanctuary the night before.

> I read the psalms in the morning and the evening and complete a cycle in a month. I also study one book of the Bible. I find inspiration in reading and writing. I give high priority to daily jogging and exercise. That is my time for God. No phones ring. I plant a single verse in my mind and meditate on it as I jog.

> My spiritual disciplines are erratic. I think I have had good intentions, but I am not a disciplined person. In the mornings at breakfast my wife and I would have prayer times. One thing we did: We took all our Christmas cards and put

them in a basket. Each morning we would pull out four cards and talk about each person who sent them and pray for those four. Then we would put the cards in a second basket. During the course of the year we worked our way through those cards three or four times. It was a very helpful way to be aware of people. One of my wife's friends in an ecumenical Bible study group sent us a card one year with a note, "Please make me one of your basket cases."

In one of my dreams a person was given a gift of a gold fish on a gold chain. Soon after that I made a shift from a parish pastor to director of a pastoral counseling center. A year later in a conference on pastoral counseling, I visited a place that made jewelry, looking for a gold fish. Instead I found a dolphin. The dolphin is a mammal that lives in water. It needs both air and water. It became for me a symbol that the spiritual and the psychological are both important. The dolphin became the analogy of one who lives in two environments and relates them in a living whole. I wore that for a number of years until I had worked through my integration of the spiritual and the psychological.

Spiritual Direction

Spiritual direction has been defined as "a covenant friendship between Christians in which one assists the other in the discernment of God's presence and the contemplative living out of God's call."[11] Six out of ten pastors in our study have had some experience with spiritual direction. More than one-fourth say that spiritual direction has been very valuable or valuable in their personal and professional development. Eleven percent include spiritual direction among their three most important forms of spiritual development. And ten percent feel it has been of little or no value to them.

Spiritual direction, as an essential part of spiritual formation, has a rich heritage in the Roman Catholic tradition. Protestant ministers are just now beginning to discover the value of having someone who regularly accompanies them on their spiritual journey and helps them identify the movement of God in their lives. The fact that so many in our study say that they have experienced spiritual direction suggests that within a few years we will see a significant growth in the number of ministers and members who find this discipline helpful in their lives and ministries. One of the Empowering Pastors says, "My spiritual growth has come from two outstanding continuing-education experiences: a two-year program in spiritual direction at the Shalem Institute for Spiritual Formation in Washington, D.C., and the doctor of ministry program."

WORKING THE ANGLES

Those who want to give more serious attention to their spiritual growth will find Eugene Peterson, *Working the Angles,* helpful. He uses the metaphor of a triangle to describe three crucial acts of ministry. The lines of the triangle are common tasks of ministry: preaching, teaching, and administration. They are held together by three angles, without which the triangle falls apart. They hold together and give meaning to our preaching, teaching, and administration. "Working the angles is what gives shape and integrity to the daily work of pastors and priests. If we get the angles right it is a simple matter to draw in the lines. But if we are careless with or dismiss the angles, no matter how long or straight we draw the lines we will not have a triangle, a pastoral ministry."[12]

What are the three angles? Peterson says:

> Three pastoral acts are so basic, so critical, that they determine the shape of everything else. The acts are praying, reading Scripture, and giving spiritual direction.
>
> The three areas constitute acts of attention: prayer is an act in which I bring myself to attention before God; reading Scripture is an act of attending to God in his speech and action across two millennia in Israel and Christ; spiritual direction is an act of giving attention to what God is doing in the person who happens to be before me at any given moment.
>
> Always it is God to whom we are paying, or trying to pay, attention. The contexts, though, vary: in prayer the context is myself; in Scripture it is the community of faith in history; in spiritual direction it is the person before me. God is the one to whom we are being primarily attentive in these contexts, but it is never God-in-himself; rather, it is God-in-relationship—with me, with his people, with this person.[13]

Here we have the heart of the power that helps us become all God wants us to be in ministry. By closing this chapter with these quotations, I seek to underscore the crucial importance to vital ministry of these spiritual resources.

7

THE POWER
IN YOUR HANDS

"What do you have there in your hand?" the Lord asked him.
And he replied, "A shepherd's rod."
The Lord said, ". . . be sure to take your rod along so that you
can perform the miracles I have shown you."
—Exod. 4:2, 17, *The Living Bible*

God always begins with what we have in our hands. What we do with that rod makes the difference. Over and over pastors inspire me with ways they discover their special gifts and develop them. Each Empowering Pastor is gifted uniquely. No two are alike. They have taken their own particular shepherd's rod in their hands. Because of their openness to change and growth, the Spirit has transformed those rods into miracle ministries that live with power in many different ways. Paul's words still ring true today:

He handed out gifts above and below, filled heaven with his gifts, filled earth with his gifts. He handed out gifts of apostle, prophet, evangelist and pastor-teacher to train Christians in skilled servant work, working within Christ's body, the church, until we're all moving rhythmically and easily with each other, efficient and graceful in response to God's Son, fully mature adults, fully developed within and without, fully alive like Christ. (Eph. 4:10–13, TM)

FIFTEEN SKILLS OF EMPOWERING PASTORS

In chapter 5 we described the distinction between *core essences* (those almost immutable characteristics at the core of one's being) and *values and beliefs* (qualities that can be learned but are so deeply ingrained that they can be changed only with great difficulty). Now we come to a third dimension involved in effectiveness: the skills that a pastor brings to ministry. *Skills* include significant behaviors and styles of working with people and with the content of ministry that have been learned or can be learned. They are acquired either in formal educational settings, self-study, or in life experiences. Because skills can be learned, they offer to every pastor potent areas for growth. Accordingly we have made a special study of the skills that seem to be important to an empowering ministry.

Many skills of Empowering Pastors flow naturally out of the personality and innate abilities with which they have been endowed. Because they are open, eager to learn, and willing to take risks, they have taken their gifts, developed them, and used them. Some skills have not come naturally to them. In response to the demands of ministry they have found ways to learn those skills, although many pastors find it difficult to identify just how they learned them.

In a follow-up study to *Congregations Alive*, we identified twenty skill areas and found that in eighteen out of twenty skill ratings made by pastors and lay leaders of especially effective churches, there were significant differences from ratings by average Presbyterian pastors and lay leaders. We used fifteen of the original twenty skills, with some refinement, in our current study. Four of the original skills proved not to be very helpful in describing differences in effectiveness. The fifth missing skill, "application of biblical and theological thought," has in this study been covered by two descriptions of pastoral activity to which we have already referred: "relates the gospel to issues people face in their personal lives and in society" and "helps people find meaning for living through worship, preaching, teaching, and so forth." As we have already seen, Empowering Pastors are much more likely than Other Pastors to describe their ministry in these ways.

The Interrelationship of Skills

In our previous study we found that effective pastors were highly resistant to rating the relative importance of the skills we had identified. They insisted that all were so important that it was almost impossible to assign a higher importance to one than to another. Recognizing that those skills were in many cases closely related to each other, we looked at them through the statistical device of factor analysis and found two major groupings: Factor A, "leadership in mission achievement," and Factor B, "responsiveness to others." Several skills did not cluster and need to be looked at separately. We call that group "energizing and facilitating skills." We have used that three-part framework in analyzing the responses in our present study.

Empowering Pastors are much more likely than Other Pastors to rate themselves as very skillful or skillful in all fifteen skills and in each of the statistically derived groupings of those skills (Factors A and B). The levels of statistical significance are so high that the differences are incontestable.

Leadership in Mission Achievement

Empowering Pastors are much more likely to be skillful or very skillful as leaders in mission achievement, Factor A. This includes planning, leading, organizing, and managing the life and activities of the congregation so that members can be productive in its mission. It involves seeing possibilities for the future and motivating others to respond to that vision; assessing the talents of self and others; and assigning tasks to them with confidence that they can accomplish their tasks. In Figure 7.1 the leadership, executive, and managing skills that make up Factor A are defined. Included in this factor are visioning, strategizing, organizing, identifying gifts, persuading, delegating, and guiding.

Fig. 7.1. Factor A: Leadership in Mission Achievement

VISIONING: The ability to see new possibilities for the future and to express this vision to others

STRATEGIZING: The ability to plan activities that lead toward accomplishment of objectives and tasks related to the congregation's mission

ORGANIZING: The ability to plan and manage the life and work of the congregation so that all elements fit together in an ordered whole

IDENTIFYING GIFTS: The ability to identify and assess one's own talents and the talents of others

PERSUADING: The ability to convince people of one's position and convictions and to motivate them to take specific courses of action

DELEGATING: The ability to assign tasks to others with clear instructions and with confidence in their ability to accomplish the task

GUIDING: The ability to guide and manage the work of session and key committees for maximum productivity

Responsiveness to Others

Empowering Pastors are more likely than Other Pastors to rate themselves higher in all the skills included in Factor B, responsiveness to others (see Fig. 7.2). These involve understanding the thoughts and feelings of others; seeing things from their perspective; accepting them as they are, without judging, manipulating, or dominating them; treating them with unconditional respect; responding to them appropriately; and placing them ahead of one's own fulfillment or advancement. Included in this factor are listening, empathizing, collaborating, and serving. Note that these are person-oriented, relationship, and group-building skills.

Energizing and Facilitating Skills

Finally there are four abilities that do not cluster with any of the others (see Fig. 7.3). Each stands alone. But careful study shows that in many ways they facilitate the use of skills involved in Factors A and B. They are energizing and facilitating skills. Empowering others, by establishing a climate in which they feel free to grow, energizes their involvement in mission and builds firm and trusting relationships. One assesses situations in order to determine the direction one's leadership should take and to respond to others' real feelings and circumstances. The ability to communicate effectively is essential to providing leadership in mission achievement and to maintaining warm relationships with others. Destructive conflict that is poorly managed can thwart mission achievement and destroy relationships. Conversely, the skills involved in leading for mission achievement and in being responsive to others contribute toward empowering, assessing situations, communicating, and resolving conflict.

Fig. 7.2. Factor B: Responsiveness to Others

LISTENING: The ability to hear other people fully, with understanding of thoughts and feelings and with unconditional respect for their opinions

EMPATHIZING: The ability to place oneself in the shoes of others, feeling what they feel, without manipulating or judging them

COLLABORATING: The ability to work cooperatively with others without need to dominate or take credit for accomplishments

SERVING: The ability to place the needs of one's congregation above the need for self-fulfillment and advancement

Fig. 7.3. Energizing and Facilitating Skills

EMPOWERING: The ability to establish a climate in which people feel free to grow, learn, explore, and use their gifts in Christian ministry without fear of retribution

ASSESSING SITUATIONS: The ability to understand what is happening in work and social situations and to relate appropriately to them

COMMUNICATING: The ability to express thoughts clearly and understandably to a broad range of individuals and groups

RESOLVING CONFLICT: The ability to help others in a conflict situation to make use of differing ideas and opinions without losing their self-esteem

SKILL RATINGS OF EMPOWERING PASTORS AND OTHER PASTORS

A look at Figure 7.4 makes clear that there are large differences in the percentages of Empowering Pastors and Other Pastors who rated themselves as very skillful or skillful on the fifteen skill scales. Empowering Lay Leaders and Other Lay Leaders rated their pastors on the same fifteen skills. Lay leaders tend to rate their pastors higher on most of these skill areas than their pastors rate themselves. Perhaps partly for that reason, differences in lay leaders' ratings of their pastors were not as great as between Empowering and Other Pastors' self-ratings, and not all the differences were statistically significant. For simplicity of interpretation lay leaders' ratings are not shown in Figure 7.4, but when differences between lay leaders' ratings are not statistically significant for any skill, that is indicated.

Four of the six greatest differences between pastors' self-ratings are in empowering, identifying gifts, delegating, and resolving conflict. These are also among the six greatest differences in lay leaders' ratings of their pastors. For pastors, the other two skill ratings with the greatest differences are on guiding and

Fig. 7.4. Pastors' Self-ratings on Skills

Percent of pastors who rated themselves as very skillful or as skillful

	Empowering Pastors (%)	Other Pastors (%)	Difference (%)
FACTOR A (COMPOSITE)	67	35	32
Identifying gifts	65	29	36
Delegating	53	18	35
Guiding[a]	69	37	32
Persuading	61	30	31
Strategizing	75	46	29
Organizing	69	40	29
Visioning	79	51	28
FACTOR B (COMPOSITE)	81	61	20
Collaborating	89	62	27
Listening[a]	80	59	21
Serving[a]	75	58	17
Empathizing[a]	80	67	13
ENERGIZING AND FACILITATING SKILLS			
Empowering[b]	100	0	100
Resolving conflict	57	26	31
Assessing situations[a]	74	46	28
Communicating	76	58	18
AVERAGE	72	43	29

[a]Indicates that on lay leaders' ratings (not shown) differences on those skills were not statistically significant.

[b]The 100% difference results from the definition of the two groups. It does not mean that Other Pastors have no skill in empowering. Empowering Pastors are defined as those who rated themselves very skillful or skillful in empowering. Other Pastors are those who rated themselves as somewhat skillful or lower than that.

persuading. For lay leaders, the other two with greatest differences are on organizing and visioning.

Five Abilities Contributing Most to Pastoral Effectiveness

We asked pastors to list five abilities that they feel contribute most to their effectiveness. Lay leaders were asked which five abilities contribute to the effectiveness of any pastor. Empowering Pastors and Empowering Lay Leaders agree on all five. Other Pastors and Other Lay Leaders agree with them on three of the five: listening, communicating, and organizing. These are the last three items in each list in Figure 7.5. Other Lay Leaders also agree on including empowering.

When Other Pastors' and Other Lay Leaders' choices differed from the choices of Empowering Pastors and Empowering Lay Leaders, that is indicated in Figure 7.5. Note that instead of visioning, Other Lay Leaders choose guiding. Other Pastors, on the other hand, do not include either visioning or empowering. Instead they choose empathizing and serving.

These differences suggest an important distinction between Empowering Pastors and Other Pastors. Visioning gives direction and motivation to members of a congregation. Empowering creates a climate in which they will feel free to grow in the direction of that vision. These are skills that activate, stimulate, and energize members. In contrast, empathizing focuses a pastor's attention on understanding members of a congregation, and serving emphasizes meeting their needs. While empathizing and serving are valuable abilities, focusing major attention on them could leave members in a more passive and potentially dependant stance than do empowering and visioning.

These interpretations are merely suggestive, since our analysis of the data does not establish clear, significant statistical differences.[1] Nevertheless, the extent of the differences in these patterns does raise two searching questions: Do Empowering Pastors tend to stimulate growth by giving people a vision and creating a climate in which they feel free to grow? In contrast, do Other Pastors give less stimulus to members' growth because they are giving more emphasis to understanding people and serving them? And since Other Lay Leaders choose guidance over visioning, we wonder if they represent congregations that are less eager to be challenged by vision and more content to seek and follow a pastors' guidance.

These findings raise some interesting additional questions that we have pursued. Has the membership size or location of the churches served by pastors in our sample contributed to these results? Others have shown that sociological differences between small towns or rural areas and suburban areas or large towns

Fig. 7.5. Five "Most Important" Abilities

Cited by Pastors		Cited by Lay Leaders	
Empowering	*Other*	*Empowering*	*Other*
Visioning	Emphathizing	Visioning	Guiding
Empowering	Serving	Empowering	Empowering
Listening	Listening	Listening	Listening
Communicating	Communicating	Communicating	Communicating
Organizing	Organizing	Organizing	Organizing

tend to shape the character of congregations in those areas. Characteristics of small churches tend to be different from large churches. Large churches with multiple staffs require some different styles of leadership than small churches served by solo pastors.

Skills Related to Church Size

When we look at all pastors in our study, combining both Empowering Pastors and Other Pastors, we find some significant differences between churches with different membership sizes (see Fig. 7.6). The larger the congregation, the greater the likelihood that its pastor will give a high self-rating on five of the seven skills related to Factor A, leadership in mission achievement. This is as one would expect, because the larger the congregation, the more emphasis is given to program and the more strenuous are the demands for leadership in mission achievement. Pastors who serve large congregations have a special need for the skills of strategizing, organizing, persuading, delegating, and guiding.

Two of the seven skills in Factor A, leadership in mission achievement, are not included in Figure 7.6. They are visioning and identifying gifts. There is a slight tendency for the proportion of high self-ratings on visioning to increase with

Fig. 7.6. Significant Differences by Membership Size

Percent of pastors who rated themselves as very skillful or as skillful

	Size of Church[a]		
	Small *(%)*	*Medium* *(%)*	*Large* *(%)*
FACTOR A: LEADERSHIP IN MISSION ACHIEVEMENT			
Strategizing	57	67	79
Organizing	50	60	73
Persuading	34	56	65
Delegating	36	42	52
Guiding	49	59	74
FACTOR B: RESPONSIVENESS TO OTHERS			
No significant differences (all are between 66% and 83%)			
ENERGIZING AND FACILITATING SKILLS			
Communicating	70	78	89

Note: Pastors' self-ratings on skills
[a]Small congregation = up to 199 members; medium congregation = 200 to 499; large congregation = 500 or more.

membership size, but the differences are not statistically significant. Again there is a slight tendency for pastors of large congregations to give themselves higher ratings on identifying gifts, but the differences are not statistically significant. This suggests that both skills may be equally important whatever the size of the congregation. Indeed, it is not difficult to see why that would be the case. These two skills are less related to management of a large operation and more related to challenging members and channeling their gifts into ministry.

There are no statistically significant differences related to church size on the skills that comprise Factor B, responsiveness to persons. At least two-thirds of all pastors rate themselves as very skilled or skilled on all of these abilities regardless of church size. Our conclusion is that listening, empathizing, collaborating, and serving form the foundation for effective ministry, and that the other skills enhance effectiveness.

Having made these observations on the total group of congregations in our study, I turn to the differences in church size between congregations served by Empowering Pastors and Other Pastors (see Fig. 7.7). Medium-sized congregations are equally represented in our group of Empowering Pastors and Other Pastors. The data suggest that a higher percentage of Other Pastors may be found in small congregations and a higher percentage of Empowering Pastors are serving large congregations. It is possible that this influences the results of our study, but that influence is not likely to be very great since the differences are not statistically significant.

Heads of Staff Compared to Solo Pastors

Since heads of staff normally serve larger congregations, we might expect to find the differences between heads of staff and solo pastors to be similar to those between large-membership churches and medium to small congregations. On this dimension our sample of Empowering Pastors is weighted more heavily with heads of staff than with solo pastors (see Fig. 7.8). Solo pastors are less likely to be represented among Empowering Pastors, and heads of staff are less likely to be represented among Other Pastors. These differences are statistically significant so we need to take them seriously.

Heads of staff rate themselves significantly higher than solo pastors in skills

Fig. 7.7. Size of Congregations in Our Samples

	Empowering Pastors (%)	Other Pastors (%)
Small congregations (up to 199 members)	28	34
Medium-sized congregations (200 to 499 members)	32	32
Large congregations (500 or more members)	39	34

Fig. 7.8. Current Position Held by Pastors in Study

	Empowering Pastors (%)	Other Pastors (%)
Solo pastor	38	54
Head of staff	32	17
Associate pastor	1	3
Co-pastor	2	1
aRetired	6	5
aOther	4	2

aThese persons were active clergy when nominated.

related to Factor A, leadership in mission achievement (see Fig. 7.9). This is even more pronounced than the differences related to membership size. It also is what one might expect. Heads of staff must give leadership to church officers and staff. They are generally expected to fulfill executive responsibilities in multiple-staff situations. The differences between solo pastors and heads of staff also are found in the energizing and facilitating skills.

But again, both solo pastors and heads of staff tend to rate themselves high in skills related to Factor B. Differences between their ratings are not statistically significant. Percentages of pastors in both groups who rate themselves high in those skills range from 69 percent to 83 percent. Once again we conclude that responsiveness to others in its various dimensions is indeed the baseline for effective pastoral ministry, whatever other skills may be involved in serving as solo pastor or as head of staff.

All this makes very clear that pastors who aspire to serve as head of staff need to assess carefully whether they are blessed with considerable skills related to leadership in mission achievement (Factor A). It also provides a clue to pastor nominating committees regarding skills they may wish to seek in potential heads of staff.

Empowering Solo Pastors Compared to Other Solo Pastors

We have concluded that skills related to Factor A are of special importance to those who serve as heads of staff. However, the converse is not true for solo pastors. Leadership in mission achievement is not unimportant for solo pastors. Empowering Solo Pastors are more skilled than Other Solo Pastors in skills related to Factor A (leadership in mission achievement). Their emphasis on empowering others makes the difference. See Figure 7.10 for data on solo pastors alone and comparisons of Empowering Solo Pastors with Other Solo Pastors. The results here confirm the importance of the Empowering dimension and demonstrate that the bias in our sample toward heads of staff does not vitiate the importance to all pastors of an emphasis on empowering others.

Fig. 7.9. Self-rating Differences between Solo Pastors and Heads of Staff

Percent of pastors who rated themselves as very skillful or as skillful

	Solo Pastors (%)	Heads of Staff (%)	Difference (%)
FACTOR A: LEADERSHIP IN MISSION ACHIEVEMENT			
Persuading	37	67	30
Strategizing	52	80	28
Guiding	45	71	26
Organizing	49	71	22
Delegating	33	53	20
Visioning	63	80	17
Identifying gifts	48	60	12
FACTOR B: RESPONSIVENESS TO OTHERS			
No significant differences (all are between 69% and 83%)			
ENERGIZING AND FACILITATING SKILLS			
Assessing situations	52	77	25
Communicating	71	89	18
Resolving conflict	39	55	16
Empowering	67	81	14

Note: Only significant differences are reported, and they are listed in descending order of differences under each factor.

In Figure 7.10 we see that Empowering Solo Pastors rate themselves as significantly more skillful than Other Solo Pastors in fourteen of the fifteen skills. Only in serving is the difference not significant. Once again Factor B ratings are high for all. But now, the differences between Empowering Solo Pastors and Other Solo Pastors are statistically significant. At the same time, the differences between Empowering Solo Pastors and Other Solo Pastors on leadership in mission achievement (Factor A) are greater than the differences on responsiveness to persons (Factor B). Since solo pastors serve mostly small and medium-sized congregations, the importance of leadership in mission achievement is confirmed for those congregations as well as for large churches.

In the next two chapters we look more closely at the fifteen individual skills with an emphasis on those that appear to be most important to the effectiveness of the Empowering Pastors.

Fig. 7.10. Self-rating Differences between Empowering Solo Pastors and Other Solo Pastors on Skills

Percent of pastors who rated themselves as very skillful or as skillful

	Empowering Solo Pastors (%)	Other Solo Pastors (%)	Difference (%)
FACTOR A: LEADERSHIP IN MISSION ACHIEVEMENT			
Persuading	64	30	34
Organizing	60	26	34
Identifying gifts	59	27	32
Strategizing	62	31	31
Visioning	73	45	28
Delegating	42	14	28
Guiding	53	30	23
FACTOR B: RESPONSIVENESS TO OTHERS			
Listening	78	61	17
Serving[a]	74	59	15
Emphathizing	80	66	14
Collaborating	86	73	13
ENERGIZING AND FACILITATING SKILLS			
Empowering[b]	100	0	100
Resolving conflict	46	24	42
Assessing situations	64	30	34
Communicating	81	50	31

[a]This difference is not statistically significant.

[b]The 100% difference results from the definition of the two groups. It does not mean that Other Pastors have no skill in empowering. Empowering Pastors are defined as those who rated themselves very skillful or skillful in empowering. Other Pastors are those who rated themselves as somewhat skillful or lower than that.

8

THE POWER IN
MISSION ACHIEVEMENT

Pastoral leaders see visions of ministry, communicate our dreams
clearly, gain consensus and commitment to common objectives,
take initiative by setting the pace in ministry actions, and multiply
our influence by transforming followers into new leaders.
—Robert D. Dale, *Pastoral Leadership*

Empowering Pastors, as we saw in chapter 7, are much more likely than
Other Pastors to be very skillful or skillful in the constellation of skills that contribute to leadership in mission achievement. These include visioning, strategizing, organizing, identifying gifts, persuading, delegating, and guiding. We now
look more closely at these skills and explore the ways in which Empowering Pastors have acquired them.

VISION ENHANCES CONGREGATIONAL VITALITY

Out my window I see a row of beautifully shaped small trees along a nearby
street. A year ago, through that same window I saw those same trees, overgrown
and misshapen. Up in them, with seeming reckless abandon, a man was rapidly
sawing off branches. As the skeleton of the almost-bare branches began to
emerge, I marveled at the skill of an artist. Obviously he had a mental picture of
what those trees might look like when nature had covered the scars of his handiwork. That man knew trees and how they grow. He had a vision of what they
could become. And because of his vision they are now more beautiful than ever
I could have imagined.

Like that tree surgeon, Empowering Pastors are women and men who are
skilled at visioning. Seldom does their vision require surgery. But, as with
Covey's second habit of effective people, they "begin with the end in mind."
They know the importance of giving the people of God a clear sense of direction.
They understand the congregations they serve and the context within which
those congregations carry out their mission. They are in tune with the Spirit and
take time to dream. They share those dreams in such a way that commitment to
a vision emerges.

In chapter 4 the importance of a shared vision to the exercise of effective servant leadership was stressed. Now we look in greater depth at the visioning skills found in Empowering Pastors. In chapter seven we observed that Empowering Pastors list visioning among the five most important skills for effective ministry, whereas Other Pastors do not. Empowering Lay Leaders also differ from Other Lay Leaders in identifying visioning among the five most important pastoral skills. In other words, a fundamental difference between Empowering Pastors and Other Pastors seems to be the priority they give to visioning and the skill with which they do it. Because of the importance they ascribe to visioning, we will look extensively at what they have to say. What do Empowering Pastors teach us about the art of visioning?

Visioning is one of a pastor's crucial responsibilities. In many ways, congregational vitality depends upon the vision that its members have for what God has called them to be and to do. And it is the pastor, more than anyone else, who bears the burden and the privilege of leading people to discover and commit themselves to that vision. One pastor correctly observes, "I have learned that few people other than the pastor can see the big picture." Another puts it this way:

> Motivation has to do with vision. It is critical. Vision is knowing where you are going and then persuading others to follow. It is having some big picture for a particular situation, for the church. Vision comes from the pastor. That is one of the responsibilities of that position. The pastor takes a vision and shares it in such a way that people believe that it is not only possible but probable. You have to articulate your vision. You must be able to tell it to others. I have seen churches where the pastor would work to have the vision come from the people. But pastors are more than managers, they are leaders. Most leaders have a vision that they share with a passion. A pastor has to be gripped by the gospel and have a passion for God's vision for the church.

But there is a paradox in visioning. While visioning is a high-priority responsibility for every pastor, vision must belong to the whole people of God. They play an important role in developing any viable vision. As this pastor says, one does not simply draw out a congregational vision from the membership. But neither does one proclaim a vision to which the people of God have not made some important contribution. Vision grows out of listening to God and listening to the people of God. The pastor must take the lead. But visioning does not depend upon the pastor alone. It is a dialogical process. The pastor shares the vision the Spirit is giving, and the people respond with their vision. Vision blossoms, grows, and is refined as members of the congregation make the vision their own. Our quotations from Empowering Pastors begin first with ways to develop our own capacity for visioning. We then move to considering how mutual visioning develops.

Trusting God to Give a Vision

Believe that God intends good things for you and for your congregation, and then start looking and listening for what that goodness might be. Articulate what you have begun to see and hear. The more you tell, the more you and others will see. Pray. Pieces of goodness that God intends are lying around in the most unlikely places. If you imagine that it exists only in your head you are lost.

It's all a matter of control. The sooner you learn that you don't have any control, the sooner you will start to have success. I think this comes with the realization that God has a vision for the church, for me, and for each Christian. It calls for sensitivity to those visions.

Remember, in Christ all things are possible, so dream big!

Developing Your Capacity for Visioning

Visioning emerges out of basic attitudes and orientations. It comes when we are open and willing to take risks. Some are gifted with curiosity, love, forgiveness, trust in God, and persistence. Discovering those gifts and using them help develop one's capacity for visioning. Others need to work at acquiring those qualities.

I'm a big-picture person, a dreamer. I grew up as an only child in a happy, hope-filled, joyous environment. Through stories and discussion I was nurtured to dream. My visioning comes from childhood "wonderment" cultivated by my parents.

Visioning? How do I do it? I don't know. I just do it. Roy Oswald's Myers-Briggs workshop helped me trust my own strong, intuitive side. I received affirmation from my executive presbyter. Session members encouraged me to set it loose.

Intentionally I have built on strengths of my Myers-Briggs intuitive type preference. Alban Institute's "Renewal of the Long Pastorate" and other seminars have helped me.

Some pastors are not naturally intuitive. They need to learn visioning from others. They have worked to develop their ability in visioning through modeling by a mentor, tutoring by lay leaders, taking courses in strategic planning, participating in workshops, and doing lots of reading on a variety of issues.

The pastor of a small congregation spells out his formula for visioning: "(1) studying and practicing creativity; (2) holy dreaming; (3) reading scripture; (4) exercising my imagination." Another says, "Visioning is a growing skill I see as being critical to church growth. Through reading, prayer, and talking it out I see my skills as a visionary growing."

Taking a Long Look into Tomorrow

The pastor of a large congregation says,

My job is to live in the future and hire good people. To look at what we are doing that is still relevant and add and subtract from it. We are on the drawing boards every day. We are radically restructuring our church in many ways. We have two tiers of management: the executive committee and those who relate directly to people we serve. We are doing away with anything in between.

I tell people the only thing that is permanent is change. The only thing that is stable is Jesus Christ and the scripture. Everything else is up for grabs. I keep a finger on the pulse of the congregation. Things are always fresh. We are always rearranging our troops. People never know what to expect in worship. Worship is built around people's needs today.

Other pastors say,

My parents were instrumental in teaching me to take the long view, to be willing to bear the burden of God's vision and the task of communicating it to others.

I would sum it up with the biblical reference to the great commission. For me, to be truly effective, the church must focus outward rather than inward. Always viewing what is out there leads us to be moving outward. When we are doing that, we are also moving forward as the body of Christ. In my experience, the churches that are growing are focused outward. Their theology may vary, but being focused outward, they capture those who are seeking a faith that is relevant to where they are living. We must go where the needs are. And this is going to be different for every church.

Investing Time to Develop Your Vision

Empowering Pastors emphasize the importance of taking time away from the bustle of activities to meditate on scripture, pray, read, and dream.

The vision must come from quiet time. It is not your own.

My biggest challenge has been maintaining the vision! Taking time away gives me the energy to sell the vision and take the necessary risks for new things.

Keep focused on the vision for ministry God gives through the scripture and conversation with others.

Biblical study helped me understand vision as a spiritual value. I have worked at reining in my intellectualization and giving free rein to my imagination.

Sabbaticals are a time for renewal and for shaping a vision through an extended period of reading, thinking, meditation, prayer, visiting other congregations, talking with other colleagues, travel, or taking courses.

Developing a Shared Vision

The importance of developing a shared vision cannot be overemphasized. There is power in the paradox of which we have been speaking. The clearer and more compelling the pastor's vision, the more urgent it is to develop a shared vision. One pastor who vigorously advocates a pastor's duty to motivate a congregation with his vision also recognizes danger there.

I can't let my agenda take precedence over people's needs. I can't manipulate them. And there is a difference between motivation and manipulation. Pastors are so busy that many things fill up a day. Sometimes I have to struggle with being so caught up in my own agenda and the programs that I envision that I can get caught in the trap of manipulating. When that begins to happen I am not as effective. Then, I am doing things in my own strength, I am not a good listener, and I tend to be insensitive. As someone has said, "Always remember, never take yourself too seriously." There is something far greater at work in the church than you and your ability. God empowers, and people need to be recognized.

In our discussion of preaching we found it helpful to think of bridge building between the Word and the lives of ordinary people. The same is true for visioning. As one's vision begins to take shape, skill in assessing situations, in listening to people and empathizing with them, sinks a pylon into the reality of congregational life. Scripture, prayer, meditation, and intuition erect the tower at the other end of the bridge. The bridge is built and the vision takes shape as communication between pastor and people takes place.

Pastors speak of this in different ways. For example, "Take the vision for ministry God gives you and communicate it to those you are called to lead. Plant seeds and nurture them; God will bless with growth." And, "Have a vision for the people and share it—encourage them to share theirs."

Communicating a pastor's vision and persuading a congregation to make it their own can be an arduous process. Two pastors tell of their struggles.

My biggest challenge has been selling the vision of a growing church that is open to new styles of worship and fellowship. I formed a committee to do nothing but envision the church's future and communicate it to the congregation. It takes too long, though, to get others to let go of the status quo. It's frustrating, but we're moving ahead.

Eighty percent of our members are over sixty-five. My biggest challenge has been getting them to imagine a future, and integrating new younger members into the same congregation with older, long-time members. I have worked at this with lots of back patting, positive reinforcement, "envisioning," and celebrating successes big and small.

Leading Others in Visioning

Whenever it is possible to involve the leaders of a congregation in a dialogical process of visioning, the task of "selling" the vision can be easier. A small church in a changing rural area is facing a typical struggle between the pillars of the past and the pilgrims of the present. Their pastor describes the process of visioning in their experience.

Through Bible study and prayer I wait and look for the vision, share it, and adapt it. It goes like this: (1) Listen to where the people are; (2) listen to God through prayer and Bible study; (3) gain a vision of what can be; (4) explain the vision and ask for responses and evaluation; (5) allow a common vision to emerge; (6) allow the congregation to take the vision and go with it; (7) evaluate annually with as many people as possible.

My biggest challenge? With growth comes new and different ideas. How can we best utilize new members and encourage them without making the pillars feel discredited? We have dealt with this by pulling new and old together in shared visions and insights, making sure that old and new interact and share in decisions.

Brainstorming

Some pastors have found that visioning in their ministry comes most fruitfully when they involve their leadership in a process of problem solving out of which visions emerge. They begin with a conviction that the congregation needs to move forward in some particular area. That conviction is their initial contribution to the vision that emerges. The need for a solution is their vision. That need becomes the focus of common inquiry. Here is how one pastor does it.

> You've got to know where you are going. I do this best in a group where we brainstorm. I have participated in many such settings. In retreats I love to take a theme and ask the group to throw out every idea we can think of in relation to that theme. We use the standard brainstorming technique where everyone contributes ideas, but judgment on those ideas is reserved until later. After brainstorming, we ask, Which of our ideas are feasible? Which of them excite you? Then we prioritize them. So visioning in my ministry is a corporate process. If I'm dreaming about something alone, I have to be the salesman. If the vision comes out of the body, they are the salesmen.
>
> Recently we did brainstorming on the assimilation of members. Then we let it sit. Nothing happened initially because it was my project. Then two weeks ago one of the elders said, "We need to get together to talk about the assimilation process."
>
> One of the keys to the work of the Holy Spirit is that what I want at a particular time may not be God's time. Sometimes it is very hard to wait. But if it's not God's time, it may not be God's project.

Another pastor in a rapidly growing middle-sized congregation advises,

> Work with the visions that all your congregation's leadership and the gospel naturally stir up by the power of the Holy Spirit. Do this instead of trying to inflict your agenda on them, as wonderful as that vision may be. In a collegial system there is plenty of space for your vision. I don't always have a vision personally. I have learned to use their energies and visions and lead a process that selects our best vision.

Developing a Mission Statement

Many pastors work with congregational leaders to develop a "mission statement" that incorporates the congregation's vision of its calling. Larger governing bodies often can make available resources that include manuals to guide boards in a self-study process that results in a statement of mission. A pastor describes such a process:

> Twenty-nine years ago when this congregation was organized, their goal was to get organized and build these buildings. When that had been accomplished they no longer had any goal or mission. We decided to do something about that,

making use of materials provided by our presbytery. It is a self-directed program guided by a manual. The process includes a congregational survey, home meetings where we examine our strengths and weaknesses, and a demographic study of the community around the church, their backgrounds and beliefs. We gathered data and then developed a mission statement.

The experience of a small congregation shows how a less formal process can work. The pastor's nominator says that the congregation was about to die or leave the denomination. They could not afford a full-time pastor so this pastor serves them part-time. Since he has been there, they have increased the enrollment and attendance in church school. Worship attendance and participation has grown, and they have raised the level of giving significantly. They have made major improvements in their church building and have just completed adding an elevator. They are now beginning to branch into community activities. "This has been a major turnaround for this congregation and it is all due to Pastor Jones!" the nominator says. Pastor Jones says, "I make a regular practice of setting aside times when I (and sometimes with others) play the 'what if' game. Out of this comes ideas that can—or cannot—work. This allows for purposeful development."

Another pastor of a small congregation describes how brainstorming has helped her develop her capacity for visioning. "Creativity is difficult to acquire," she says. "Visioning is an extension of an active imagination. Brainstorming that activates right-brain thinking helps."

HOW DREAMS COME TRUE

Visions are essential. They motivate people. But dreams rarely come true unless someone makes them come to life. Careful planning must lead to concrete action taken by specific people. Without a specific blueprint for implementation, a mission statement will stay in the files and make no difference whatever. We turn again to research into effective schools. "School effectiveness resulted from concrete actions taken in response to the premise that students could and would learn. In each case, successful schools had action plans that involved setting clear goals, devising specific ways to reach the goals, directing school resources toward achieving the goals, and creating a school environment supporting goal attainment."[1]

It is a rare congregation indeed that does not involve the pastor in implementing their vision. Even in that congregation, it is the pastor who permits vigorous, committed, and capable lay leadership to make the plans and carry them out. Usually the pastor needs to play a much more central role than that. At minimum, the selection of effective lay leadership is often a key responsibility of the pastor. And in most cases the pastor must give strong leadership in developing strategies and organizing resources for implementation. Pastors usually have the time that lay leaders cannot give. They usually preside at meetings of the congregation and of the boards that make decisions. And most church leaders look to the pastor for that kind of leadership. Those expectations are so strong that it would be difficult to change them, even if that were desirable. This does not mean that the pastor should do the work of making the plans and carrying them out. It does mean that the pastor must take the lead in seeing that goals are set, plans are made, tasks are assigned to individuals or committees, and someone is monitoring progress toward goals that have been agreed upon.

As evidence for this we point to the agreement of all pastors and lay leaders in our study that among the five most important skills for a pastor is the skill of *organizing:* There is agreement that, as one pastor said, it is the pastor's responsibility "to plan and manage the life and work of the congregation so that all elements fit together in an ordered whole."

From Strategy to Fulfillment

Once a congregation has developed a clear sense of its particular mission, the next step is to decide what specific things need to happen in order to fulfill that mission. Some call those specific tasks goals. Others call them objectives. Whatever nomenclature one uses, goals or objectives answer the question, *What* needs to happen if our congregation is to move meaningfully toward carrying out our mission?

Strategizing, as we have defined it, is "the ability to plan activities that lead toward accomplishment of objectives and tasks related to the congregation's mission." Whereas *organizing* involves the coordination of the total life and work of the congregation, *strategizing* is more specifically related to the development of plans that will achieve goals or objectives. It spells out specific tasks, projects, or programs and identifies what individual(s) or group(s) will be responsible for carrying them out.

Delegating is closely related to strategizing. Part of any strategy needs to be a decision as to *who* will carry out various tasks. Many a beautiful idea has been framed in deathless prose as an objective. Everyone agrees that something should happen, but nothing does happen. Why? Because no one was designated to carry it out or see that it was carried out. *Delegating* is "the ability to assign tasks to others with clear instructions and with confidence in their ability to accomplish the task."

The last part of the definition is as important as the first. If a pastor or board has assigned someone a responsibility, lack of confidence in their ability to carry out the task may lead to interfering with their doing so. Nothing can be more demoralizing to lay leaders or staff members than for a pastor to overdirect their performance, to interfere with that performance, or to rescue them from dropping the ball, unless the consequences would otherwise be devastating to the whole life of the church. As we have already observed, being willing to let someone fail can be difficult for the delegator, but in the long run it will build more solid working relationships. The pastor can provide resources and give guidance to those who need help in carrying out their assignments. But having done that, the accountability needs to rest squarely on their shoulders.

Identifying gifts is "the ability to identify and assess one's own talents and the talents of others." Skill at identifying one's own gifts enables a pastor to decide whether it is really important to perform a task himself. Skill at identifying the gifts of others enables a pastor to delegate tasks to those who have the capacity to carry them out. Someone who is assigned to a task that makes use of her or his particular gifts will usually be more easily motivated to carry out the task.

Given the foregoing framework for accomplishing goals, it is not difficult to see why Empowering Pastors are more effective than Other Pastors in giving leadership in mission achievement. In order of magnitude, the greatest differences in their self-ratings are in the skills of identifying gifts, delegating, guiding, and resolving conflict. The percentages of Empowering Pastors who rate themselves as very skillful or skillful in these abilities are from 31 to 36 percent higher than the self-ratings of Other Pastors. The greatest differences in lay leaders' ratings of their pastors (in order of magnitude) are in delegating, identifying gifts, resolving conflict, and organizing.

LEARNING TO LEAD IN MISSION ACHIEVEMENT

There is good news for pastors who are eager to grow in their ability to lead in mission achievement. Most of the skills that contribute to such leadership can be learned in many different ways. One can readily find helpful resources for the task. There are many workshops on planning and management. Many pastors will find in their congregations executives who have high levels of these leadership skills. They use them every day in their professions or places of business. Once they are convinced that those skills are appropriately used in the church, most will be more than willing to use them there. And most of them will eagerly respond to a request to serve as a mentor to the pastor who wants to develop those skills.

Learning to Organize and Strategize

Among the means by which Empowering Pastors have developed skills in organizing and strategizing are:

Various D.Min. courses
A D.Min. devoted to practical strategies for ministry
Planning seminars
Army chaplaincy training
Planning processes carried out by larger governing bodies
Workshops, both secular and religious
Mentors in Early Days of Ministry
Mentoring by a chief executive officer of a corporation
Mentoring by a professional planner
Tutoring by a business person in the congregation
Learning from educators who use these skills in their work
Working as a team teacher and leading a teacher's organization

Working with community leaders and observing how they organize and administer programs
Understanding of politics in the nation, state, city, and larger church

Learning to Identify Gifts

Pastors have developed their skills in identifying gifts through:

Learning to understand and use the Myers-Briggs Type Indicator
Training by Marlene Wilson on working with volunteers
Learning to listen to people's wishes for accomplishment as well as to their present achievements
Home visitation to every member, with an effort to identify personal gifts
Emphasizing the ministry of the laity and working to strengthen their talents, self-esteem, and self-worth

Learning to Delegate

A number of pastors have learned to delegate by these means:

Accepting a biblical and theological understanding of gifts (e.g., Ephesians 4)
Recognizing that others have skills that they do not possess
Learning (sometimes the hard way) that they cannot do everything themselves
Pastoring so large a congregation that it is impossible not to delegate
Learning from businesspeople in the congregation
Accepting that the work does not depend only on them
Modeling by a mentor or senior pastor who said, "You have an area of responsibility; do it!"

Delegating does not mean abdicating all responsibility for what has been assigned to someone else. Rather it provides an opportunity to support and encourage members as they grow in their ability to undertake tasks for which they have accepted responsibility. Two pastors describe their style of delegating:

I delegate and turn people loose. I do not secretly try to control while pretending I am not. But I do not turn people loose to sink or swim. I am available as a resource person. I am there to listen, to explore options, to suggest resources, and to troubleshoot. For example, we recently had a meeting of the session on Saturday and another on Sunday. Between them the clerk of session asked if I wanted to review the Saturday minutes. I said, "No, I trust you." But if she had had a problem with the minutes I would have consulted with her.

I like "letting loose" my staff and members to "do their thing." Set people free. Avoid impulses to control those you trust.

Delegating can be very fulfilling to the delegator who sees someone blossom into a more confident and effective person through successfully carrying out responsibilities. "I get great joy from seeing others take tasks and do a good job with them," a pastor said. "An idea, a work, belongs to another when they know the desired end result and they develop the plans to reach it."

Learning to Guide

Guiding is a skill that can give a pastor the assurance that delegated tasks are indeed being carried out. Guiding is the ability to shepherd the work of church boards and key committees for maximum productivity. It involves a process of general oversight of what is happening. It includes serving as a consultant to committee chairs and as a resource to committees and individuals when they need a boost. Guiding is like mentoring. A mentor keeps in touch with his protégé, answers questions, and offers timely suggestions, sharing the wisdom the mentor has accumulated over the years. Several Empowering Pastors explain how they do this.

We have forty-five minutes of church officer training with each session meeting. They learn how to make decisions and are ready to do so.

I am a borrower of other people's good ideas of how to do something effectively. I am always providing organizational oversight and new ways of doing our work. I talk frequently with colleagues and evaluate regularly with committees, session, and trustees. Because I do not control what the work or mission is, the church welcomes this.

I'm intentional about guiding without dictating. I want session to decide on key issues (though always with my input). To do this I attend committees or give my suggestions to the committee moderator. I work as a "team" with our committees and sit in with them. After that, in session they make the decisions for church direction.

THE INTERDEPENDENCE OF SKILLS

As we have reviewed the seven skills that contribute to leadership in mission achievement, it will have become clear that these skills are closely interrelated. That is why they clustered statistically in the same factor. The relationship between Factor A, leadership in mission achievement, and Factor B, responsiveness to persons, will become clearer as we move to chapter 9, where we observe the "power in people skills." As we do so, we remind ourselves that skills in Factor B (responsiveness to persons) form the essential foundation for good personal relationships without which mission achievement is significantly hampered, if not thwarted altogether.

9

THE POWER
IN PEOPLE SKILLS

At the heart of skill in dealing with people is social perceptive-
ness—the ability to appraise accurately the readiness or resistance
of followers to move in a given direction, to know when dissension
or confusion is undermining the group's will to act, to make the
most of the motives that are there, and to understand the sensitiv-
ities.

—John Gardner, *On Leadership*

I am the Good Shepherd. I know my own sheep and my own sheep
know me. . . . I put the sheep before myself, sacrificing myself if
necessary.

—John 10:14–15, TM

Two fellows who were out hunting encountered an angry bull. They ran
for their lives. One climbed a tree and sat on a limb out of reach of the bull. The
other dived into a narrow cave where the bull could not reach him. The man on
the limb saw his friend come out of the cave. The bull went after him. He dived
back into the cave. He kept doing this until the limb sitter called out to him, "If
you would just stay inside the cave, the bull can't get you." His friend cried back,
"But you don't know about the bear in the cave!" From the safety of our limbs
we never know about the bears in people's caves.[1] As someone said to me many
years ago, "Be kind; you never know what the other person is going through."

Responsiveness to others involves understanding their thoughts and feelings;
seeing things from their perspective; accepting them as they are without judging,
manipulating, or dominating them; treating them with unconditional respect; responding to them appropriately; and placing them ahead of one's own fulfillment or advancement.

Empowering Pastors are particularly adept in such "responsiveness to others" (Factor B). Between 75 and 89 percent of both pastors and lay leaders rate
them as very skillful or skillful in listening, empathizing, collaborating, and serving. On all of these skills they are much more likely than Other Pastors to rate
themselves that high.

In chapter 8 we saw that the largest differences between skill ratings of Empowering Pastors and Other Pastors are in those that relate to leadership in mission achievement. That emphasis on differences obscured the fact that Empowering Pastors are more likely to rate higher on responsiveness to others than on leadership in mission achievement.

This is as it should be. The focus of mission is always people. People skills provide the firm foundation on which pastors build as they lead congregations. If pastors have limited people skills, they are in very deep trouble, as we discover over and over again when conflicts force them to leave their churches. Those congregations suffer even if their pastors do not leave.

When asked what advice he would give to a pastor who wanted to grow in effectiveness, one pastor summarized succinctly: "Don't do dumb things in working with people." We all do "dumb things" once in a while in relating to others. So it behooves us to continually sharpen our people skills.

LISTENING

In chapter 3 we looked briefly at the skill of listening. We saw that pastors free people to grow when they seek to understand them empathetically. (Before proceeding, you may wish to review what was said there.) Chapter 4 developed the concept of servant leadership as a way to empower congregations. In his treatment of servant leadership Robert Greenleaf stresses the importance of listening. He assures us that listening can be learned and advocates training in listening as prerequisite to servant leadership.

> I have a bias about this which suggests that only a true natural servant automatically responds to any problem by listening first. When one is a leader, this disposition causes one to be seen as servant first. This suggests that a nonservant who wants to be a servant, might become a natural servant through a long arduous discipline of learning to listen, a discipline sufficiently sustained that the automatic response to any problem is to listen first. I have seen enough remarkable transformations in people who have been trained to listen to have some confidence in this approach.[2]

In chapter 7 we observed that all pastors and lay leaders in our study place listening as one of the five most important skills for effectiveness as a pastor. One pastor speaks for many others, "Listening is the basis of everything! No listening—no trust or authority. Listening is based in respect for the other."

Assessing Your Listening Skills

Both Empowering Pastors and Other Pastors rate their skills in listening and empathizing among their four highest skill self-ratings. Both Empowering Lay Leaders and Other Lay Leaders also rate their pastors high in listening. But interestingly, neither group of lay leaders ranks their pastors' skills in listening and empathizing among their top four ratings. For Empowering Lay Leaders those skills rank ninth and thirteenth among fifteen ratings and for Other Lay Leaders they rank fifth and tenth respectively. In other words, in the hierarchy of their abilities, pastors tend to place their skills in listening and empathizing higher than lay leaders do. This suggests that pastors may not be as skillful in listening as they would like to think. Whether or not that is true, the importance of empathetic listening skills is commonly recognized. And because pastors usually are quite skilled in speaking, they will be tempted to speak more than they listen. If so, they will need continually to give high priority to listening and give special attention to developing their skills in listening.

Helps and Hindrances to Listening

Those who want to check their listening skills can use the lists of questions that follow.[3] Answer them for yourself and by yourself. Or better yet, ask your spouse, or someone else who will be honest with you, to help you with at least some of the answers.

Helps to listening

Do you listen to understand the person who is speaking? Both content and feelings are important.

Do you give your full attention to a speaker? Do you concentrate on listening and avoid mental distractions or outside interruptions? Good listening requires focus and energy.

Do you take time to listen? Hurried listening can short-circuit the process.

Do you observe gestures, posture, facial expression, and tone of voice so that you can really understand the person behind the words and what he or she is trying to communicate?

Are you eager to learn all you can from what others may have to say? Or do you listen because you have to?

Do you remember that words can mean something very different to someone else than they mean to you? Meanings are conditioned by the experiences of each individual rather than by what the dictionary says. They vary in the minds of user and listener.

Do you try to understand what the speaker is really saying behind the words used?

Do you ask questions to clarify what a speaker really means? For example, "Is this what you mean?" Do you try to find out whether you are "on target" in your understanding of the speaker?

Do you try to put the feeling you observe into your own words? Do you reflect your understanding of the person, rather than simply rewording the content of what you have heard him or her say?

Do you sum up what a speaker has said to make certain you have really heard him or her?

Hindrances to listening

Do you tend to dominate conversations in social situations? in pastoral calls? Good pastors listen more than they talk. As one pastor put it, "We have two ears and one mouth to be used proportionately."

Do you get impatient with speakers who take too long to say what they are saying?

Does your mind wander or dart ahead as you listen? If so, you may miss what the speaker is really saying. The average rate of speech is about 125 words a minute; the average person thinks at a rate nearly four times faster. What do you do with the extra time?

As someone is speaking, are you preparing your answers? Get the whole message before you decide what to say.

Do you jump to conclusions? Do you sometimes interrupt because you are sure you know what the speaker is saying? If so, you may actually miss the point.

Do you sometimes feel defensive when someone makes a suggestion or criticism? This may alert you to the fact that you are not as open to hearing another as you would like to think.

Do you find it difficult to listen to ideas with which you disagree? Do your own convictions and values block your ability to listen?

Do some words, laden with emotion from your past, turn off your hearing?

Do you label people by their occupations? If so, there is a danger you are filtering what they say by your image of those occupations.

Reflections on Listening

There is . . . a grace of kind listening, as well as a grace of kind speaking. . . . Some interrupt, and will not hear you to the end. Some hear you to the end, and then forthwith begin to talk to you about a similar experience which has befallen [them], making your case only an illustration of their own. Some, meaning to be kind, listen with such a determined, lively, violent attention that you are at once made uncomfortable, and the charm of conversation is at an end. Many persons whose manners will stand the test of speaking break down under the trial of listening. (Frederick W. Faber)[4]

When I ask you to listen to me and you start giving advice, you have not done what I asked.

When I ask you to listen to me and you begin to tell me why I shouldn't feel that way, you are trampling on my feelings.

When I ask you to listen to me and you feel you have to do something to solve my problem, you have failed me, strange as that may seem.

Listen. All I ask is that you listen, not talk or do—just hear me. When you do something for me that I can and need to do for myself, you contribute to my fear and inadequacy.

But when you accept as a simple fact that I do feel what I feel, no matter how irrational, then I can quit trying to convince you, and can get about the business of understanding what is behind them.

So, please listen and just hear me. And if you want to talk, wait a minute for your turn and I'll listen to you. (Anonymous)[5]

HOW PASTORS DEVELOP THEIR
LISTENING SKILLS

Few of us could reflect on the last several pages without feeling the need to polish up our listening skills. Empowering Pastors have found ways to develop those skills. For each of them the path has been different. But the following summary of their personal experiences may offer suggestions.

Some pastors are naturally gifted and have developed those gifts for listening. A pastor who rates herself as very skilled in listening and empathizing says that she is by nature nonjudgmental and accepting. "I was like this before seminary. With training and practice, I've become more skilled." Another pastor, who retired from a large pastorate, is serving a small congregation. He says, "I have a strong enough sense of my own worth that I do not to need to impose my ideas and thoughts on others. So I am able to hear them."

Some pastors have learned because good listeners have listened to them.

The times I've felt most nourished and loved are times folks have seriously listened to me. I've tried to make this a centerpiece of my ministry and have received training in active listening.

I suppose I learned to listen by being listened to. I think it is the first step to most everything we do as a church. Empathizing is perhaps a product of listening. If you really hear what is being said you will empathize.

A semi-retired minister was my mentor and counselor. His example of listening to me and raising questions with me has modeled listening for me.

Experience has taught some pastors the value of listening.

We've had multicultured congregations where listening was necessary. We have appreciated multicultural as well as multidenominational folk from whom to learn.

I learned to appreciate what people say and feel and think about life and ministry. I have learned that others know far more than I do. Sometimes I do get a little impatient when they have a lot to say but are not saying very much. There are times when I feel like interrupting, but I discipline myself.

I discipline myself to focus on others and what they say and how they say it. I try to observe group dynamics and responses rather than interrupting or thinking about my response.

To relate effectively with a wife, a husband, children, friends, or working associates, we must learn to listen. And this requires emotional strength. Listening involves patience, openness, and the desire to understand—highly developed qualities of character. It's so much easier to operate from a low emotional level and to give high-level advice.

Other pastors have learned from courses, seminars, and workshops.

I have had clinical pastoral training, have kept those skills, and added to them.

Many experiences have helped me learn to listen. A seminary professor taught me to listen. His reality therapy model was closely tied to scripture. Two workshops were helpful. One was called an introduction to Reality Therapy Training. The second was called Clergy Effectiveness Training. It is a model developed out of Parent Effectiveness Training. Stephen Ministry training has helped, and the recognition of the value of each individual person.

I developed the skill through making it a priority and through one or two workshops for resident assistants in dorms when I served as a campus minister.

My seminary concentration was in pastoral care.

Some counseling training and family systems study helped me learn to listen.

Workshops, Stephen Ministry, my own counseling, observation, and the recognition of the value of the individual person.

I attended a seminar on active listening in my first year of ministry. I caught the gist of it. I practiced it in thousands of one-on-ones and in many small groups. I feel honored and stirred when I hear the discourse of another's soul.

I was helped by training in a Young Pastors' Seminar, D.Min., collegium group, and a variety of small-group settings.

I developed my listening skill by reading books on active listening.

COLLABORATING AND SERVING

We have read Robert Greenleaf's convictions about the importance of listening. In chapter 4 Greenleaf told us that a servant leader is one who serves the highest priority needs of others; and who prizes the contributions of each individual to the whole. We saw how servant leaders inspire a shared vision of what the church is called to be and to do and how they celebrate diversity, inspire unity, and actively share power with others. Servant leaders do this as they develop collegiality with lay leadership and staff, have the courage to call capable colleagues, and then prepare and support them in their responsibilities.

Now we see that collaborating and serving are the skills that make possible that kind of effective servant leadership. For this study, *collaborating* is defined as "the ability to work cooperatively with others without need to dominate or take credit for accomplishments." It is the skill of interdependence. It is closely related to *serving*, "the ability to place the needs of one's congregation above the need for self-fulfillment and advancement."

Empowering Pastors are especially skilled in collaborating. Eighty-nine percent of them compared to only 62 percent of Other Pastors say they are very skillful or skillful in collaborating. For both this is their second-highest rating. Empowering Lay Leaders are also more likely than Other Lay Leaders to say that their pastors are very skillful or skillful in collaborating. How can a pastor grow in the skill of collaborating? That skill has deep roots in a pastor's sense of personal security and integrity. Personal security makes it possible to share power and put the achievements of others first. Those who would grow in their skill of collaborating must start with themselves. To collaborate with others requires a capacity for interdependence. Independent people do not feel the need for collaboration, and dependent people are unable to carry their part in the necessary interaction. This brings us back to *Seven Habits of Highly Effective People*. In his habits three, four, and five Stephen Covey describes ways to grow in our ability to collaborate effectively.

Beginning with a chapter on interdependence, Covey asserts that "effective interdependence can only be built on a foundation of true independence. Private victory precedes Public Victory. . . . You can't be successful with other people if you haven't paid the price of success with yourself."[6] In this, he is referring to the foundation laid with the first three "habits of highly effective people." Personal independence comes when one is *proactive* (choosing how one relates to life); *begins with the end in mind* (knowing oneself well enough to decide what is really important in one's life); and exercising one's independent will to pursue that end by *putting first things first* in one's life.

To greatly oversimplify Covey's thesis, these things give one the foundation on which cooperative relationships can be built. "Self-mastery and self-discipline are the foundation of good relationships with others. . . . Independence is an achievement. Interdependence is a choice only independent people can make."[7]

Collaboration and interdependence depend upon trust of self and trust of those with whom one collaborates. We build up trust, Covey tells us, by making deposits on what he calls an Emotional Bank Account. We do this through courtesy, kindness, honesty, and keeping commitments to others. We can draw on this trust reserve when we make mistakes or otherwise disappoint others.[8]

Win/Win Collaboration

A win/win approach to problem solving is the foundation of collaboration. There are, Covey tells us, five different approaches to our interaction with others.[9]

1. A *win/win* approach tries to find mutual benefit in our interaction with others. This is the philosophy of collaboration. It assumes there is plenty for everybody so I can afford to seek ways to share the abundance. Such an "abundance mentality" depends upon a deep sense of personal security.
2. A *win/lose* approach assumes that if I am going to win you must lose. This is the philosophy of competition that dominates our culture. It assumes there is not enough for everyone, so I must come out on top. There is only one winner of a race or of a ball game, so I must win. This scarcity / competitive mentality makes it difficult to collaborate. We can not afford to share power, recognition, and credit.
3. *Lose/Win* is the approach that assumes I must lose because you are going to win. It is the approach of those who are convinced they are born losers or who, above all, want to please others. They will keep peace at any cost and are quick to appease. As leaders they are indulgent and permissive.

4. A *lose/lose* situation arises when two win/lose people clash. Both lose.
5. Finally there is the *think win* approach. This philosophy does not assume that you must lose if I am to win. But it does emphasize that I must win, whether or not you lose.

Covey gives examples of circumstances where each of these philosophies may prove helpful. But in most situations he concludes, "Win/Win is really the only viable alternative." Furthermore, it opens the door to creative collaboration.

Because of their commitment to service, pastors may be tempted to assume a lose/win approach to ministry. As we have seen, this is not the strong servant leadership style of Empowering Pastors. In speaking of collaboration, one of our Empowering Pastors tells of his struggle to overcome his own lose/win mentality while serving a congregation of high-powered leaders.

> Mainly I have had to learn to assert myself, and not to give myself away. This was when I served in the unfriendly environment of a church filled with prestige-people who assumed they would prevail and dominate—always. I was helped by readings and study of Servant Leadership (the writings of Robert Greenleaf), and the Church of the Savior in Washington, D.C. Faith at Work Institutes were invaluable.

It takes maturity to embrace a win/win style of living. Covey describes maturity as a balance between courage and consideration. A mature person has the ability to express feelings and convictions with courage while showing consideration for the feelings and convictions of others. One who is high on courage and low on consideration lives by win/lose. One who is low on courage and high on consideration lives lose/win.

Win/Win relationships depend upon trust that is built up in our emotional bank accounts. They are not easily arrived at. Without trust, only compromise is possible. With trust relationships, it usually becomes possible to discover win/win solutions. Trust relationships make *partnership agreements* possible. These spell out desired results, guidelines for accomplishing them, resources needed, accountability standards, and consequences at time of evaluation.

Creative Cooperation

We discover the power of collaboration in Covey's discussion of "the miracle of synergy." Synergy, for Covey, "means that the whole is greater than the sum of its parts."[10] Empathetic communication and a win/win approach to others release a level of creativity that uses differences to build strengths and compensate for weaknesses. That creativity involves mutual learning, which creates "a momentum toward more and more insights, learnings and growth." But because the outcome of a synergistic process is unknown, "it requires enormous personal security and openness and a spirit of adventure." Here is where the earlier habits come in. They help create the requisite sense of personal security that makes participation in synergy possible. "Most all creative endeavors are somewhat unpredictable. They often seem ambiguous, hit-or-miss, trial and error. And unless people have a high tolerance for ambiguity and get their security from integrity to principles and inner values they find it unnerving and unpleasant to be involved in highly creative enterprises. Their need for structure, certainty, and predictability is too high."[11]

THE NEED FOR CONFLICT MANAGEMENT

The longer I study pastoral effectiveness, the more convinced I am that pastors need to give much greater attention to developing skills in conflict management. Both Empowering Lay Leaders and Other Lay Leaders give their pastors the lowest of fifteen skill ratings on conflict resolution. Self-ratings on conflict resolution by Empowering Pastors and Other Pastors ranked fourteenth and thirteenth respectively among fifteen skill ratings.

It is true that Empowering Pastors are more likely than Other Pastors to rate themselves as effective or very effective in conflict resolution. But only 57 percent of Empowering Pastors did so. And just 26 percent of Other Pastors felt they were effective or very effective in that skill. It seems clear that many pastors recognize that they have a long way to go in managing conflict.

There is a significant amount of serious and destructive conflict in Presbyterian churches. I suspect this is equally true in congregations of other denominations. In the study that led to *How to Attract and Keep Active Church Members*, 439 Presbyterian churches responded to questions about conflict. Of these, 53 percent said they had experienced serious conflict at some time during the previous five years. A significant number of these conflicts resulted in the loss of members and/or the departure of pastors.[12]

The need for pastoral skill in conflict management is emphasized by the fact that the largest single cause of conflict mentioned by respondents was interpersonal differences between pastors and members. Because conflicts in any organization are inevitable, pastors need to have the people skills necessary to deal with them creatively. Conflicts that are well managed can energize a congregation. Conflicts that are poorly managed can lead to serious problems.

HOW EMPOWERING PASTORS MINIMIZE
DESTRUCTIVE CONFLICT

Before looking at the management of conflict, let us first observe that most of the characteristics of Empowering Pastors will tend to minimize the development of destructive conflict. Perhaps this explains a difference in the perceptions of lay leaders and of pastors on the skills that a pastor possesses in conflict management. Seventy-four percent of Empowering Lay Leaders say that their pastors are skillful or very skillful in resolving conflict. This is much higher than the 57 percent of Empowering Pastors who rate themselves as being that skillful. Why the difference? To begin with, pastors are keenly aware of the times when they feel they have not done a good job in handling a developing conflict. Could it be that Empowering Lay Leaders have observed little conflict in their congregations? If so, they would assume that their pastors are skillfully dealing with conflict. This could be true, if as we intend to show, an empowering pastoral leadership style does lead to less conflict in a congregation. In this study we did not ask how much conflict these congregations had experienced, so we do not have factual evidence to back up our hypothesis. But we can look again at some of the leadership characteristics of Empowering Pastors in the light of the reasons that people fight.

In his answer to why people fight, Speed Leas identifies three reasons. They fight (1) over specific substantive issues on which they disagree, (2) because their personal needs for importance, attention, and power are unmet, or (3) because of "the deterioration of interpersonal relationships," such as when someone wants revenge for "a confidence betrayed, a trust broken, or an attack endured."[13]

In what ways do the leadership styles of Empowering Pastors minimize these reasons for church fights? Empowering Pastors minimize destructive conflict (1) by involving members in decision making in such a way that they can resolve or accept the differences they have over substantive issues, (2) by meeting many of members' needs for importance and attention, which otherwise would erupt into conflict, and (3) through their skills in interpersonal relations. We can see this by a quick review of characteristics we have identified in previous chapters.

1. They share power persistently. A servant leadership style involves people in decision making. As decisions are being hammered out, members have opportunities to express their substantive concerns. When this happens, they are more likely to own decisions and less likely to rebel against them. Participation in decisions meets some of people's needs for recognition. When those needs are being met, members are less likely to get into fights. (See chap. 4.)

2. They empower people. Members will be less likely to fight when their congregations provide a climate in which they feel free to grow, learn, explore, and use their gifts in Christian ministry. People find fulfillment when they are loved, respected, and accepted unconditionally. (See chap. 3.)

3. They help discover and channel people's gifts into service. Members find fulfillment when their gifts are recognized, developed, and channeled into meaningful service and when leadership responds positively to their dreams and initiatives. Members who feel fulfilled are less likely to engage in destructive conflicts. (See chap. 3.)

4. They help people find meaning for living. People will be less likely to fight when they are discovering meaning for living. (See chap. 2.)

5. They celebrate diversity. Empowering Pastors who celebrate diversity within a strong bond of unity in Christ provide broad opportunities for

people to meet their diverse needs. An emphasis on tolerance for theological diversity and an insistence on fairness and respect for those with whom one disagrees develops a climate in which members feel that they can differ without being put down. This makes it possible for them to feel important. They are less likely to fight. (See chap. 4.)

6. They create a caring context. Empowering Pastors express genuine caring for people and inspire people to develop caring communities. When people experience deep caring for their needs, they are less likely to get into fights. (See chap. 4.)

7. They are authentic persons. Since Empowering Pastors refuse to wear masks, play games, or manipulate behind the scenes, people are more likely to see them as genuine human beings and to know where they stand. Fewer misunderstandings reduce the need for fights. (See chap.5.)

8. They develop and use their own people skills. Empowering Pastors use their people skills to model and maintain good interpersonal relations. When they can listen empathetically, champion creative cooperation, and work for win/win solutions to problems, they help keep destructive interpersonal conflict to a minimum.

CLARIFYING EXPECTATIONS MINIMIZES DESTRUCTIVE CONFLICT

Empowering Pastors remind us that clarifying expectations can minimize destructive conflict. Half of them, in comparison with 31 percent of Other Pastors, say they rarely or never experience conflicting or ambiguous expectations for their work. At the other extreme, only 11 percent of them, compared with 25 percent of Other Pastors, say they often experience stress from conflicting or ambiguous expectations for their work.

When expectations for a pastor's performance differ, we have role conflict. When there is confusion in expectations, we have role ambiguity. The differing expectations can be between the pastor and one or more members of the congregation. They can be differences between the pastoral expectations of different members. Or role conflict and ambiguity can even exist when a pastor's self-expectations of himself or herself are conflicted or confused. To minimize role conflict and ambiguity it is essential to clarify expectations continually.

Shattered expectations invite conflict. High hopes for a new pastor turn to bitter disappointment when expectations are not met. And in many pastor/parish relationships most expectations that matter are never articulated. Neither pastor nor people have ever expressed them clearly to themselves, much less to each other. Every member's expectations of the pastor differ from every other member's expectations. They have been shaped by their own personal needs, dreams, and past experiences with pastors, both positive and negative. All pastors have expectations for congregations that have called them. They too have been shaped by personal needs, dreams, and past experiences with congregations, both positive and negative.

Develop dependable relationships. Fulfilled expectations are the basis of trust and bonding. Clarified expectations improve the chances of their fulfillment. Implicit or ambiguous expectations are time bombs waiting to go off.

Expectations are not static. They are continually changing. People change. The congregation, its membership, its situation, and its needs change. What both pastor and people look for in relationships may change, or they may become more aware of what they really want. So a stable, trusting, productive relationship depends upon constant clarification of expectations. In any relationship people experience disappointments when expectations are not met. When that happens those disappointments must be shared in order to maintain healthy relationships. So timely clarification of expectations helps renew trust and repair fractured relationships before they deteriorate into hostile conflict. Here are some helpful hints.

Clarify Expectations at the Beginning of a Pastorate

At the beginning of a pastorate (1) articulate mutual expectations, (2) negotiate a description of the pastor's responsibilities to the congregation and to the governing board, (3) negotiate a description of the congregation's responsibility and the board's responsibility to the pastor, and (4) agree on ways you will keep expectations alive and flexible. Plan to set interrelated annual goals for the pastor and for church boards. Decide on how you will review the performance of each, and provide for regular review of the mutual responsibility statements of the pastor and the board.

Clarify New Members' Expectations

Tell new members what the congregation expects of them. Remember that high expectations can build faithful members when they are expressed at the beginning of a member's relationship with the church and are built into the fabric of the ongoing life of the church.

Ask new members to share their expectations of the congregation. This helps them to make a commitment to the church and helps the leadership of the congregation to know what to expect of them. For example, if a nurse must work on two Sundays a month, her absence from worship will not be interpreted as a declining commitment to the church.

Provide Ways for Members
to Communicate Their Disappointments

It is inevitable that members will be disappointed with their pastor or their congregation. Tell them you know that all their expectations will not be fulfilled. Ask them to commit themselves to share those disappointments through appropriate channels. More than one congregation has used John Savage's pinch-hearer approach to legitimize the renegotiation of violated expectations.[14] A pinch is one's reaction to a violation of an expectation. Carefully selected members are trained with listening skills. They are designated as "pinch-hearers."

New members are asked to commit themselves to share their pinches with the pastor or with one of the pinch-hearers. Pinch-hearers take turns in being available for a month at a time. In the newsletter and in the Sunday bulletin, on-duty pinch-hearers are announced and members are urged to use them to express their disappointments.

Carry Out Review Processes

A process for review that is not carried out is worse than no process at all. Remember, expectations must be renegotiated frequently.

HOW TO GROW IN YOUR ABILITY
TO MANAGE CONFLICT

A Lay Person's Guide to Conflict Management, by Speed B. Leas,[15] should be required reading for every pastor. It succinctly summarizes valuable insights into the nature of conflict and some of the more helpful approaches to it. Several other of Leas's publications on conflict management are listed in Resources for Further Study. Through Alban Institute, Leas offers workshops on conflict management. The suggestions that follow draw heavily on the work of Speed Leas and incorporate some insights from my own work on role conflict, which was published in *Clergy in the Cross Fire.*

Understand Yourself

As I have said repeatedly, self-knowledge is the foundation for effective ministry. Know the possibiliies and pitfalls that you bring to the practice of ministry. What roles do you play effectively? Communicate this to all concerned and encourage others to play roles that supplement your weaknesses.

How do you feel about conflict? Are you afraid of it? Your attitudes make a difference in how you handle conflict. Leas cites four beliefs that enhance the management of conflict. (1) Believe that mutually acceptable solutions to problems are available. Give people hope that satisfactory joint outcomes can be found. (2) Believe in cooperation rather than competition. (3) Believe that statements of the opposition are legitimate descriptions of their position. (4) Recognize the potential value of differences.

Know your conflict-management styles. Do you have a broad range of styles, or do you deal with every conflict in the same way? A Speed Leas work that can help pastors understand their preferred styles of conflict management is *Discover Your Conflict Management Style.* By answering forty-five forced-choice questions, one can identify one's preference for persuasion, compelling or forcing, avoiding/ignoring/accommodating/fleeing, collaboration, bargaining or negotiating, or support (active listening). In an accompanying guide Leas helps us see the potential impact of each of these styles of conflict management.

Clarify the congruence of your goals with those of the church. What is the mission of the congregation, and what are its goals? To what extent do your expectations contribute toward these goals? To what extent are they incompatible with those goals? If so, how can you reconcile them? Are actual or potential conflicts the result of unexpressed incompatibilities?

Check your perceptions. Do you really know what others expect of you? The results of several studies suggest that ministers do not accurately assess the feelings of their people about their work. So they need feedback from others they can trust.

Study your role. How deeply involved are those who expect things of you in those expectations? How powerful are they in enforcing them? How observable to them are the role conflicts? How legitimate are the different claims they make on you?

Understand Conflict

Understanding the nature of conflict is a prerequisite for dealing with it effectively. We have already referred to Leas's analysis of why people fight. He goes on to outline things people do that are not helpful when they fight in church. Some drop out without doing enough to challenge the system. Blame, attack, and character assassination are common in the church. People tend to move too quickly from the specific to overgeneralization. "The more general the conflict, the more difficult it is to handle. The more specific, the easier."[16] So it helps to get people to be specific in defining the problem. Distorted communications, rumors, and anonymous communications aggravate tensions. Encourage people to communicate their concerns directly to one another. Go with them if they need support in doing so. Or at least agree to pass on their concerns only if they are willing to let you use their names.

Learn the different levels of conflict. Speed Leas worked with a task force in the Presbyterian Church (U.S.A.) to develop a resource that promotes understanding of the nature and severity of disagreement and conflict in congregations. This "Conflict Intensity Chart"[17] describes different levels of conflict. At the risk of oversimplification, I summarize the levels as follows:

Level One: Problem to Solve. Problems involve differing goals, values, and needs and do not tend to be person-oriented. Short-lived anger is quickly controlled.

Level Two: Disagreement. Issues are personalized and difficult to define; distrust begins and information is withheld from opponents.

Level Three: Contest. Win/lose dynamics begin among developing factions. Problems get distorted, "enemies" resist solutions and engage in personal attacks.

Level Four: Fight/flight. Struggle shifts from winning to hurting opponents and getting rid of people. Factions are solidified and will not speak to each other. There is a high probability of a church split.

Level Five: Intractable. Personalities have become the issue, and conflict is unmanageable. The goal is to destroy other factions or people. May require ecclesiastical adjudication and rebuilding of the congregation.

Face Conflict Squarely and Quickly

Be proactive in dealing with conflict. This does not always mean that you take immediate action. Sometimes there is wisdom in monitoring a conflict for a while and waiting. Being proactive does mean that you should not procrastinate. Face it squarely and understand what is going on. Decide whether it may be advantageous to help the conflict surface so it can be dealt with openly. Whether openly or quietly, more often than not a pastor must deal with emerging conflicts quickly before they escalate.

Empowering Pastors speak of the importance of being open, accepting, and reconciling but not afraid to deal with controversy. A pastor's responsibility for dealing with conflict is clear.

How to Attract and Keep Active Church Members[18] reported that out of 439 churches that responded to questions on conflict, 58 percent named pastoral leadership and interpersonal differences with the pastor as a cause of their conflict. Conflict that centers in the pastor is particularly difficult to deal with. But it also is especially important. Do not run away from it! Under concerted role conflict, ministers tend to withdraw psychologically. This tendency is more pronounced when pastors feel that others question the quality of their performance. But withdrawal is a self-defeating mechanism. Ambiguity increases and conflicts escalate. Instead, increase your communication with others involved.

So when differences in expectations put you in a bind, do not be passive. Actively renegotiate your roles. When conflicts center in you, deal with them. And, insofar as possible, do so in such a way that the needs of everyone are met.

Communicate

Conflicts often arise because of a failure in communication. They are aggravated in conflict situations when communication shuts down. So find ways to keep channels of communication open with church officers and with members of the congregation. This can be particularly important when differences in expectations are the cause of conflicts.

Discuss your role with your board and let them interpret it to the congregation. There is evidence that discussion of the minister's role by clergy and laity increases consensus among all concerned.

When others disagree among themselves on what they expect of you, help them to face it together. Let it be their problem, not yours. As they struggle to resolve their differences, they may better realize the bind they have been putting you in.

Work Closely with Others

Have a pastor-parish committee or personnel committee whose members you can trust. Work closely with them before conflicts develop. Encourage them to bring problems to you promptly. Let them help you understand how your style of ministry is affecting members of your congregation. They need to support you but also to challenge you when you need challenging. When pastors wear no clothes, someone had better tell them!

It is sometimes helpful to get the church board to deal with seemingly intractable conflicts involving a pastor and a member or small group of members. The pastor of a medium-sized congregation in a suburban community illustrates this.

> The biggest challenge to my ministry in the last five years has been the presence of a gifted, committed young couple who seemed determined to undermine my leadership and disrupt or destroy our life together as a family of faith. Initially I tried to deal with these folk personally and pastorally and on my own. After some years of attempting to encourage and accommodate them, to redirect their energies, I shared this painful matter with the session, who confirmed the destructiveness of their behavior and voted to visit them in a pastoral spirit, but with a clear message to end such unhelpful and unhealthy activities. The couple refused to be visited and left the church.

Be big enough to call in an outside consultant when the situation requires it. A lay leader who operates a judicatory-sponsored mediation service finds that ministers often do not call for mediation when they need it. "Their attitude seems to be, 'If I can't handle it, neither can you.' "

HOW TO MANAGE CONFLICT WHEN IT ERUPTS

It takes significant levels of skill to manage conflicts once they erupt. A trained pastor can learn to deal with the early stages of disagreement before differences escalate into personal conflicts. Leas makes many helpful suggestions. It is impossible to cover them adequately here, but he suggests that the goals of conflict management are "to move from enmity to amity, to move from malevolence to benevolence." He gives five penultimate goals for a conflict-management process: (1) making clear decisions, (2) increasing tolerance for difference, (3) reducing aggression, (4) reducing passive behavior, and (5) reducing covert, manipulative behavior.[19] Leas then outlines some actions any pastor can take to help manage conflict.[20]

1. Help your board make decisions. In descending order of their value, Leas lists five possible decision strategies. *Collaboration* is difficult and time-consuming but effective. Leas gives illustrations of how to do it. *Negotiation* is useful when collaboration is not possible. *Voting* or *hierarchical decisions* are last resorts. They can be better than allowing conflict to fester and grow.

Sometimes *avoidance* is appropriate, and Leas gives illustrations of when that is helpful.

2. Help all parties stay in the action.
3. Find out what each side wants.
4. Help all groups feel stronger, which will diminish the likelihood of verbal or physical violence.
5. Work for joint problem definitions.
6. Remind the group of ties that bind them together.
7. Deal with feelings.
8. Provide a structure for the process that spells out who will attend meetings, what the agenda will be, steps in the resolution process, who will make what decisions and how, rules of fair and open discussion, and so forth.
9. Help people open up communication. Leas suggests ways to do so.

CARING FOR PEOPLE

Beyond the conflict-management skills that pastors need to learn is the central importance of maintaining a loving but firm relationship with those with whom one is involved in conflict. A pastor who serves a medium-sized congregation in a small town and a pastor of a small congregation in a rural community give illustrations of this.

Caring for people as persons, and loving them even when disagreeing with them, has helped in conflict resolution. It is an attitude more than skills that seems to have worked. I have had the attitude that people are important. People's attitudes are conditioned by a lot of baggage they carry with them. Somewhere I had heard "Everybody you meet is fighting a battle. Remember to be kind."

When I came here over thirty years ago, the church was divided. An administrative commission of the presbytery asked me to come here for six months. A group of people were running the church. They would caucus before congregational meetings to develop a strategy for getting their own people elected to the boards of the church. There was a nasty conflict situation. It was partly theological. The group wanted to go back to the old Westminster views of the 1700s and to convert everybody with a Damascus experience before accepting them as Christians. They had a brittle theology. One of the leaders was finding it difficult to cope with change.

The second year I was there the local TV station had a program of lectures that ran for six to eight weeks, presented by Hamilton, the God-is-dead theologian. We put a television set in the church and people came to listen and discuss. The first of those lectures was on the role of God in the world and human problems. In that context, Hamilton quoted Freud.

This leader was not at the meeting until five or ten minutes after the program had finished. He slipped into the back of the room. Finally he interrupted. He just had to speak out. He could not understand how we would bring this modernist into the church who quoted a writer of dirty books. The group quietly continued the discussion.

After the meeting we had a conversation. I asked him why he felt the way he did. He replied that he had had an experience of Christ, and didn't want to lose it. That gave me insight as to why he was so combative and helped me accept him as he was. I continued to do that in spite of things that happened. He left the church and went to an independent Baptist church. When he was ill, I went to see him at the hospital. Several years later he came to see me and said he couldn't understand how I could love him when we disagreed so much. Underneath that personality there were some deep burdens.

My biggest challenge has been trying to pastor a dysfunctional, victimized congregation. This congregation had experienced a severe betrayal (clergy sexual misconduct) approximately a decade before my arrival. They needed someone gifted in discernment and conflict management. I did not know of the incident until after arrival. (It was deliberately kept secret.) I was able to discern their pain, help process their grief, and have learned much about conflict. But because of their displaced anger and denial, I have not been as effective as possible.

I have tried my best to give them an image of a pastor who loves them, whom they can trust, who pastors with integrity and offers them ways to deal appropriately and constructively with their hurts, while moving toward their future as a church of Jesus Christ. Also I have tried to provide as much information as possible about the behavior of congregations.

Having looked at the impact of the ability to listen, collaborate, and manage conflict on ministry, it is not difficult to realize why people skills are the bedrock of pastoral effectiveness. Without them, the achievement of congregational mission is severely hampered, and a pastor is doomed to increased stress, unhappiness, and even failure. A high level of people skills opens wide doors to opportunity.

10

POWER TO
LIVE WITH STRESS

The more significant our ministry, the greater the possibility that
we may be faced with ministry burnout. To avoid this problem we
need to know ourselves and our motives deeply *and* well and we
need to be guided by the deepest wisdom of our souls.
—Morton Kelsey, in *Ministry Burnout* by John A. Sanford

The pastoral ministry is a stressful calling. Air traffic controllers, pilots,
and others who carry instant responsibility for the life or death of many people
experience greater stress of a different kind while they are on the job. But, along
with therapists, physicians, nurses, and others in the helping professions, a pastor's work involves greater stress than perhaps is required in many other ways
of life. A study of nearly five thousand parish ministers from twenty-one denominations concluded that 75 percent of pastors experience stress at one or
more times in their careers. One-fifth of them reported stress during three or
more periods and one-fourth during two such periods.[1] Although this study was
published in 1971, there is no reason to believe that the incidence of stress has
significantly changed since then.
    Burnout among pastors is not at all uncommon. In fact, more than 44 percent
of both Empowering Pastors and Other Pastors in our study say that they have
suffered burnout at some time. And we do not know how many ministers have
left the pastorate because of burnout. Other research suggests that those loses are
not high. In fact, after studying stress in the ministry, Seward Hiltner, a professor of pastoral counseling, concluded that pastors deal with stress better than
most professionals. Charles Rassieur observed that "Few pastors are over-
whelmed by the pressures of ministry, and even fewer are leaving the professional ministry.[2] But all agree that the management of stress is important for sustained effective ministry.
    Given the highly stressful demands of ministry, how does a pastor sustain vi-
tality and creativity over the years? To answer this, we begin with a definition of
stress and burnout. Next we interpret some of the causes of stress and burnout.
Finally we look at ways that Empowering Pastors sustain their power over the
years.

A friend and I were discussing pastoral stress and burnout. With some feeling he said, "I can't understand why so many ministers today are always talking about burnout. When I was young I preached several times on Sunday, conducted a Bible class, worked with the young people in the evening. I called in several regional hospitals, had a midweek service, and otherwise carried a very heavy schedule. I had never even heard of such a thing as burnout. I was called to be a pastor, and I did it round the clock."

My friend was identifying burnout with carrying a heavy workload. And that can be a cause of burnout. But as we talked, he began to recognize that burnout involves much more than that. He had been working in a homogeneous Midwest community where everyone was committed to the church. He knew exactly what his people expected of him. His wife was highly supportive and fulfilled all the normal expectations of a pastor's wife in those days. As the "dominie," he was looked up to by everyone. He was a highly important person in the community. He had a deep dedication to his calling. Of course, he had his problems. Like any young pastor, he made his mistakes. But the people were kind and forgiving. Under such circumstances it is not difficult to carry a heavy load.

For most pastors today there is much that is different. There is tremendous diversity in many communities. In most communities the church no longer plays such an important role in society. The status of the pastor in most communities has eroded. Most pastors now face a wide variety of ambiguous and conflicting expectations.

STRESS AND BURNOUT

Stress is the response within us to all the demands made upon us at any given time. These demands may come from others or from ourselves. Stress is not necessarily destructive. In fact, without stress life would be drab and unbearable. To live is to experience stress. It can stimulate tremendous creativity or it can lead to our downfall professionally or personally.

The amount and nature of stress makes a big difference. Excessive stress may cause burnout, whatever we do. Stress that impacts areas of our special vulnerability can be particularly difficult to handle. But normally, the outcome depends on what we do with the stress we are experiencing. Many pastors handle stress effectively. We must recognize our stressors, know and use sources of renewal, and take time for that renewal. Perhaps you have used as a sermon illustration the fable of the young buck who went to an old sage with the intention of trapping him with a riddle. "O man of great wisdom, tell me. In my hand is a bird. Is it alive or is it dead?" If the old man were to say, "It is dead," the young fellow would open his hand and let the bird fly free. If, on the other hand, the wise man were to say, "It is alive," the challenger would crush the bird. Said the sage, "As you will, my son." In many ways, what happens to us under stress depends upon us.

Burnout is the loss of energy, purpose, and idealism that results from excessive unmanaged stress in our work. The image is of fire that burns up vitality and leaves one empty, disillusioned, and apathetic. Its symptoms include exhaustion, fatigue, frequent headaches, gastrointestinal disturbances, weight loss, sleeplessness, depression, and shortness of breath.[3]

Two books are particularly helpful in understanding burnout and the nature of stress in the ministry: John Sanford's *Ministry Burnout* and Charles Rassieur's *Stress Management for Ministers*. Largely from those two sources I draw the following seven major areas of stress in the pastoral ministry:[4]

Overwork
Dealing with too many conflicting or ambiguous expectations
Working constantly with needy people
Confusing the masks we wear with the persons we are
Not knowing whether we have really accomplished anything
Groping for a relevant faith
Living with pressing personal or family needs

Overwork

Like the work of the proverbial housewife, a pastor's work is never done. Not all pastors are overworked, but most of them probably are. Because of the demands of their calling and for a variety of other reasons, many are probably workaholics. Fifty-seven percent of all pastors in our study say that they experience stress often or very often from too many demands on their time. When asked in what areas of their life and ministry they wish they were more effective, the most frequent response was "time management." Among the five most frequently mentioned problems of pastors who sought help from the Menninger Foundation is *overextension*, defined as "the feeling of having too many commitments that vied for time and energy."[5]

There is no significant difference between Empowering Pastors and Other Pastors in the stress they experience from too many demands on their time. However, we found significant differences between solo pastors and heads of staff and between pastors of different-sized congregations.

The larger the congregation, the more likely pastors are to say that they experience stress often or very often from too many demands on their time. In like manner, heads of staff are much more likely than solo pastors to say that they experience such stress. Some will find these results obvious. In addition to preaching and some pastoral care, heads of staff must give leadership to church officers and staffs while they manage a large complex organization. Others will wonder at our findings. They would expect solo pastors of medium-sized congregations to experience more stress from time pressures than heads of staff. Solo pastors bear the load alone. They do not have colleague pastors to share their ministries.

But no matter what the size of the congregation, a pastor's work is never done. Over and over again come the weekly demands for a fresh, inspiring sermon. Advent, Christmas, Lent, Holy Week, and Easter come, ready or not. And pastors face the same people and the same problems again and again and again. John

Sanford makes an apt comparison: "The ministering person is like Sisyphus in Greek mythology, whose fate it was to have to push a great stone up a mountain only to have it roll down again just before reaching the top. This feeling that a job is endless, that you never quite reach the top of the mountain no matter how hard you try, can lead to exhaustion."[6]

Role Conflict and Ambiguity

In chapter 9, I reported that Empowering Pastors are more likely than Other Pastors to say that they never or rarely experience stress from conflicting or ambiguous expectations for their work. In contrast, one in four Other Pastors experience such stress often or very often. Sanford identifies the multiplicity of expectations as an important cause of stress: "Perhaps in no other profession," he says, "except maybe that of the politician, is a person facing so many expectations from so many people, and, to make the situation more complicated, the expectations people place upon the ministering person vary enormously."[7]

Needy People Who Drain Our Energy

"Someone touched me. I felt power discharging from me" (Luke 8:46, TM), Jesus insisted when the hemorrhaging woman touched the edge of his robe. Even our Master lost energy when he worked with needy people. Even he needed to renew that energy constantly by times of solitude and prayer. Who are we to be any different? Sanford points out:

> The energy drain that comes from working with people who are in need is subtle. One hardly uses one's physical energy in working with such people, but mentally and spiritually one becomes depleted. It is like having a small but constant loss of blood. When a ministering person once complained of how tired he was getting, a colleague remarked, "Well, how many blood transfusions a day can you give to people?"[8]

Not only does a pastor work with needy people; their needs vary widely and those needs are often hidden. The most difficult people are usually needy and intractable. Sometimes you must simply let them go, and recognize that your help is not going to be enough. But letting go also can be very stressful to one who is committed to helping others.

Confusing Persona with Identity

Chapter 5 looked at the importance of being yourself while being a pastor. It told of the determination of Empowering Pastors to be genuine human beings and how one pastor balances the desire to be authentic with the need to fulfill pastoral expectations. Sanford pursues the issue to a deeper level as he deals with the stress pastors feel when so much of their work requires that they wear a professional mask or "persona." "The persona is often useful and necessary," he says. "It enables us to be effective in our dealings with the world, and also to protect ourselves when that is necessary." Wearing a mask helps pastors keep parts of themselves hidden from others while it allows them to project their personalities to those around them. Pastors may choose a persona or it may be handed to them by others.[9] Stress comes when pastors confuse their persona with their identity. To try to be someone one is not is exhausting, and one risks losing touch with the real self. It "will also impoverish our personality, and, in the long run, also impoverish our congregation."[10]

Lloyd Rediger, a pastoral counselor with wide experience, is really dealing with the same issue when he says that "the pastor's personal and professional identities, and the pastor's religious faith, are all combined in the single pastoral role, thus causing a continuing identity crisis."[11]

Nebulous Accomplishments

Two of the five stressors cited by pastors at the Menninger Foundation are closely related. "Imprecise competence" and "lack of accomplishment" are part of a common need to feel that one's ministry is really making a difference. Pastors can feel good about tangible accomplishments if their congregations are growing numerically, budgets are increasing, or a building program has been completed. But most pastors are not serving congregations where they experience those tangible results. And, even if their congregations are booming, much of a pastor's work yields unmeasurable results. One can gain satisfaction from lives of individuals where obvious transformation has taken place. But those results are not always evident, even when they are taking place. So pastors ask, What difference has my preaching really made in the lives of pew sitters? Perfunctory appreciation routinely expressed as members exit the sanctuary is easy to ignore. What difference has a Bible class made? Has a pastoral call really accomplished anything? On and on the doubts roll along. There are usually more questions about results than answers.

All of us need to feel that we are competent and that our efforts are productive. We need genuine affirmation. Without affirmation of accomplishments it is easy for pastors to wonder what their ministry adds up to. Without evidence to the contrary it is easy for pastors to feel they may be failing. And many pastors get no formal feedback. Nor do they know how to evaluate the informal feedback they do get.

Groping for Relevant Religious Faith

One of the five "most representative problems" pastors at the Menninger Foundation presented was "a desperate groping for relevant religious faith." "Pastors themselves are subject to so many demands from others that they begin to feel in need of a pastor themselves," Donald Houts said in a *Pastoral Psychology* article. "Many experienced this as a gradual sense of losing the reality of the faith that they proclaimed, ... playing their roles with decreasing involvement, commitment, and integrity."[12]

At a deeper level of understanding, insights from Jürgen Moltmann suggest that many pastors in our day have been caught in the double crises of relevance and Christian identity. He says, "These two crises are complementary. The more theology and the church attempt to become relevant to the problems of the present day, the more deeply they are drawn into the crisis of their own Christian identity. The more they attempt to assert their identity in traditional dogmas, rights and moral notions, the more irrelevant and unbelievable they become."[13]

Moltmann shows how the tension between relevance and Christian identity has polarized the church. Social activists, in their commitment to solidarity with others in the struggle against injustice, run the risk of drifting from their Christian identity. Fundamentalists, in their passion to defend orthodoxy from the assaults of social change, are in danger of becoming irrelevant to the structures that oppress suffering humanity. And, I might add, the large body of mainline pastors who seek the middle ground easily become victims of the tension between the two as they struggle to articulate and live out a relevant faith. Frequently, they face in their congregations advocates of both polarities who find it difficult to relate to those at the other extreme or to recognize the validity of the dynamic interaction between the two.

Moltmann challenges the absurdity of this polarity, saying that evangelization must inevitably lead to social and political involvement, and "the humanization of social circumstances leads either to a crisis of identity, or inevitably to evangelization or pastoral care."[14] He concludes that "the 'identity-involvement dilemma' of Christian life at the present day is consequently not a dilemma, but the inevitable tension of Christian faith."[15]

Once again we are confronted with the imperative of discovering ways to build bridges from biblical/theological verities to the issues that confront individuals and the structures of society.

If all this is true, pastors must learn to live with the tension involved in seeking to communicate a relevant faith. And that can be stressful. As one bears the pain of needy souls, and as one wonders whether one's ministry is bearing fruit, it is not strange that ultimate questions arise. Faith and doubt are constant companions. It is only through continued renewal of the spirit that relevant faith can continually sustain us. Even our Lord experienced the ebb and flow of doubt and faith. In his darkest hour upon the cross his anguish expressed itself in two seemingly contradictory cries. First, "My God, my God, why have you forsaken me?" (Matt. 27:46), and then "Father, into your hands I commend my spirit" (Luke 23:46).

Pressing Personal and Family Needs

In describing stress in the ministry, Rassieur likens ordination to the marriage contract.[16] Ordination is normally for life and involves deep emotional commitments just as marriage does. Life commitments, whether to marriage or to the church, exert strong pressures on the soul. Both have explicit and implicit expectations, which he analyzes. Deeply dedicated, able young ministers bring their idealism to their first parish. When they made their decision to enter the ministry, recognition and praise came to them. Now they find themselves in the reality of the parish where pastors are often "admired extravagantly" or "criticized severely." Just as the nonverbal marital contract may require renegotiation in marriage counseling, pastors will need to renegotiate the expectations of their congregations.

Most professionals and business persons spend a great deal of time and energy in their early years seeking to establish themselves in their calling. The demands that they ascribe to their work take away from time to meet their own needs and to spend with their families. Pastors are no different. Although a workaholic may be driven by many forces aside from "legitimate" reasons, the results on personal and family life are the same, whether the perceived job demands are legitimate or not. For pastors, this common tendency of young professionals is further complicated by the religious motivation that drives them and theological rationalization that justifies their neglect of self and family.

As one example of personal neglect, we cite the fact that 29 percent of Empowering Pastors and 43 percent of Other Pastors say they are ineffective or somewhat ineffective in taking time for exercise and recreation. On the positive side, 41 percent of Empowering Pastors and 27 percent of Other Pastors say that they are effective or very effective at taking such time.

Ninety percent of the pastors in our study are married. Roughly 5 percent are single and have never been married. The other 5 percent are separated, divorced, or widowed. There are stresses related to all these conditions.

Families of pastors face many sources of potential stress. As we have said, they share with families of other busy professionals severely limited time with spouse and father or mother. However, pastors and their spouses and children face some unique problems. Among them are the expectations many congregations place upon the wife to participate fully in the life of the congregation. Some wives may not choose to do so. Many congregations have begun to recognize that they are not employing the wife along with her husband. But some, at least in subtle ways, still expect that a wife will be part of the pastoral team. She is expected to take messages for her husband and to be knowledgeable about what is going on in the church. Most members still expect a pastor's children to be models of decorum.

The spouses of most ministers today have their own professions or occupations. This is both by choice for professional fulfillment and by necessity. The family needs to make ends meet financially. Thus most spouses are out of the home during regular weekday working hours. Many families in our culture enjoy weekends as the time when children are out of school and parents do not have to go to work. This can be family time. Couples can enjoy each other, and parents can support their children in the swirl of sports and other activities. But for pastors, weekends are the most demanding days of the week. So when spouse and children are free, the pastor must work. When the pastor is able to take off a weekday, children are at school and the spouse is at work. A few disciplined pastors manage to take Saturdays off. But retreats and other unavoidable responsibilities frequently make that impossible. Many pastors rarely have a free evening during the week. Spouse and children are also caught up in myriad activities. Like many other families in our culture, they may manage an occasional evening meal together. But finding time together for the pastor's family can be complicated and is frequently neglected.

The parallel Rassieur makes between the marriage contract and ordination is in line with the common accusation that pastors' marriages break up because their marriage to the church gets more attention than their marriage to the spouse. The growing incidence of divorce among pastors is eloquent testimony to the stresses pastors and their spouses are experiencing.

Our present study made no effort to measure stresses that spouses endure. We have mentioned some of them. Barbara Gilbert, in *Who Ministers to Ministers?*[17] includes many others that pastors' wives experience. Among them are expectations that she will be the "resident holy woman" because she lives with the resident holy man, and that she can substitute for her husband as listener and counselor. She often finds herself caught in the middle between her husband and parishioners who register their complaints with her. She is then trapped into bringing bad news to her husband. Wives are frustrated when they are expected to play an active role in the congregation but restricted from ever holding an office or taking prominent leadership. That would lead to a perceived conflict of interest. And with all these stresses, a pastor's wife has no pastor of her own.

Both Empowering Pastors and Other Pastors in our study report a remarkably low incidence of family stress. Roughly half of the pastors in our study say they rarely or never experience stress in their personal or family situations. One wonders if the spouses of these pastors would give the same answer to that question. It is likely that more of them would report stress in their personal and family lives than their minister wives or husbands report.

Giving Priority to Family Time

Pastors in our study were asked to select five activities from a list of sixteen to which they give the highest priority. Empowering Pastors mentioned "taking time for family" more frequently than any other activity except "preaching and preparing sermons." Other Pastors also included this among their top five. How well do pastors actually do in maintaining that high priority level for family time? On this, there is a significant difference between our two groups. Fifty-six percent of Empowering Pastors compared with 38 percent of Other Pastors say they are effective or very effective in taking time for their families. Would spouses and children confirm their estimate? We don't know.

Before leaving consideration of family, we should consider the 5 percent of our pastors who are single and have never been married. They do not have the benefit of a spouse to give them support. They have freedom from responsibilities to spouse and children, but they may have responsibilities for parents or others. Congregations can react differently to a single pastor than to one who is married. Some single pastors are quite lonely. This can be a special problem for women pastors whose parishes are far from other women colleagues. Alone, and without that source of support, they must make their way in a profession that has until recently been reserved for men only.

Financial Stress

For some pastors and their families, limited financial resources and low compensation can create considerable stress. This can be especially severe for pastors with children of high school or college age who are serving struggling congregations with limited resources.

There is no significant difference between Empowering Pastors and Other Pastors in the stress they experience from inadequate compensation or finances. However, there are significant differences in the incidence of financial stress between solo pastors and heads of staff and between pastors of different-sized congregations. Our study found that the smaller the congregation, the more likely pastors are to say they experience stress often or very often from inadequate compensation or finances. Solo pastors are also more likely than heads of staff to feel financial stress. Both of these findings are what one might expect. Pastors who say they rarely or never experience stress from inadequate compensation or finances range from a low of 47 percent with pastors of small congregations to a high of 74 percent with pastors of large churches. In like manner and in similar proportions, heads of staff are more likely than solo pastors to say they experience such stress rarely or not at all.

Aside from work overload and financial stress, church size or position as solo pastor or head of staff seems to have no other significant difference in the incidence of other sources of stress that we sought to measure.

HOW TO HANDLE BURNOUT

We asked pastors who had suffered burnout at some time how they had dealt with it. One or more answers were selected by 185 responding pastors. Forty percent said they had in some way revised their priorities to spend more time for rest, exercise, recreation, to be with family or friends, or to engage in outside activities. Twenty-eight percent turned to some form of spiritual renewal. They spent more time in prayer, retreats, Bible reading, or fasting. Some sought a spiritual director. The third largest group of responses was of those who chose to take time away from the parish for an extended leave, vacation, or sabbatical. Other responses are shown in Figure 10.1.

In comparing the responses of Empowering Pastors with those of Other Pastors we found that they may be more likely to seek spiritual renewal and less likely to solve their problems by leaving their positions. The differences in these areas of response are large enough to suggest real differences. However, the numbers of respondents are too small to determine whether those differences are statistically significant. The data also suggest that Empowering Pastors may be more likely to deal with burnout by finding sources of support or engaging in study activities.

Both groups seem to be almost equally likely to take time away from the parish or to revise their priorities. Time away from the parish may give the most immediate relief from burnout. But revised priorities, spiritual renewal activities,

Fig. 10.1 How Pastors Dealt with Burnout

Revised priorities (rest, exercise, recreation, family/friends, outside activities)	40%
Spiritual renewal (prayer, retreats, spiritual director, Bible reading, fasting)	28%
Time away (time off, time out of town, vacation, sabbatical, extended leave)	26%
Counseling, psychotherapy, career counseling	18%
Left position (retired, took another parish, interim work, nonpastoral position)	18%
Found support (colleagues, family, friends, congregation, support group)	16%
Study activities (continuing education, study leave, academic program, reading)	13%
Kept keeping on (time passed, did not deal with it, still suffering)	8%
Worked with personnel committee and/or judicatory staff	4%
Miscellaneous personal growth endeavors	2%
Other and no response	6%

Note: N = 185; percentages do not add to 100 percent because some pastors gave multiple responses.

discovering support resources, and counseling or therapy probably give more lasting results.

Two-thirds of all pastors in the study took an average of at least four weeks of vacation over the previous three years. Only 4 percent took less than two weeks of vacation.

Forty-seven percent of all pastors in our study took an average of at least one day off each week. (See Fig. 10.2.) At the other extreme, 12 percent took less than one day off every other week. Forty-one percent took at least one day off every other week.

Living by Grace

Given the relatively high incidence of stress in the pastoral ministry, pastors who seek to be effective will profit from understanding some of the ways in which stress may be dealt with creatively.

Overwork is a real and present danger from all the unavoidable demands of the pastorate. But it also can be the result of a deeper personal or spiritual problem. Burnout can be the result of single-yoke ministries, of carrying the load alone. That, in turn, can come from our own insecurity. If we are unsure of ourselves, we fear failure, doubt the competence of others, and do it all ourselves. It can come from an exaggerated effort to control our lives rather than resting in

Fig. 10.2. Average Number of Vacation Days Used per Year Spent

Number of Days	Percentage of All Respondents
1–6	1
7–13	3
14–20	16
21–27	13
28–30	55
31 or more	12

God's grace. W. Benjamin Pratt, in "Burnout: A Spiritual Pilgrimage," describes his own experience with burnout and concludes that

> burnout is the symptom of sin—the attempt to justify one's own existence. . . . When a minister seeks to establish the grounds of his self-esteem, prove his value and worth as a person, and secure his life by his zealous, unrelenting work, he is omnipotently, pridefully, denying the grace of God in Christ and living to work out his own salvation. Such an effort will be plagued by constant stress and anxiety about the success of the effort or project.[18]

When we overwork, do we know why? How much of our overload is of our own making? Are we trying to prove something to ourselves or to others? Are we living by grace or by works? These are questions we need to face when too much work overwhelms us.

Strengthening Self-esteem

Our Lord's call to deny ourselves, take up our cross, and follow him is unmistakable. But what does this mean? Does it mean that we should denigrate self? Does it mean that we can neglect a reasonable care of our bodies and our spirits as we pour ourselves out, until there is nothing left but an empty shell? Unfortunately, that is the way some pastors have lived, until they lost their effectiveness altogether. Rassieur shows how the popular understanding of self-denial leads to burnout.

> Authentic and effective ministry which reflects biblical servanthood cannot be based upon the popular notion of the "denial of one's self." On the contrary, ministry that has as its purpose to express the love of God and the love of neighbor requires the basic affirmation of one's self and care for one's self. Ministry in the parish for Jesus Christ must begin with the recovery of self by the individual pastor.[19]

In the discussion of servant leadership I tried to show that self-affirmation and self-denial are not mutually exclusive alternatives. Paradoxically they live in creative tension with each other as one engages in strong servant ministry. We find this dramatically portrayed in the life of our Lord, and finally in the passion narrative. That which enabled our Lord to live his life as servant, and finally to take up his cross, was his strong sense of personal identity as Son of the Father. This consciousness of who he was dominated his life and ministry. His affirmation of self was as strong as it could possibly be. As a boy of twelve he said to his parents, "Why were you searching for me? Did you not know that I must be in my Father's house?" (Luke 2:49). His strong sense of self-identity was reinforced by temptations in the wilderness, by his baptism, and by the transfiguration experience. On the night of his passion, our Lord's discourse in the upper room focused both on his own unity with God and on his calling to suffer on the cross. In the garden, his struggle with the prospect of crucifixion was sustained by his unshakable relationship to the Father. He prayed, "Father, if you are willing, remove this cup from me; yet not my will but yours be done" (Luke 22:42).

Just as his identity enabled Jesus to take up his cross, so our identities as servants of the Father can sustain us when we answer the call to take up our cross daily and follow him. Rassieur is right when he asserts that what is most needed is for pastors to recover a strong positive sense of their own identity. "Ministry," he says, "that joyfully copes with stress is grounded in centered self-identity. The recovery of self is the essential prerequisite for all ministry."[20]

Spirit, or self, he maintains, is the organizing center of one's life. Our spirit-self stands above body, emotions, intellect, and desires. It exercises the power of choice that makes wholeness as a person possible. "For effective stress management, [pastors] need to claim for themselves the power of a spiritual existence that strengthens their own selfhood." This leads to strengthening of one's self-identity and self-responsibility as a choice maker. With a strengthened sense of self, one is no longer driven by one's own needs. Ministry is no longer reactive. It is intentional. He concludes that "self that is spirit means having a mind of your own that knows it is in the service of Another."[21]

"The root of the crisis in ministry today is with each individual pastor. The question of how to deal with stress will be decided privately as each pastor works toward a clear sense of identity and personal affirmation. And at bottom, the question of dealing with stress in pastoral ministry is a spiritual problem."[22]

The pastor of a medium-sized congregation, who also directs a counseling center, is convinced that many pastors need to grow in their self-esteem.

A significant number of pastors are chronically depressed. Part of that comes from the expectation that ministers have to do it all. Also from the expectation that they can't take time for their own refreshment. This is related to low self-esteem. If you don't think you deserve to take time for yourself, it is not worth doing. If you are not able to validate yourself, your self-esteem is dependent on what others think and do. You will continue to try to please people. Then if others change their thinking about you, your self-esteem suffers. You have had it!

We need to acquire self-validation rather than other validation. Validation by others should be little more than icing on the cake. If it becomes the major way we seek the feeding of self-esteem, then we are in trouble.

To grow in self-esteem often means therapy. But to be realistic, a lot of pastors are not going to seek it. We grow in self-esteem indirectly. I tell my patients that if you begin to do what you need to do, your self-esteem will go up. Accomplishing little things you have been trying to avoid helps you feel better about yourself. Functioning even when you do not want to function results in an enhancement of self-esteem.

How can pastors grow in their self-esteem? Governing bodies need to exercise care for pastors by placing a strong emphasis upon their taking time to care for themselves, improve their skills, nurture themselves, and take care of their families.

Taking Control of Time

For busy pastors under pressure, the management of time is a critical skill. Our data suggest that Other Pastors may be more likely than Empowering Pastors to identify time management as an important need. However, the number of responses is too small to determine whether those differences are statistically significant. In any case, because of the pressures pastors face, most of us can probably increase our effectiveness if we grow in our ability to take creative control of our time. How do we do that?

Once again we turn to Stephen Covey's *Seven Habits of Highly Effective People* for a brief summary of some important principles. Anyone who is concerned about improving the use of time should read, digest, and put into practice the principles he develops there. He summarizes the secret of time management in five words: "Organize and execute around priorities."

He speaks of four successive waves in approaching the management of time. The first is "notes and checklists," which enable one to see the demands on one's time. The second is "calendars and appointment books," by which one seeks to look ahead and schedule activities. The third is "prioritization," by which one seeks to clarify the relative value of activities and set both long-term and short-term goals. The fourth wave focuses on managing ourselves rather than managing our time. "Rather than focusing on *things* and *time,* fourth generation expectations focus on preserving and enhancing *relationships* and on accomplishing *results.*"[23]

Covey says that activities are either urgent or not urgent. They also are either important or unimportant. Combining these four possibilities, he develops a "Time Management Matrix" that divides activities into four quadrants:

1. Urgent and important
2. Not urgent and important
3. Urgent and unimportant
4. Not urgent and unimportant

Urgent matters are usually visible. They press on us; they insist on action. They're often popular with others. They're usually right in front of us. And often they are pleasant, easy, fun to do. But so often they are unimportant!

Importance, on the other hand, has to do with results. If something is important, it contributes to your mission, your values, your high priority goals.

We react to urgent matters. Important matters that are not urgent require more initiative, more proactivity. We must act to seize opportunity, to make things happen.[24]

When we spend most of our time reacting to what is urgent, we fail to deal adequately with what is important. We need therefore to deliberately neglect the unimportant, whether or not it is urgent, and focus on what is important. If we focus only on what is both urgent and important, it soon dominates our lives. If, however, we proactively spend as much of our time as possible on the important that is not urgent, we are ultimately able to reduce the amount of time we must spend simply reacting to the urgent.

Covey sharpens the issue by proposing the question, "What one thing could you do in your personal and professional life that, if you did on a regular basis, *would make a tremendous positive difference in your life?*"[25]

To understand the full impact of what Covey is saying, we go back to his "Habit 2: Begin with the End in Mind."[26] There he says that "all things are created twice." Leadership in our own lives develops self-awareness and vision of what we want to be and do. That is our first creation. Then managing our lives in response to that vision is the second creation.

In order to identify and clarify our priorities, Covey advocates having each person develop a personal mission statement. This will flow out of our "center or core paradigm." He identifies and describes a number of such centers. For example we can center in spouse, family, money, work, possession, pleasure, friend/enemy, church, or self. He describes how to develop your own personal mission statement and shows how that can lead to goals and priorities. These, in turn, guide our use of time. Pastors who take this approach seriously could clarify what is really of greatest importance in their lives and in their work. This would help them maintain a balance between their calling as pastors and their responsibilities to their families and to themselves.

In a chapter titled "Time for Things That Matter," Donald McCullough illustrates many of Covey's principles. First, he tells how he has become proactive about taking control of his time (Covey's habit one). "One day it occurred to me: even though many, many people have ideas about how I ought to use my time, I alone bear responsibility for it."[27] Second, McCullough clarifies his mission as a pastor and sets his goals and priorities accordingly (Covey's habit two). He "begins with the end in mind." Then he uses his vision as criteria for "putting first things first" (Covey's habit three). We see all this in the following passage.

A few years ago I had one of those "Aha!" experiences that can dramatically influence one's life. I was reading Peter Drucker's book, *The Effective Executive,* and came across this: "The effective executive focuses on contribution. He looks up from his work and outward toward goals. He asks: 'What can I contribute that will significantly affect the performance and the results of the institution I serve?'"

Suddenly the lights went on for me. I realized I have things to contribute to the church that no one else has, and if I don't contribute what I'm called to contribute, no one else is likely to. Given these facts, I asked myself, *What can I contribute?*

I had to come back to the twin consideration of *who* I am and *where* I am. Soon it became clear that what I could contribute to my church were four things: (1) communicate the gospel as effectively as I'm able through preaching, teaching, and writing; (2) develop an effective leadership team; (3) articulate a vision for the congregation; (4) create an open, positive atmosphere in which a diverse community can flourish.

With these goals in mind, I plan my activities for each week. I set aside time for study in order to have something worthwhile to communicate (for goal one). I meet with the members of my staff and discuss issues with key lay leaders (for goal two). I plan to repeat certain themes in sermons and committee meetings and private conversations (for goals three and four.).

I try not to get distracted from these goals. Because I do not feel called to do much pastoral care, I do little counseling and visitation. I'm blessed with others on staff who do these things and do them better than I. But I do some pastoral care, at least in part to fulfill my first goal, because communicators of the gospel must stay in touch with people's needs.[28]

A look at Don McCullough's weekly schedule may be instructive to other pastors who are struggling with ways to organize their time. Note that in scheduling, he sets a regular time each week to deal with important responsibilities that are urgent, like preparation for preaching and working with staff and committee chairs. He makes certain that everyone knows when he is unavailable because he is doing this. Then he blocks out time to work on important things that are not urgent, such as working on long-range plans and time for regular study that is not directly related to his preaching and teaching. By doing this he is able to decline invitations or requests that conflict with study or planning time by explaining that he is already committed at that particular hour.

His week goes like this: On Friday he plans for the following week, blocking out time to work on long-range goals. For each day he lists detailed activities he intends to accomplish. On Monday he answers mail—nearly all mail can wait until the next Monday for a reply, he says—and he spends time on the telephone "talking with committee chairpersons, recruiting, lighting fires under slow movers, and putting out the fires of the agitated."[29] Sermon exegesis comes Tuesday morning, followed by staff meetings in the afternoon and preparation of the worship service. Wednesday is a "flexible" day when he writes for publication or prepares for teaching. Sermon preparation begins on Thursday, with brainstorming and outlining. On Friday morning when he writes his sermon, all telephone calls are held, and the staff members know he can be interrupted only for true emergencies. On Friday afternoon he cleans off his desk and plans another week. Counseling is scheduled on week days in late afternoons. This is convenient for those who work and keeps mornings free for study.

All pastors know that unexpected calls destroy many a schedule. Interruptions can be kept to a minimum by protecting blocks of time and letting everyone know when they are. But some interruptions cannot be avoided. McCullough deals with this problem head-on.

> Two things have helped me cope with this. First, in my study of the gospels, I discovered how much of Jesus' ministry happened because of interruptions. His miracles and teaching often took place in response to unscheduled pleas for help and questions.
>   The second thing that helped me deal with intrusions in my day was learning how to schedule them on my calendar. I know they will happen, I expect good things in ministry to result from them, and so I now make room for them. I try never to plan a day too tightly; I keep my to-do list manageable enough so that when Mrs Smith calls and "really must" see me, well, she can.[30]

McCullough maintains his proactive stance by delaying any response to requests for him to undertake new responsibilities. "I never say yes or no at the time I'm asked to do something," he says. "I take at least twenty-four hours to pray and think about it. I generally say something like, 'So far as I can see, my calendar looks clear, but I want to pray about it. I want to make sure this would be a good use of my gifts. I will call you in a day or two to inform you of my decision.'"[31]

Negotiating and Communicating Expectations

We have already described the necessity for pastors to negotiate their priorities with officers of the church. As we have said, pastors must share their goals and self-expectations and church officers must do the same. When mutual expectations have been agreed upon they can govern time allocation. When communicated to the congregation these expectations give a rationale for what the pastor is doing and failing to do. (See chap. 9 for discussion of skills that assist such negotiations.)

One particular issue—inadequate compensation—can sometimes be dealt with if pastors are willing to negotiate with their congregations for more adequate compensation. This requires enough self-esteem to believe one is deserving of higher remuneration and a proactive stance when it comes to compensation. Nevertheless, in spite of the most effective of negotiations, some congregations will be unable to pay what pastors and their families deserve and need. Middle judicatories may then need to intervene with arrangements to move toward part-time service in more than one congregation, for example. Again, the pastor's initiative in working out such arrangements will often be crucial.

Finding Out How Well You Are Doing

Earlier in this chapter we identified the strong need all of us have to feel that we are accomplishing something. Yet it is difficult for pastors to know how well they are doing. There are some ways pastors can secure feedback on their ministries. For example:

Informal discussion with a trusted confidant. This is the "safest," most informal, and least conspicuous way to secure feedback.

Informal discussion with a personnel committee. This may often follow prior discussion by the committee of the pastor's performance based upon committee members' personal observation and upon comments they have received from members of the congregation. In a multiple-staff situation, the committee's preliminary discussion would have dealt with the performance of the whole staff.

Review with a personnel committee of separate written statements of accomplishments prepared by the pastor and by the committee. These are based upon goals for the pastor's work that had been mutually agreed upon at the beginning of the previous year.

Discussion of a summary of effectiveness followed by planning for improvement. The pastor and personnel committee members each fill out a form with three open-ended questions on (1) areas in which a minister's work has been most effective, (2) areas in which a minister's work is satisfactory, and (3) areas in which the minister's work needs improvement. The committee's responses are summarized in advance and are then compared with the pastor's responses. Discussion then focuses on ways the pastor may improve his or her performance.

Indirect feedback received in a review by the board of its goals and accomplishments, and of the church's program.

For evaluating their ministries, some pastors have used materials from the "Toward Improvement of Ministry" series. This series includes a "Pastoral Activities Index" that describes all the activities a pastor might be expected to perform and a "Pastoral Performance Profile" that provides descriptions of different levels of pastoral performance in several areas of activity, such as preaching, conducting worship, pastoral calling, and so forth. To use this material a pastor identifies in each area the statement that best describes the way she or he performs ministry. A church officer and a ministerial colleague, who serves as consultant, then meet with the pastor to confirm or modify the pastor's perceptions of performance.

The Academy of Parish Clergy encourages the establishing of colleague groups that help members evaluate their ministry by commonly accepted professional standards. Members of the Academy must fulfill requirements for annual study, and so forth.

Wearing Your Triple Yoke

We have already dealt with the imperative of wearing triple yokes. Pastors cannot expect to carry their loads alone. And it is not helpful to congregations or good for pastors' own health for them to try. In addition to dependence on God's resources, learning to delegate responsibilities to lay leaders and to any available staff is essential.

We have left for consideration three fundamental secrets of sustaining power in the pastoral ministry. First is a deep and abiding conviction that God continues to call one to pastoral ministry and to service in a particular congregation. Second is a vital and growing spiritual life. Third is an active network of supporting relationships within the congregation, in one's family, and with one's colleagues. These we will explore in chapter 11.

11

THREE SECRETS
OF SUSTAINING POWER

You did not choose me but I chose you. And I appointed you to go
and bear fruit, fruit that will last, so that the Father will give you
whatever you ask him in my name. I am giving you these com-
mands so that you may love one another.

—John 15:16

Just as the branch cannot bear fruit by itself unless it abides in the
vine, neither can you unless you abide in me.

—John 15:4

How do Empowering Pastors sustain their power over many years?
What can we learn from them? We have already explored some of the ways they
live creatively with stress. Now we turn to three dynamic sources of sustaining
power that undergird their lives and ministries, sources of stability available to
every Christian. In a special way they are crucial to faithfulness in the ordained
ministry. One is the deep conviction of God's call to ministry. The second is an
active spiritual life stimulated by the abiding presence of the Holy Spirit. The
third is the loving support that we give and receive from others. These three are
what sustained the early disciples when they suddenly found themselves bereft
of the One who meant everything to them. As he left them, he said, "All authority in heaven and on earth has been given to me. Go therefore and make disciples of all nations, baptizing them in the name of the Father and of the Son and
of the Holy Spirit, and teaching them to obey everything that I have commanded
you. And remember, I am with you always to the end of the age" (Matt. 28:18–20).

These words are so familiar they have lost much of their meaning for many of
us. What does it mean that the sovereign of heaven and earth has sent us forth to
carry out God's mission in the world? We did not choose God; God chose us. As
we go, God is with us constantly with all God's power. Our Savior's commandment of love draws us into the intimate community of our upper rooms where
we support one another in the particular ministries he gives each of us.

ASSURANCE OF GOD'S CALL

In the midst of all kinds of stress one of the most important stabilizing forces in pastors' lives can be the deep conviction that God has called us to ordained ministry and more specially to the particular place where we are serving.

> I know I am where I am because God wants me to be here. I am always asking myself what God expects me to do and to be. I think this has more to do with my effectiveness than particular skills or abilities. I am in love with these people, and they find countless ways to affirm me. I'm constantly grateful for what they bring to our ministry. I think this kind of mutual affirmation is essential.

Most Empowering Pastors would resonate to those words, spoken by one of them. Fruitful ministry is more than a function of a minister's giftedness. It grows out of a profound conviction that God has called one to be a pastor, has guided that pastor to a particular congregation, and continues to affirm that calling.

Eighty-one percent of Empowering Pastors compared with 69 percent of Other Pastors report that their sense of call when they decided to enter the ministry was very strong or strong. Their sense of calling has grown over the years so that 91 percent of them compared with 86 percent of Other Pastors have that strong sense of calling today.[1]

For some, the calling to the pastorate has been a natural process over many years, going back to nurturing experiences in childhood and youth. They say such things as:

> Early faith experiences were very formative to me in my sense of call to the ministry. My experiences in the church affirmed my call. The caring of pastors and congregations was very helpful. My pastor was a good role model and a greater encourager. Opportunities for leadership in high school youth fellowships and in summer conferences strengthened my sense of calling. A college mentor was another example of what it meant to be a caring pastor. I have experienced the presence of God, transforming my life at critical times. Responding to these gifts has helped shape my sense of call to ministry.

Others have been called in unlikely ways. An Empowering Pastor of a large congregation describes his journey.

> I am in the ministry by surprise. I never expected to be called to ministry and was least likely to be chosen to be a pastor. In college I wanted to be a jet pilot. By my senior year I wanted to go to seminary. Having been raised in a legalistic atmosphere, I rediscovered grace and decided I could get excited telling people about God's grace. But starting in seminary I had agoraphobia, with panic attacks. I was afraid of everything in any place. I was not in control of my panic. I could hardly go to graduation. I felt trapped even for an hour. So it seemed to be a joke that God was calling me to ministry. This greatly influenced my life and philosophy of ministry.
>
> My first call was to youth ministry and not to the pulpit. My divorce came at that time. My wife was anorexic and got down to sixty-three pounds and was

pregnant. After the birth she was almost homicidal. She needed therapy and I had therapy because of the divorce. After my divorce, a minister told me that my ministry was over. But a neighboring pastor helped me rediscover grace. I became very dependent upon the Lord and upon prayer. I knew what brokenness was, and my ministry has always been a surprise to me. My first pastorate was in a church of forty-five members. I figured if I could stand up in front of several hundred youth, I could preach to forty-five. The Lord blessed that ministry and I came here.

The Elements of a Call

We find in the experiences of these pastors the four elements of a call to professional leadership that H. Richard Niebuhr has identified:[2]

1. *The call to minister* that all Christians receive. As we have seen, many of the Empowering Pastors were challenged by early experiences in vital congregations to give their lives to Christ's service. Caring pastors and faithful lay leaders opened the doors of young lives to this call.
2. *The secret call,* that inner imperative to serve God through a church occupation. Pastor after pastor in our interviews described this personal sense of urgency to which they attribute the source of their effectiveness. Their calling has sustained them through all the vicissitudes of their pastoral ministries. As one of them put it, "Effective ministry begins on one's knees. It begins with the fire in the inner parts that says this is the most important message on earth."
3. *The providential call,* which threads through a lifetime of special people and circumstances , and people who initiate or confirm the secret call by identifying and developing their particular gifts for pastoral ministry.
4. *The ecclesiastical call,* which comes when a congregation, governing body, or church agency invites one to a particular ministry. It is this call that confirms all other calls. It is this call that, for most pastors, comes several times as they move from one parish to another. Transitions are critical moments for enhancing effectiveness. To stay in a present call or move to another is a question with significant potential. Responsiveness to the initiatives of others and careful exploration of each possibility can confirm and reenergize a present ministry or open new opportunities to use a pastor's best gifts and accumulated skills.

It may not be too much to say that without all four of these elements in a pastor's calling, effectiveness in ministry will be hampered.

Matching Gifts to Needs

Effectiveness is likely to be enhanced if a pastor proves to be the right person with the right gifts in the right congregation at the right time. Conversely, a mismatch of pastor and congregation can severely limit effectiveness. Furthermore, a pastor who is effective in one congregation may well be ineffective in another. A ministry that withers in one congregation may blossom in another. Therefore, the ability to discern God's initial or continuing call to a particular congregation is crucial. One of the Empowering Pastors puts it this way:

> Determining God's call usually involves a prosaic wrestling with two factors: We come to understand what God wants us to do by evaluating *who* we are and *where* we are placed.
>
> Here's my general rule: Unless struck by lightning, I assume that what God wants of me will be consistent with how he created me. So I pay attention to my desires and gifts. This evaluation, however, must be balanced with the demands of our circumstances. We don't always enjoy a perfect match between who we are and where we minister. God sometimes calls us to places that need our gifts but don't yet realize it, and thus we offer ministries that aren't fully received or appreciated.
>
> So we make adjustments. . . . Still, if too many compromises must be made, if there is too great a conflict between gifts and congregational needs, a change may be necessary. Normally, though, a sense of God's will usually emerges in the intersection between who I am and where I am.[3]

Most Empowering Pastors feel that their gifts match the needs of the congregations they serve. We found them more likely than Other Pastors to agree or strongly agree with the following statements:

My gifts and style of ministry meet the needs and expectations of my present congregation.
I feel very good about myself and my ministry.
I feel I am accomplishing more in my ministry than I did five or ten years ago.
Leaders of the congregation where I serve are very responsive to my ideas.

These answers suggest respondents' feelings, both about the fit of their gifts with the needs of their congregations, and about their levels of self-esteem. In many ways the two can be closely related. Even pastors with relatively high levels of self-esteem, when frustrated by a congregational mismatch, may become discouraged or depressed and lose some of their self-esteem.

It appears that Empowering Pastors have either a better match with their congregations or a higher level of self-esteem or both. Two-thirds of Empowering Pastors, compared with slightly more than half of Other Pastors, say they rarely or never experience stress from a feeling of powerlessness in their work.

A good match between pastor and congregation can be wonderfully energizing to both pastor and people. The Empowering Pastor of a large city church says, "The congregation I serve is incredibly responsive to its co-pastors, as well as supportive. There is a climate of real openness to new ideas, as well as mutual trust, and I find that my genuine admiration of the gifts of these people energizes my own ministry in return. It seems that we are well suited to each other."

A pastor who has served a small rural congregation for nine years puts it this way: "I may never serve another church that will respond to the gifts I bring: excitement about the Lord; openness to God's challenges for living; insatiable intellectual curiosity about scripture; willingness to 'live on the edge.' We have changed, grieved over the past, expanded our vision. There aren't many congregations out there that would be open to this kind of discontinuity."

Patient Proactivity

The next several paragraphs apply particularly to pastors who are not members of denominations with an episcopal form of polity. They deal with the exploratory process through which pastor-nominating committees and prospective pastors go before a congregation extends a call that is accepted by the pastor. For those whose appointment to a congregation is made by the bishop, this analysis may help in understanding the dynamics of their relationship with congregations to which they are being assigned.

Pastors who are exploring whether God is calling them to a new parish need a high degree of patient proactivity. On the one hand, they must take vigorous initiative in learning as much as possible about the prospective congregation. As they are being interviewed by the pastor-nominating committee, they will skillfully interview that committee and anyone else who is likely to know the congregation. They will take the initiative to explore every possible lead. An effective pastor's frame of reference will be to seek God's guidance, not to seek a call. So this is not a time for passivity.

But this is also a time of waiting. A pastor must wait for responses from committees and especially for a clear signal of God's call. In the midst of frustrating delays, pastors need a double measure of faith to believe that God will guide them to the right place of service. It takes infinite patience to wait for that guidance while actively exploring one's fit with one or more potential pastorates. When there are more pastors seeking a parish than there are openings, it takes a great deal of courage to say no to a congregation for which one's gifts are not suited. But effectiveness as a pastor may well depend on it. "Fulfillment in ministry comes when gifts and needs identified meet. A match between pastor and congregation happens best when both pastors and congregations know what they are looking for. Hidden agendas of the congregation or of the pastor are what get those relationships into trouble."

Honesty with Self and with Committees

Finding the right congregation starts with knowing yourself and honestly revealing who you are to pastor-nominating committees. When you do not know your strengths and limitations, you cannot tell where you will be most effective. In chapter 12 we will look at various ways in which pastors can gain a better understanding of themselves. Meanwhile, one pastor advises this:

> To have a good match, pastors need to evaluate their strengths and weaknesses. Career counseling can help pastors become clear about what they are good at and what they would like to do. Of course it is possible that you may think you

are good at something that you are not. You need to get feedback somewhere and somehow. Colleague support groups or members of the church you are in can help you in self-evaluation.

If you do not share yourself openly, a search committee has no way of knowing whether you will meet their needs and expectations. If you are so intent on getting a job that you distort who you are, you may be successful in getting a call and fail as a pastor. One pastor observes that "If you are going to move, it helps not to be wanting to move. If you don't need to move, there is not as much hanging on that. You don't have to be trying to sell yourself, and so forth." A pastor who teaches a class in polity at a well-known seminary speaks to the importance of self-revelation.

When I am teaching my students about the call process, I tell them not to worry about being honest on their personal information forms. "There are places out there where you don't want to work," I say. Ministers need to come to terms with what they are good at and what they want to do. There will be congregations that value those same things. I have been fortunate in having had congregations where I fit well, though they have been very different. I am sure there are congregations where I would not be effective. However, I do not believe in an extremely narrow view of a match. I don't agree with those who believe that there is only one person on earth who would be their star-made lover. There are pastors who have gotten into the wrong church for some kind of reason. Perhaps they were not honest with themselves or they were desperate for a job. But there are lots of churches in which an effective pastor can serve effectively.

I tell my students, "To get a good match, trust the process and use it. We have about as complicated a process for calling a pastor as anybody. But the positive side of it is that there are lots of ways to get input about the appropriateness of any particular call. Problems come when pastors don't listen when people raise questions. If they don't pay attention to the signals, they get what they deserve. It boils down to being truly open to being led."

Reading between the Lines

The church needs to have spent time in evaluating its strengths and weaknesses. If it has failed to do this, it will be difficult for pastors to know whether their gifts will match its needs. Even when pastor-nominating committees have done their homework, like pastors, they want to put their best foot forward. In an attempt to combine honesty with salesmanship they may skillfully hide their flaws, giving, at best, only subtle clues to problems they feel would discourage a potential pastor. Those clues may easily be overlooked if one does not read between the lines on whatever information the congregation gives. If a pastor-nominating committee is getting desperate to find a pastor, they may even fail to give any clues to booby traps that later will explode in the pastor's face. Therefore pastors need to follow up on any clues that come to them and to seek sources of information in addition to those provided by the congregation itself. Executives and former pastors can be helpful in this quest. The effort should be to understand a congregation's character and history. One pastor develops this analogy at length.

I believe every church has a type of spiritual genetics. Forefathers and foremothers in every congregation set a behavioral tone that is inherited generation after generation. This congregation's desire is to be the hub of its community, to be open to all people who are called by God to participate in this church. So it is easy to incorporate and assimilate new people. The foundations for this were laid many years ago.

It is important to know the spiritual genetics of a congregation. A pastor needs to know the congregation's expectations. Read carefully the church information forms. Don't just look at the functions they want the pastor to perform. But look at what those functions say about the family atmosphere of that church.

After I came here I began to research the history of this congregation. I found three common threads of what they had always wanted: good preaching, great music, and a ministry to youth. I had not realized this when I accepted the call. But when I reviewed the church information form, those expectations were right there without my knowing it. And during my ministry here, that is what they have created.

When I came, the congregation had no ministry to children and youth. There were fifteen children in the Sunday school. But the congregation has always had a passion for children and their families. I shared that passion. What has evolved is tremendous. I give major time to those ministries. Our congregation has fewer than 300 members but ministers to 750 people in the community. They look to our congregation for counseling, marriage, burial, and comfort.

I have refused to burn out in the ministry. So there are certain areas left undone. I can't do it all. Older members who have believed in youth and young families realize this, and are willing to take a minimum of my time. This is the result of the genetic makeup of this congregation. For example, when a woman's husband died, I called to ask if I could visit her. She said, "Please don't come. Give your time to the young families." That's where her heart was. Both she and her husband had been praying for them.

In seeking to discover a match with a congregation during the call process, a minister should study the church information form carefully and ask the pastor-nominating committee, "How do these goals that you set forth for ministry reflect where the church has been in the past?" If they are new things, they are potential red flags. Then the question is, "Does the congregation really want to make those changes?"

Exploring Your Fit to the Congregation

When pastors are considering a call, they may want to be aware of several demographic and cultural factors that seem to have a bearing on how well their gifts will match the demands and possibilities in any particular congregation.

Our findings strongly suggest that pastors tend to serve the same size congregation in the same type of community in which they grew up. We assume that this is because they feel more comfortable in familiar settings of community and congregation. All other things being equal, pastors will have less to learn about ministry if they serve in a community whose culture they instinctively understand, and in a congregation whose size and dynamics they have experienced under able pastoral leadership. Of course this should not be a determinative factor in any decision, because there are many exceptions.

Pastors of congregations with five hundred or more members are more likely than pastors of smaller congregations to have grown up through high school in congregations of five hundred or more members and to have served their first parish in a large congregation. Pastors of congregations with fewer than two hundred members are more likely than pastors of larger churches to have grown up through eighth grade in congregations with fewer than two hundred members and much less likely than pastors of larger congregations to have grown up through high school in a congregation of five hundred or more members.

Forty-eight percent of solo pastors compared with 11 percent of heads of staff serve congregations in small towns or rural areas. Solo pastors also are much more likely than heads of staff to have grown up through high school in small towns or rural areas. Sixty-two percent of heads of staff compared with 32 percent of solo pastors serve congregations in suburban areas or large cities. Heads of staff also are much more likely to have grown up through high school in suburbs, small cities, or large cities. They are more likely to have served their first congregation in the suburbs.

These demographic factors seem to have no influence on the issue of empowering. We have found no significant differences between Empowering Pastors and Other Pastors on the type of community or size of congregation in which they grew up.

Understanding the Congregation's Culture and Identity

Regional cultural characteristics can also be very important in matching pastors and congregations, especially in small towns or rural areas. A study of congregational identities by Carroll and Roozen[4] provides valuable tools for understanding the culture and identity of a congregation. Beyond questions of size and community, the premise of the study was that congregations, as collectives of individuals, have identities just as individuals do. This identity, or reason for being, they defined as

a set of shared perceptions of members about themselves, their congregation and its mission. Such an identity arises . . . out of the interaction of the internal characteristics and dynamics of a congregation—its history, beliefs, symbols, rituals, norms and relational patterns—with various aspects of its external environment, including the social worlds of its members.

The researchers developed nine pairs of descriptive statements at each end of a seven-point scale. By choosing one of the seven possibilities on each of the nine scales, 6,362 elders from 615 congregations described characteristics of their churches. We used five of these descriptive scales in our study (see Fig.11.1). The four scales that we did not use in our study are presented in chapter 11, note 5.[5] This is not the place to describe the results of the congregational identify study, which developed six congregational identity descriptions.[6]

The five descriptive scales we used provide a tool by which pastors might explore with nominating committees several important dimensions of congregational identity. If you wish to do this, you might take one of two possible approaches. A formal process might include the following steps: First, place a check

Table 11.1. Dimensions of a Congregation's Identity

Listed below are several pairs of alternatives that relate to important dimensions of a congregation's identity. Using the seven-point scale between each pair of alternatives, please circle the appropriate number to indicate which statement best describes your congregation. ("1" = most like the characteristic on the left, "7" = most like the characteristic on the right, "4" = an equal mix of both characteristics)

The congregation is influenced more by history and tradition.	1 2 3 4 5 6 7	The congregation is influenced more by contemporary ideas and trends.
Members are similar in values and lifestyle to the people who live around the church.	1 2 3 4 5 6 7	Members are very different in values and life style from the people who live around the church.
The congregation's approach to social issues is basically educational, leaving any action to individual conscience.	1 2 3 4 5 6 7	The congregation's approach to social issues is decidedly "activist." We have a proven history of taking a stand as a congregation.
The congregation's approach to individual salvation emphasizes education, nurture, and gradual growth in the faith.	1 2 3 4 5 6 7	The congregation stresses a "born again" conversion experience in its approach to salvation of individuals.
The congregation has a high tolerance for theological diversity.	1 2 3 4 5 6 7	The congregation has a low tolerance for theological diversity.

Source: Jackson W. Carroll and David A. Roozen, "Congregational Identity in the Presbyterian Church," *Review of Religious Research* 31, no. 4 (June 1990): 351–69.

mark at the appropriate point on each of the five scales to represent your feeling regarding those characteristics of an "ideal" congregation. Second, ask members of the pastor-nominating committee or of the congregation's governing body to describe their congregation using the same scales. Finally, compare the composite responses of those church members with your own responses. This comparison could become the basis for discussion with the pastor-nominating committee.

Alternatively, you could simply use the five dimensions as a basis for interview questions you would ask to get a clearer picture of the congregation's identity. Either process should help identify areas of compatibility and potential pitfalls in a pastoral relationship.

Where differences emerge, you and the nominating committee could make a judgment as to the relative importance of those differences. For example, if you have a very strong commitment to social activism you might decide that you could not be effective in a congregation where social activism might be frowned upon. Or if your convictions insist upon a "born again" emphasis in your approach to individual salvation, you might not expect to be effective in a congregation that is strongly opposed to such an emphasis.

Dealing with a Less-Than-Perfect Fit

In spite of all that pastors may do in seeking to match their gifts with the needs and expectations of a congregation, a pastor will often find significant differences in perspective with which he must deal. When asked what was the biggest challenge in his ministry over the past five years, the pastor of a large suburban church replied:

> To blend my views of church and ministry with an existing staff, session, and congregation, all of whom understood church and ministry in different ways. What have I done? (1) Blundered into conflict with the associate pastors . . . worked it through with the help of a counselor/consultant, hammered out a covenant to guide our relationships, and worked hard and humbly (most of the time) to make the covenant work. It has! (2) Encouraged the nominating committee to seek elders in terms of their gifts for ministry . . . trained those elders . . . set them free to be creative and risk taking.

Another pastor of a small congregation found that his congregation's view differed significantly from his own perspective on three of the scales. The congregation was much more inclined to be influenced by history and tradition, less inclined toward social activism, and had a much lower tolerance for theological diversity. He put his "greatest challenge" this way:

> Having come from a congregation that more closely paralleled my "ideal," I have struggled to find my niche in this congregation that perceives the church much differently. I miss a greater degree of openness and theological tolerance.
> The biggest challenge I have faced has been working with a congregation that is much more conservative and distrusting of the denomination. I have at-

tempted to deal with this by building trusting relationships and providing an open forum in which to talk. It seems at times that we are making progress together in learning some new ways and entertaining some new ideas. I hope that over time this approach will be beneficial.

This Empowering Pastor must be doing something right because his nominator summarized his effectiveness as a pastor by saying, "He does all things well. He has ended conflict in a divided church, led them to be more involved in mission to the local community, and solidified a growing rapport with presbytery and the wider church. In the last two years their mission giving to [the mission fund of more inclusive governing bodies] has increased 228 percent."

A third pastor comments on his experience of entry into a large congregation where his fit proved to be somewhat marginal. He moved slowly to allow time for adjustments to take place.

> The pastor-nominating committee felt that I fit the theology and style of ministry the congregation was seeking. However, I was more conservative than the pastor who preceded me. He was neoorthodox. My first year here, the president of the board of trustees left the church because he said I was a "fundamentalist." I guess there were a lot of people who didn't think that I fit. But I was very careful in that first year not to make changes and to fit in with their culture. I visited people to get to know them, and I didn't react quickly to what happened. That is part of my self-esteem. As time goes on in a congregation, people who join the church do so because they relate well to you. Then you fit very easily.

In commenting on fit, this pastor identifies two important dimensions. "One is theology. If a pastor is too conservative or too liberal for a congregation, we are asking for trouble.... The second is leadership style." In the illustration he gives, we once more see the importance of initially adapting to the culture and expectations of the congregation. He continues,

> For example, two contrasting styles are the country parson and the chairman of the board [Schaller's categories]. Those are leadership styles that are culturally appropriate in different congregations. A pastor I know came to a two-hundred-member congregation that wanted a parson. There was no office in the church, and the people did not think in terms of office hours. He demanded an office. That was inconsistent with their culture for he was the parson. That pastorate failed miserably. An interim pastor who understands their culture followed him. He visited everybody. Even though he was a liberal, he was doing Bible stories and parables to fit their culture. Once you have established a reasonable fit, you can begin to move the congregation in new ways. But you must begin where they are.

When pastors question whether their gifts fit with the needs of the congregations they are serving, a time of deep soul searching may come. At such times they need to seek God's guidance through prayer and meditation, and seek the counsel of others whom they trust. It is at such points that a trusting community of one's peers can be especially helpful. It is also at such times that one's conviction of God's call may be more important than one's feelings. One pastor confessed to such a situation. "The fit doesn't feel as comfortable as I believe it is. That is, my response is based on conviction and faith that God has called me to be here because he wants to use my gifts here now. But I don't feel my gifts are able to be used here as fully and freely as I would like."

Reevaluating a Call

The pastor of a medium-sized congregation has had an extended, successful pastorate. His nominator said, "His pastoral leadership is characterized by a keen-minded, articulate understanding of the faith, and in full accord with the Reformed tradition, a passionate understanding of the need to apply the faith to issues of daily life and community. This leadership shows clearly in the life of what has become a vital community of faith with a strong awareness of its mission." Not only does this pastor affirm a good fit, he is asking himself if it is too easy a fit and is seeking clues as to what should be the next steps in his ministry. Should he stay in a comfortable spot or move to a new challenge? Or is there still challenge in his present pastorate? "I am trying to discern whether I've overstayed my effective years here. I've asked colleagues (pastors and executives) and sought instruments of evaluation that don't create their own agendas. Right now we're trying a strategic planning process suggested by Roy Oswald. It looks promising. I—we—hope the outcome is mutual growth and renewal without separation!"

An Ongoing Dynamic Process

All this suggests five things pastors may do to renew and affirm their calling to a particular congregation: (1) initially to discern with clarity God's call to the pastoral ministry and to a particular congregation; (2) constantly to assess the needs of their people and the gifts with which they meet those needs; (3) annually to clarify their own and their congregations' expectations for their ministry; (4) periodically to revisit their calling with honesty and openness to change, adapting their approach to ministry as guided by the Spirit; (5) regularly to develop those gifts that will meet the demands of their calling.

LIVING BY THE SPIRIT'S POWER

The second, and perhaps most important, source of sustenance in ministry is to live by the Spirit's power. In chapter 6 I described patterns of spiritual development found among all pastors in our study. I showed how varied approaches to prayer and meditation seem to meet the diverse spiritual needs of different personalities, and reported that Empowering Pastors are more likely than Other Pastors to feel that they succeed in giving time to prayer and meditation.

We return to a consideration of spiritual disciplines because of the crucial importance they play in generating sustaining power for a pastor's ministry over the long haul. Without a close connection to the vine, our branches wither and our fruit is shriveled or disappears.

Pastors in our study were asked to rate the value of eight different spiritual disciplines to their personal and professional development. Because we know that most pastors consider preparation for preaching, teaching, or worship among important areas of their personal and spiritual life, we included it in the list along with Bible study and exegesis. Of course the two activities overlap for most pastors.

Figure 11.2 shows that more than nine out of ten Empowering Pastors feel that preparation for preaching, teaching, or worship, along with Bible study and exegesis, are very valuable or valuable for their personal or professional development. We also note, as has already been mentioned, that Empowering Pastors are more likely than Other Pastors to feel that Bible study and exegesis together with lectionary study with church members has been very valuable or valuable for them.

Figure 11.3 shows that two out of three pastors spend from three to ten days per year in retreats. Our wording of this question does not make clear whether such retreat time was for the pastor's own spiritual enrichment or was spent in leading retreats for their congregations. In terms of a pastor's own spiritual

Fig. 11.2. Spiritual Disciplines Rated Valuable or Very Valuable

Preparation for preaching, teaching, or worship	96%
Bible study and exegesis[a]	91%
Prayer and meditation	81%
Spiritual direction	28%
Lectionary study with other ministers	20%
Lectionary study with church members[a]	17%
Journaling	16%
Fasting	5%

Note: Responses are from Empowering Pastors only.
[a]Significantly higher than for Other Pastors

Fig. 11.3. Average Number of Retreat Days Taken per Year

None	8%
1 to 2 days	13%
3 to 5 days	36%
6 to 10 days	30%
11 or more days	14%

Note: Responses are from Empowering Pastors only. Rounded numbers do not equal 100 percent.

growth, differences in their interpretation of this question might be important. In either event, this finding does indicate that pastors attach some importance to retreats as a source of spiritual growth.

CULTIVATING SOURCES OF SUPPORT

The third secret of a pastor's sustaining power is to cultivate a strong network of personal, spiritual, and professional support. Pastors desperately need such support to cope with their stressful lives and minimize the possibility of burnout.

In *How to Build a Support System for Your Ministry*, Roy Oswald gives two dramatic illustrations of our human need for support from others.[7] A study of survivors of the Coconut Grove nightclub fire in which 129 people died found that some of them recovered quickly from the fire. Others did not. The first group had many people who checked with them frequently and just listened to them. The other group did not. Some of those who were cared for even developed a higher level of well-being than before the fire. And some of those without support never really recovered. A nine-year study of seven thousand people in Alameda County, California, found that those "with many social ties (such as marriage, close friendships, extended families, church membership, and other group associations) have far lower mortality rates" than those who did not. Anton Antonovsky, who cites this study, also points out that the ostracism of tribal people in voodoo rites can result in death. What kills them is being cut off from contact with community.

Oswald concludes that "if support is so essential to human life, it certainly must be essential to professional competence and well-being." He goes on to show how critical it is to a pastor's effectiveness and survival to have "a critical mass" of supporters within the congregation.[8] "Little of significance will happen inside a parish without a high degree of support there. Yet effectiveness will also be proportional to the quality of support we have outside our congregations. We need that support for our health and self-esteem. We also need it for perspective."[9]

A few pastors may be blessed with sources of support to which they need only to respond with receptivity and full involvement. Others find themselves in circumstances in which little or no support seems to be available. Most will need to discover or generate support opportunities if they are to avoid burnout and achieve full effectiveness.

From a list of nine sources of support, pastors in our study were asked to select three that have been most helpful to them in their ministry. They then identified any sources of support that have been helpful in their spiritual life, family life, and personal life. In all their responses we found no significant difference between Empowering Pastors or Other Pastors. There is a remarkable congruence among both groups regarding the kinds of support they have found helpful for different aspects of their life and ministry. Figure 11.4 summarizes the responses of all pastors in the study. In all categories the five sources of support mentioned most frequently were (1) one's spouse, (2) a member or group of the congrega-

Fig. 11.4. Sources of Support That Are Helpful to Pastors

	Their Ministry (%)	Spiritual Life (%)	Family Life (%)	Personal Life (%)
Spouse	76	61	86	78
Member or group of the congregation	55	69	48	61
Ministerial colleague or support group	52	65	31	52
Member of session or personnel committee	39	40	30	41
Friend outside the congregation	22	33	37	50
Executive or committee of presbytery	13	18	11	23
Mentor	11	20	9	16
Pastoral or marital counselor or therapist	11	14	27	26
Spiritual director	6	13	5	7
Other	7	10	9	11

Note: Responses are from all respondents. Items are listed in order of frequency of response for help in pastors' ministries.

tion, (3) a ministerial colleague or support group, (4) a member of the board or personnel committee, and (5) a friend outside the congregation.

For a pastor's ministry itself, the frequency with which sources of support were selected followed the order we have just used. For the other three categories, the frequency of mention followed the same order, with one exception for each. For support of spiritual life, the spouse came third. For family life, a friend outside the congregation came third. And for personal life, a friend outside the congregation came fourth.

Let us examine each source of support to weigh its possibilities and pitfalls and to explore ways to take the initiative in developing that source of support.

Spouses

For the 90 percent of pastors in this study who are married, a spouse is by far their most important source of support. This is true for their ministry, for their family life, and for their personal life. The only exception is for their spiritual life, where the spouse is a close third. For pastors who have a relatively healthy marriage the spouse may be one of few to whom pastors feel free to express their frustrations with the parish.

Oswald, who arguably has done more work than anyone else with pastors' support systems, feels that pastors tend to overuse their families. He has found that "burnout scores of the spouses are consistently higher than those of clergy themselves."

More than people in any other profession, we bring our problems home with us and unload them on our families. Possibly one reason for this is that we have so few places where we can go to talk candidly about what is happening to us within our parish. In addition to overburdening our families with all those problems, we show them a side of the church that no one else sees. Yet they are unable to do much about it, which is hardly fair to them. This burdening and impotence may account for the alienation of many clergy spouses from the church.[10]

Oswald concludes that ministers must find other places of support in order to reduce the pressure they place on their families. The rest of this chapter suggests other sources of support. Ministers will wish to select and develop those that are likely to meet their needs and that may be possible in their particular situations.

Our study did not explore the issue of how clergy couples deal with their needs for support. In view of the increasing numbers of husband-and-wife teams in the ordained ministry, several questions come to mind. When they work with the same congregation, do the pressures intensify and require release elsewhere, or do couples then provide increased support for one another? In view of the likelihood that most will always need to deal with the specter of competition and jealousy, it would seem that their need for outside support would be magnified. When the clergy couple serve different congregations, does this enhance the possibilities of mutual support or decrease them? A clergy couple support group, if available, would seem to be an ideal way to secure appropriate support for couples serving in either of these patterns.

A study of 150 American Baptist Convention ministers' wives concluded that their husbands spend about twenty-five waking hours a week at home regardless of the number of their children or the size of the congregation served.[11] In light of scheduling complexities in most ministers' families, the problem of finding quality time for pastors to spend with their spouses is a real one. Some pastors and their wives solve this problem by planning well in advance to set aside time to be together. When asked to do something at those times, pastors can simply say, "I already have an engagement then." One of the wives in the Baptist study said, "I get hold of his engagement book, compare it with mine, and plan a month in advance on the 'blank spaces.' Planning together helps to bring about those enjoyable times when we can be together as a family."[12]

Another way in which some pastors and their wives develop their own support system is to get together regularly with other pastors and wives for fun and conversation. They also plan activities that include their families. Governing bodies or groups of clergy can plan opportunities for wives to get together in supportive relationships. For additional ideas on support of clergy spouses, see "Resources for Further Study," especially Barbara Gilbert.

Single pastors who have never been married will need to be particularly creative in how they develop support for their personal lives. If they are fortunate enough to be near other single pastors with whom they can develop a close relationship, that may provide the outlet they need. Otherwise, friendships and support groups within and outside the congregation may be the answer.

The Congregation

Several kinds of support are available to pastors within a congregation. The first is that foundational level of general support which makes ministry possible. Without it failure is inevitable. Oswald makes clear that a "critical mass" of support within the congregation is essential if a pastor is to remain healthy and effective. For developing a basic level of congregational support, he refers to the "Clergy in Transition" seminars conducted by Alban Institute.

> Our rule of thumb is that for the first nine to twelve months in a new parish the primary role of the incoming pastor is to be a lover and a historian. This involves finding something to love in everyone in the parish and finding out how this parish has functioned in the past, especially with former clergy. Only after a year of building a support base, especially with the power people in the parish, can one move on to becoming a change agent.[13]

The pastor of a medium-sized congregation shares his secret for the support he and his family have experienced in a small town. It is openness to his parishioners and openness to receiving ministry from them.

> We moved here from a small town similar to this. We talked to the family about the fact that people would be concerned about us. We needed to interpret their expression of concern as love and not as meddling in our lives. We felt we were part of their family. We did not feel the need for privacy and had a lot of friendships. I grew up in the city, and Nancy in a suburb. Through our previous experience in a small town, we found it was a pleasant place to be. Openness was very real for us, not something we had to work at or develop.
>   Be grateful to people. Have the grace of gratitude. Appreciate what people do for you and allow them to do it for you. A minister and his wife were new in a country area. The farmers and folks around used to bring them a bag of apples. Promptly, the wife would bake an apple pie and send it back to the farmer. After a while the church had some problems. When they sat down to work them out, the people complained, "We can't do anything for them without their doing something in return." We all need to learn to say thank you and not try to get back.

A second level of congregational support is that which pastors receive as they teach classes, engage in pastoral care, and meet with various groups in their ongoing work of ministry. The most frequently mentioned source of support for pastors' spiritual life is a member or group of the congregation. In the other three categories shown in Figure 11.4 (ministry, family life, and personal life), a member or group within the congregation receives the second highest ratings. In previous chapters we have seen that Empowering Pastors are likely to be more skillful than Other Pastors in empathetic listening. They are eager to grow, open to change, and willing to take risks. As mature persons, they refuse to wear masks. Their high levels of self-esteem enable them to receive from others as well as to give. All these qualities, and more, result in a level of openness that attracts others and generates a supporting response in all they do.

A third level of congregational support is experienced by pastors who involve themselves in koinonia or Connecting Christian groups within the congregation. As they lead these groups or simply belong to them, they participate fully. Their willingness to share their own humanity helps others share their vulnerability. As they share their faith and their doubts, a strong bond of comradeship develops. In prayer with and for one another there is mutual support. The pastor of a small congregation tells of the support she receives from a group in her congregation.

> A group of about a dozen in the congregation meets as a support group for each other. Some are elders, some are not. I have drawn some boundaries in what I share. For example, I don't share any misunderstanding I have with another member of the congregation.
> A couple of years in this weekly covenant group have been truly productive for spiritual growth in knowing myself better and being challenged to think theologically about people's concerns.
> Only as I have allowed myself to be vulnerable would members come to me with their problems. In some ways I've functioned like a spiritual director with some members. I'm not certified but have taken a couple of workshops. I get a lot of fulfillment from the growth of members of the congregation.

A fourth level of congregational support is that which a pastor receives from individuals because the pastor is genuinely open to mutual ministry with members of the congregation. Several Empowering Pastors in our interviews were outspoken on the importance of receiving ministry from their members. The pastor of a small congregation tells of an unforgettable experience of ministry received.

> Pastors need to allow their congregations to care for them, pray for them, and minister to them. When I was a student I went back to visit three churches that my father had served as a pastor. We came roaring up from one of the other churches to this tiny church no bigger than a living room. As I stood in the vestibule and looked at the congregation, my escort said, "When you get up to preach, remember that the people of the church will be praying for you." I have never forgotten that.
> One of the negative influences that inhibits pastors from receiving ministry from within the congregation is the serious negative bias toward congregations given to students in some seminaries. New ministers come out of their education with a negative concept of the parish. Somehow congregations are portrayed as sick, stupid, blind, and ignorant of theology. So students come out being the answer people, rescuers, and messiahs. It is really difficult to let people minister to you if you have a negative view of congregations. Being a child of the manse, I have a very positive view of congregations. They have been my womb and my family. It is hard to trust yourself to people you deem unworthy.

Several pastors testify to the ways that their people have ministered to them in times of crisis and to ways they continue to support them.

A friend and elder in my church has helped me confront things in myself I did not see. Untold parishioners have explored with me in depth my soul and theirs. They have said words of grace and blessing that healed. They brought me through marital crisis, divorce, and new life. They rejected me. They accepted me despite everything. They have insisted that I "live" my gifts.

My present church lived grace for me during a divorce when they expected to minister to me and I allowed them to minister. This is my first ordained pastorate, and they gently and thoroughly taught me about ministry in love and grace.

This church is ministering to me as I minister to them. It may be a hug or a smile, or "How are you doing, Jim?" The personnel advisory committee supports me and I had a salary raise! I have been here five years and the people are getting concerned that I might be leaving. I get reinforcement and feel appreciated when I have been absent and people say, "We really missed you!"

A fifth level of support is experienced by those who have intimate friendships within the congregation. In my generation, most of us in seminary were taught that we should not have friends in the congregation. Such intimacy, they said, would destroy our effectiveness. Today, many Empowering Pastors are proving that advice to be too restrictive. It cuts the pastor off from meaningful support within the caring fellowship of the congregation. Three voices speak of the value of friendships within a congregation. The first is from a pastor who was taught not to have close friends in his congregation. He learned the hard way the inadequacy of that restriction.

When I resigned I had a failing marriage. There were thirty-one deacons present. They had no idea that I was having marital trouble, though I had been having therapy for two years. I felt like a hypocrite. That taught me the fallacy of keeping my distance from the congregation. Now I have close friends in the congregation. I hunt and fish with them and we do other social things together. They are among my closest friends. Now I know that one can get support informally within the congregation one serves.

In my first parish the senior minister warned me not to make friends in the congregation. I decided not to take that advice. I have always had friends in the congregation. In the Young Pastors' Seminars they spoke of the loneliness of ministers. I have never been lonely with friends in the church.

I believe it is wrong to think pastors should not be friends with congregation members. I mean good friends. How can you be effective with no relationship with the people?

We will explore the issue of friendships at greater depth after consideration of one other source of congregational support.

A sixth form of support within the congregation is of a very different kind than the other five. It is the pastor-parish committee, or personnel committee. When members of that committee are wisely chosen, pastors have a tremendous resource that can provide support in honest, objective, and caring evaluation of their work. For feedback from a personnel committee to be helpful, there is one important prerequisite. Pastors must be able to really listen and to take seriously what they hear. Within a relationship of mutual trust, confidentiality, and openness, pastors can identify areas for growth and secure resources for study or professional counseling that they need. Personnel committees can play an invaluable role in interpreting the pastor's priorities and use of time to governing boards and to the congregation as a whole. This builds support in the whole congregation.

Friends from Outside the Congregation

Half the pastors in our study say that friends outside the congregation are one of the four most helpful sources of support in their personal lives. A third or more find such friends as valuable sources of support for their spiritual and family life. Added to these "outside" friends are the friends who are members of the congregation. Clearly, friendships are an important source of support. Because most of a pastor's interpersonal relationships are through professional contacts, genuine friendships are all the more important.

In an essay called "Friends for the One at the Top," Donald McCullough assesses a pastor's need for and sources of friendship. Because of his insights, forged in the fires of a large congregation, I yield to the temptation to quote him extensively.

> Pastors need friends. There may be risks whenever pastors get close to people, but we were never called to a risk-free life! We were called to follow Jesus Christ. The model for our shepherding is the Great Shepherd himself. Without doubt, he had friends: Peter, James, and John in particular.
>
> Sometimes we find ourselves caught between two problems: insecurity and arrogance. We are in positions where being liked by others bears significantly on our success, and thus we inevitably worry about our approval rating. . . .
>
> Without friends a low self-esteem gets beaten down even lower. *If I have no friends,* I begin to think, *I must be unfriendly. If no one loves me, I must be unlovable.* Loneliness and insecurity interact in a downward spiral of emotional death.
>
> Furthermore, without friends we don't have the necessary counterweight to arrogance. When you're not too sure about yourself anyway, it's tempting to grasp eagerly at every affirmation that comes your way. Before long you start believing it all; you really must be extraordinary if this many people think you're hot stuff.[14]

Friends within the Congregation

McCullough is realistic about the problem that ministers face in finding time for everything they must do. This makes them neglect their personal lives. He stresses the necessity of friendship by pointing out that he deliberately schedules time for them to develop. He cultivates friendships at weekly breakfasts and lunches, in denominational meetings, and during study leaves. He believes it is

important to have friendships within the congregation, illustrating the new attitude toward such friendships to which I have already referred. Pastors who shun
friendships within the congregation are likely to be lonely because they have little opportunity to make friends elsewhere. Friendships within the congregation
are possible and are important provided a pastor takes certain precautions,
McCullough says.

> First, I don't hurry. There is no real friendship without trust. Before sailing out
> into the relational depths, I poke and probe the other's character: Will he keep
> a secret? Will she graciously sift through the chaff of my depressed days? Will
> he know what's appropriate when he tells stories about me? Will she provide
> wise counsel?
>
> Second, I don't flaunt it. You shouldn't have to hide your friendships, but
> neither should your congregation have to deal needlessly with feelings of jeal-
> ousy. So I steer clear of close friends in congregational settings; I am everyone's
> pastor and official "friend" on those occasions. Though I have breakfast every
> week with Ken Regan, on Sunday mornings I rarely even wave to him.[15]

McCullough faces squarely the costs of deep friendships. They require self-
giving and self-sacrifice. One must be willing to reveal oneself. "Self-disclosure
takes time and requires patience. It always seeks the balance between revelation
and concealment. Jesus didn't tell the disciples everything on their first day together." Encouraging friends to maximize their gifts can lead to a lower recognition for oneself. One must be willing to endure and forgive the shortcomings
of a friend. And one must be willing to give significant time to a friend. "Finding
the time required to maintain a friendship isn't easy. But when a friend calls, you
make time for a conversation. . . . Sometimes friendship will demand a significant sacrifice of time, far more than an hour telephone conversation."[16]

Colleagues and Colleague Groups

Theoretically, one of the best sources of support should be one's ministerial
colleagues. They are much more likely to understand what you are up against in
your life and work than anyone else. Presumably they are skilled in helping others. However, many pastors question the possibility of receiving helpful support
from fellow ministers, especially if they are of the same denomination. Pastors
are notorious for being "lone rangers." When they get together they tend to be
competitive, if only in subtle ways. And one never knows when a fellow pastor
will be in a position to influence one's career possibilities. So the thinking is that
it is best to play it safe. One can talk modestly of one's achievements, but it is best
to reveal as little as possible of one's problems. The experience of one pastor illustrates a common feeling.

> The most stressful time in my ministry was when I was most successful de-
> nominationally. I was pastor of a large and successful church for eight years.
> The last two years of my ministry I was pretty sick. My marriage was breaking
> up. One of the contributing problems was that I had no one to talk with about

it. I made a feeble attempt to gather a peer group that gathered for breakfast on Monday morning. But it never went very deep. We only talked about how Sunday had gone.

I don't believe a denominational support group will work. There is too much competition. Most successful groups cross denominational lines.

Nonetheless there are those who have found colleagues in the same denomination or ecumenically who individually have been supportive or who have joined with them in effective support groups. As one pastor put it,

I have always had a support group of clergy where I was. In my first solo pastorate a group of ministers from the presbytery met for one and a half hours each week, year-round, winter and summer, for coffee, with no agenda. The group included a university professor and other ministers who were intellectually stimulating, so the agenda emerged out of the group as they talked informally. This also served as a support group. We had a strong trust relationship so we could bare our souls to each other. If it came up, we might focus on how to be better pastors. There was no one in the group who dominated the discussion.

In my present situation there is an ecumenical clergy group that meets three times a year for two days to study lectionary texts for preaching and teaching. Sometimes people would bring lectures or sermons on tapes and we would listen. We discovered that we needed to allow time when we were not working on the task to share "what's happening to me" and support one another.

The group has continued since 1980 with four of us from the original group. There never have been more than seven, and the ideal is not to have more than six. We are very careful how we select ministers to invite to the group. Some moved. The Methodist minister who did not move far away (through two successive parishes) is still a part of the group. We have contacts with one another between these meetings. One of the original members is my best friend. We play golf together.

Others agree with his experience. One pastor said, "I have friends in the presbytery who are supportive, both men and women. The issue of competition is not a problem for me because I am happy where I am." Another reported, "The ongoing encouragement and support of colleagues has been effective in helping me analyze and understand what the church does and needs. It taught me a lot about current issues, challenged me to take risks and grow."

Roy Oswald describes an extended experiment in Carlisle Presbytery that resulted in four new support groups that continued for an extended time.[17] He believes a similar approach in other middle judicatory governing bodies could be fruitful in meeting the great need for more clergy support systems. The process began with a two-day retreat to which all ministers of the presbytery were invited. About half attended. Oswald, as retreat facilitator, administered three inventories that measured life changes, strain response, and burnout.[18] Oswald made presentations on clergy self-care, on the value of support communities, and on the obstacles to effective clergy support groups. The following advantages of peer support groups were explained:

1. Only pastors can really understand the complexities of the pastoral role. So only they can provide professional support to other pastors.
2. A peer group is in the best position to respond to the complexities of role conflict, role ambiguity, and role overload in the ministry.
3. In addition to support from within the congregation, clergy need outside support that brings objectivity to evaluation of their ministry. Other pastors can provide that objectivity.
4. A peer support group can be especially helpful in dealing with morale problems.

Participants in the retreat were then asked "to mill around and congregate with persons with whom they might like to explore the possibility of an ongoing support group." Six groups began forming and they were encouraged to invite others who were not at the retreat to join them. Some groups began meeting soon after the October retreat. Others got under way by the first of the year. Group facilitators had been selected in advance to be offered to the groups that formed. They were selected for their competence in facilitating group process, for their sensitivity "to the unique complexities of pastoral ministry," and for their safety. "They should not be in a position to influence the career of the clergy involved." Three of the four groups accepted clearly designated leaders who possessed these qualities.

Oswald says, "Most clergy support groups don't work. They fail to form enough trust so that pain and vulnerability can be revealed. The key ingredient missing is leadership." He advocates paying for that leadership, although the Carlisle groups did not do so.

This is not the place to go into the Grubb Theory of Oscillation between extradependence and intradependence, which Oswald uses to explain the way support groups need to work. Anyone who wishes to consider developing a support group would be well advised to study his book.[19]

Oswald gives specific help in how a pastor can initiate a support group. He suggests the following steps:

1. Think about one other clergy person in your area with whom you would be willing to trust your pain and vulnerability. Take time to choose this person carefully.
2. Invite that person to lunch. Share your need for a support group and your vision of what it could do for you.
3. Find out if this person also feels the need for a support group and together decide whether the group should deal only with professional issues or with both personal and professional issues.
4. If you agree on having a group to meet specific goals, together think of three or four others "with whom you could be open about pain, vulnerability, and confusion." Select these people carefully. Limit your group to not more than six.

5. Decide on possible group facilitators whose ability you trust to guide you through the roadblocks you are likely to encounter in becoming a trusting community.
6. Sketch out a possible covenant for the group, dealing with how often you would meet, for how long, whether attendance would be optional, length of the covenant period, basic format of the meetings, and so forth.
7. Plan the first meeting and invite the other potential participants.

Models and Mentors

A study of ministry and stress found that greatest times of stress in a pastor's career come in the first, second, and third years of ministry. One-fourth come in the first or second year. Forty-two percent occur in the first five years of ministry.[20]

In this early period of ministry a new pastor is making the adjustment from being a student to serving a parish. This is the time when competent, experienced pastors, who serve as models and mentors, can make a permanent impact on the quality of a young pastor's ministry. Fifty-eight percent of Empowering Pastors compared with 48 percent of Other Pastors say that a positive role model early in their ministry has been very important or important to the development of their effectiveness in the ministry.[21] One-third of Empowering Pastors say that a mentor in the first three years of their ministry was very important or important for their effectiveness.

Perhaps the most frequent experience of mentoring occurs when a new pastor serves as an associate pastor or minister of youth in a large congregation. In fact our data suggest that this is how many pastors of large congregations have prepared themselves to serve as senior pastors. Forty percent of large-church pastors began their ministries serving in large congregations. One can assume that many of the heads of staff under whom these pastors once served were not only gifted in pastoral ministry but also were good mentors. Of course some may have learned what to avoid by serving with negative role models. But only 18 percent of pastors in our study think a negative role model was important in their formation. Empowering Pastors who had helpful experiences with role models or mentors had this to say:

> Before going to seminary I worked as a director of Christian education. The head of staff there was a real formative influence with me. I admired his scholarship and theological integrity. Where we disagreed, we had a good dialogue. He had a "hands off" leadership style. He set clear parameters, then the staff was on its own. He gave me freedom to try my own things. He was there to give guidance.

> The senior pastor with whom I served for five years out of seminary was a very positive role model, especially in relation to his sensitivity, skill in conflict management, and use of his time.

> I began as assistant minister to youth and families. The senior pastor was a strong preacher and administrator who encouraged me and granted freedom to be the pastor to the five hundred youth in our congregation.

Early in my ministry an older neighboring pastor was a model of pastoral care, effective preaching, and bold leadership.

This last comment reminds us that models and mentors can also be pastors of neighboring congregations with whom a pastor is able to establish an intimate, ongoing mentoring relationship.

Pastors must choose their own mentors if the relationship is to be a meaningful source of support. In my judgment every young pastor should seek a role model or mentor. But having a mentor is an option at any time in one's career. Indeed that is the advice of one pastor of a large congregation to all pastors who wish to increase their effectiveness. He suggests a simple, straightforward approach: "Find someone whose ministry you respect, a 'role model.' Ask for a meeting each month with that person to discuss your ministry."

Spiritual Directors

In chapter 6 we looked at the significant potential of spiritual direction for a pastor's spiritual growth. Those who wish to begin this pilgrimage in their own lives may well find a spiritual director nearby. Many Roman Catholic-trained spiritual directors are available across the nation, and a growing number of Protestant pastors are prepared or are preparing to serve as spiritual directors.

Those who wish to prepare themselves to serve as spiritual directors as part of their ministry might consider programs such as those offered by the Shalem Institute for Spiritual Formation in Washington, D.C.,[22] or San Francisco Theological Seminary.[23]

Judicatory Support

Out of nine different sources of support mentioned in our questionnaire, judicatory support by an executive or committee ranks seventh. This is not surprising since most supporting relationships require a level of trust that enables us to openly share our deepest problems. If ministerial colleagues are threatening because they have the potential of impacting a pastor's future, executives and committees of presbytery can be doubly threatening. They decide much that affects a pastor's present and future. However, I know of executives whose personalities and pastoral skills enable them to be supportive in ordinary circumstances. But the administrative power they exercise makes this a rare exception rather than the rule.

In spite of these limitations, there are times and circumstances when the intervention of a committee on ministry or a judicatory executive can be supportive indeed. Those times are usually when situations within a congregation are in danger of getting out of control or have already become unmanageable. It is then that a wise and caring executive can make the difference between a pastor's being broken by the situation or surviving. Middle governing bodies can provide ecclesiastical and financial resources that no one else is able to provide. It is then that a skilled committee on ministry can itself help to manage conflict and rescue a bad situation, or can make available expert consultants who can make a positive difference.

It is also judicatories that plan many retreats and continuing education events that bring pastors together for spiritual and intellectual growth and for developing personal relationships with other pastors that provide later opportunities for support. The Carlisle Presbytery experiment described by Oswald is a prime example.

I have already noted that pastors of the same denomination have great difficulty in providing support to one another. But within almost any judicatory one will find pastors whose chemistry makes possible a close and trusting relationship. And judicatory events, which give pastors an opportunity to know each other in greater depth, are likely to increase the number of those natural affiliations.

Pastoral and Marital Counselors or Therapists

One-fourth of the pastors in our study listed pastoral or marital counselors or therapists among their top three sources of support. Since we allowed pastors only three choices, this is not an insignificant response.

We have seen that a high proportion of those whom we interviewed referred to counseling and therapy as having transformed their ministries. Perhaps their testimony may encourage other pastors to seek the counseling help they need without feeling that this is a negative reflection on their ability to serve as a pastor.

A 1971 study of stress and ministry found that 7 percent of pastors experiencing stress sought medical help and 6 percent sought help from mental health practitioners.[24] In our study, 27 percent of pastors say that a pastoral counselor, marital counselor, or therapist has been helpful for support of their family life. Twenty-six percent identified the same source as helpful for support in their personal lives. The total of 13 percent in the earlier study contrasts sharply with our findings. That earlier study also found that 24 percent of pastors dealt with stress by changing jobs. Again, this contrasts with our finding that 18 percent of pastors under stress left their positions. There is no way to tell whether either of these differences is statistically significant, but it would appear that our group of pastors felt more freedom to seek counseling and therapy than did pastors nearly twenty-five years ago. Possibly this reflects a slight change in the popular acceptance of counseling and therapy during that period. It is also possible that a tighter job market may have reduced the percentage of pastors who left their positions in response to stress. Either of these differences could affect the other. On the one hand, some pastors may have felt forced to seek therapy because they were unable to move. On the other hand, pastors who received counseling may have been able to deal with their stress and remain in their posts. Whatever reasons there may be for these differences, it is encouraging to see that pastors seem to be increasingly willing to face their problems and seek the professional help that will make them more effective in their ministries.

As we close this chapter we look back at all the examples of clergy support with the deep conviction that pastors themselves must be responsible for making certain that they receive all the support they need to be effective in ministry. Pastors must discover and appropriate sources of support that are available, or they must generate support when it is not available. It is the pastor's openness and eagerness to grow that makes the difference.

12

THE DISCIPLINED PATH TO GROWING POWER

This one thing I do: forgetting what lies behind and straining forward to what lies ahead, I press on toward the goal for the prize of the heavenly call of God in Christ Jesus.

—Philippians 3:13–14

Strip down, start running—and never quit! No extra spiritual fat, no parasitic sins. Keep your eyes on Jesus, who both began and finished this race we're in.

—Hebrews 12:1–2, TM

So, you want to grow in your effectiveness as a pastor. You have caught a vision of what it might mean for you to be more like the Empowering Pastors you have been reading about. You have seen in your ministry ways in which you already are much like the Empowering Pastors described in this book. You are already doing many of the things that they do. But you want to grow beyond where you are today. How do you get on with it?

Olympic athletes arrive at the big games because they have disciplined themselves over many years in a tough training program. They keep their eye on the prize and stretch every fiber of their being to get to their goal. This chapter invites you to take a disciplined path to growing power in your ministry. You will begin by taking a fresh look at yourself. You will look at the strengths that you already bring to pastoral ministry. Then you will explore areas in which you may want to grow. You will set your own growth goals and decide what it will take to reach them. You will determine what you want to do about it. Finally you will get started and develop ways to keep going. This is a personal path that leads you step by step through possible courses of action.

This race is yours to run. No one can run it for you. So be proactive, not reactive. This might best be called a "discipled" path, because your will to grow must always be guided by the Spirit, who is to "teach us all things." So take hold of your possibilities and move forward, empowered by the author and perfecter of our faith.

Take a few days of retreat time to begin your pilgrimage to power. Spend time in reflection and prayer as you examine your life and your calling to the pastorate. You will find here a series of exercises in which you can engage during that retreat, or you can spread them out over an extended period by completing one task at a time.

You alone are responsible for your journey. But the appraisal of your strengths and limitations will be greatly enhanced if you engage trusted others in confirming or modifying your judgments and giving you support along the way. If you have a supportive pastor-parish committee or personnel committee, you may want to involve them in your pilgrimage at key points. A ministerial colleague may help. Or there may be one or more intimate friends in the congregation who will be honest with you and maintain confidentiality.

I suggest that you keep a loose-leaf "growth notebook." Make a photocopy of this chapter and keep it there to use while doing the proposed exercises. When you want someone else to answer the same questions in an exercise, make an additional copy of that exercise for that person to use. Each step suggests questions you may wish to answer. It may be helpful to write your answer to questions that seem most important to you. Add material you write and relevant quotations from other sources to the notebook. There will be times along the way when you will want to refer to work you have completed.

There are four big tasks before you: (1) clarify your vision of ministry, (2) take a new look at yourself, (3) develop your growth plan, and (4) get going and keep growing. These tasks will take time, so decide if you are willing to spend it. For each task there are steps to take, questions to answer, and conclusions to draw. Many of the questions you will be answering are those that pastors in our study answered. A number of them expressed appreciation for the challenge of thinking through their ministries in fresh ways.

TASK ONE
CLARIFY YOUR VISION OF MINISTRY

Your first task is to clarify your vision of ministry. This is a task in personal theology. What is your understanding of your ministry? What does your calling mean to you? What is your understanding of faithful and effective ministry?

STEP 1
Confirm Your Call to the Ordained Ministry

God's call to ministry sustains us on our journey. It keeps us on the path to faithful and productive service. So spend some time meditating on that call.

REFLECT on whether your sense of call has been growing, weakening, or staying the same. To get started, answer the questions in Exercise 12.A. If it has changed, what has happened in your life and ministry that has influenced that change? Does that sense of call sustain you in your ministry? If you feel it needs to be strengthened, what can you do about that? How well do your gifts match the needs of your present congregation?

RECORD the ways you might want to strengthen your sense of call.

Exercise 12.A

Answer the following questions, using the code:
  1 = weak; 2 = fairly week; 3 = fairly strong; 4 = strong; 5 = very strong.

How strong was/is your sense of call to the ministry

When you decided to enter the ministry?	1	2	3	4	5
When you received your M.Div./B.D.?	1	2	3	4	5
Five years ago?	1	2	3	4	5
Today?	1	2	3	4	5
How strong is your sense of call to your present parish?	1	2	3	4	5

STEP 2
Revisit Your Theology of Ministry

Write a brief statement of your theology or philosophy of ministry. In one or two paragraphs summarize your rationale for who you are as a pastor and what you do.

REFLECT on how your view of ministry has impacted the way you carry out your ministry. How does it relate to

the concept of empowering (as described in chap. 1)?
the goal of giving meaning for living (chap. 2)?
the concept of servant ministry (chap. 3)?

RECORD any actions you might take to sharpen or change your concept of ministry.

STEP 3
Clarify Your Picture of an Effective Pastor

Our image of faithful and effective ministry guides the day-to-day actions we take. We may not be conscious of what it is. It shapes us subtly because we seldom reflect on it. Be intentional in planning your path toward increased competence. Clarify your own picture of effectiveness.

To get started look at the "Preliminary Definition of an Effective Pastor," Figure 12.1. As you read it,

Place a plus mark (+) in the margin opposite each statement with which you agree.
Place a minus mark (−) in the margin opposite each statement with which you disagree.
Place a question mark (?) in the margin opposite each statement about which you have some question.

REFLECT on your marks. Compare the descriptions marked with a plus with descriptions marked with a minus. As you do this, *remember that no pastor could*

Fig. 12.1. Preliminary Definition of an Effective Pastor

1. Helps people find meaning for living through worship, preaching, teaching, and informal contacts. Relates biblical and theological truth to issues people face in their personal lives and in society. Expresses thoughts understandably to a broad range of individuals and groups. Generates enthusiasm for the gospel. Promotes varied educational opportunities in the congregation.

2. Serves the diverse needs of parishioners, in partnership with other leaders of the congregation. Helps people develop their spiritual lives by communicating God's grace, forgiveness, and power. Empowers them for their ministries by helping them discover, develop, and channel their varied gifts into opportunities for service that match those gifts. Makes creative use of diversity and avoids unhealthy conflicts.

3. Leads in achieving the congregation's particular mission within the context of the larger church and of a global mission consciousness. Assesses the congregation's character and context, and relates the demands of the gospel to its unique situation. Trusts church officers and staff, actively sharing power and accountability with them. Together they articulate and inspire commitment to a growing vision of what the congregation should be and do. Together they develop strategies for achieving that vision. Together they secure needed resources, organize the work, delegate responsibility, give guidance, and insure administrative follow-up.

4. Inspires the congregation to grow into a caring community by spontaneously modeling acts of caring love. Makes counseling skills readily available to parishioners under stress. Helps people increase their ability to care for one another, and stimulates the creation of caring opportunities for members. Challenges them to reach out beyond the congregation in service to others, in sharing the good news, and in shaping society.

5. Lives with consistency, integrity, and spiritual authenticity. Is centered and secure, with a level of self-esteem that makes it possible to trust self, others, and the environment. Empowers others by focusing on building up their self-esteem. Knows and acknowledges own strengths and limitations. Uses these to shape her or his ministry. Is eager to grow, open to change, positive in approach, and willing to take risks. Listens skillfully, empathizes appropriately, and collaborates with others.

6. Lives with a deep personal-faith commitment that relies on God's grace. Is confident of God's calling to the ministry of the Word and Sacrament. Through personal study, significant involvement in continuing education, and an active devotional life is growing in ministerial competence and in the gifts of the Spirit.

possibly meet all these ideals. Taken together, what kind of picture of effectiveness do you have? Why do you disagree with certain statements? Is it on some biblical, theological, or philosophical grounds? Is it because your own gifts do not make that kind of ministry possible? Do your answers give you any clues as to areas in which you have particular strengths for effective ministry? To areas in which you would like to grow?

RECORD any observations that might help you plan areas of ministry in which you may want to develop your effectiveness. Mark the two most important areas in which you would like to grow.

TASK TWO
TAKE A NEW LOOK AT YOURSELF

You have already dipped your toe into the water of self-examination. Remember, to be effective as pastors we need to understand ourselves. What kind of persons are we? What are our strengths and limitations? What attitudes and beliefs do we bring with us into ministry? What skills do we have? Which of these do we need to improve and capitalize on? What new skills do we need to acquire in order to be more effective?

No one has all the gifts that lead to effective ministry. When we know ourselves, we can plan ways to use and develop our strengths and develop our potential in areas where our limitations are holding us back. And we can plan and negotiate our particular ministry situations so that they maximize our strengths and minimize our weaknesses. We can organize our ministries so that the strengths others bring to the congregation can blossom in areas of our limitations. So take another look at yourself.

STEP 1
Reflect on Your Formative Experiences

We are all products of our heritage and of our past experiences. Others have made indelible impacts on our lives. The choices we have made along the way in response to those impacts have shaped who we are. Use Exercise 12.B to help you remember those who have made a special contribution to your personal, spiritual, and professional development.

REFLECT on how others have helped to shape who you are and how you carry on your ministry. How have you shaped your own development by ways you have responded to your life experiences? How can you make more effective use of your positive heritage as you carry on ministry today?

RECORD ways you might make more effective use of your heritage in your ministry.

STEP 2
Identify Your Core Essences, Values, and Beliefs

Remember that all of us have personalities and style preferences that are part of our uniqueness. Now is the time to reflect on who you are. To get started do Exercise 12.C.

Exercise 12.B

How important have each of the following been to the development of your effectiveness as a pastor? Use the following code:
1 = not important; 2 = not very important; 3 = somewhat important;
4 = important; 5 = very important.

Growing up in a happy home	1	2	3	4	5
Faith discussions with a Christian parent	1	2	3	4	5
Church experience as a child or young person	1	2	3	4	5
Early faith relationship with a Christian layperson	1	2	3	4	5
A pastor role model during childhood or youth	1	2	3	4	5
A high school youth group or college fellowship	1	2	3	4	5
Summer conferences or work camps as a youth	1	2	3	4	5
A conversion experience at age _____	1	2	3	4	5
Seminary courses, professors, and field work	1	2	3	4	5
Other graduate work	1	2	3	4	5
Continuing education	1	2	3	4	5
A role model or mentor early in your ministry	1	2	3	4	5

Exercise 12.C

To what extent do the following statements accurately describe you? Answer, using the following code:
1 = not at all; 2 = to a very limited extent; 3 = to some extent;
4 = to a great extent; 5 = to a very great extent.

I am basically a trusting person, trusting self and others.	1	2	3	4	5
I am centered and secure and willing to be vulnerable.	1	2	3	4	5
My sense of personal security enables me to receive from others.	1	2	3	4	5
I naturally tend to empower others.	1	2	3	4	5
I am eager to grow and open to change.	1	2	3	4	5
I value interdependence more than independence.	1	2	3	4	5
I see change as an opportunity rather than a threat.	1	2	3	4	5
It is important for me to share power and profession with others.	1	2	3	4	5
I am basically a risk taker and encourage others to take risks.	1	2	3	4	5
I am almost always optimistic about the potential of people.	1	2	3	4	5

REFLECT on the answers you recorded for Exercise 12.C. What does the "unique you" bring to ministry?

RECORD in one or two paragraphs a description of your core essences, values, and beliefs. Then describe how you might best use those unique gifts in ministry.

STEP 3
Reflect on Your Myers-Briggs Type Preferences

Many pastors have taken the Myers Briggs Type Inventory (MBTI) and have found it helpful in understanding themselves and others. If you are one of those who knows the meaning of your Myers-Briggs type, take time to reflect on the way your type preference affects your style of ministry, your family relationships, and your needs for recreation and renewal. You might do this by reading *Please Understand Me*, by David Keirsey and Marilyn Bates.[1] Especially reflect on the section that describes your particular temperament. A source that is especially helpful for pastors is *Personality Type and Religious Leadership*, by Roy Oswald and Otto Kroeger.[2]

If you are not acquainted with the MBTI, find a trained administrator who will give it to you and interpret it for you. Your judicatory probably can direct you to someone who is qualified to do this. If you can't find such a person, use the "Keirsey Temperament Sorter" in *Please Understand Me* to give you a rough idea of your type.

The purpose of the MBTI is not to pigeonhole people, but to help them understand themselves and develop their undeveloped preferences. For that reason it can be particularly helpful in setting growth objectives. It is also very useful in developing good working relationships between pastor, staff, and church officers. When colleagues know one another's Myers-Briggs types, they can learn to use their complementary strengths to build a more effective team.

The MBTI is based on Jungian psychology. It holds that each of us has certain natural preferences for ways in which to understand and respond to the world around us. Isabel Briggs Myers developed a relatively simple series of questions that reveal the respondent's type preferences. Extensive research has proven its reliability and validity. In fact, most of those who have taken the instrument are amazed at how well it describes them. One of its big advantages is that it emphasizes positive attributes, is nonthreatening, and is affirming of the person who takes it.

The MBTI has four pairs of preferences for opposites. Extraversion (designated by the letter E) is contrasted with Introversion (I), though these terms are not used in the popular sense. Sensing (S) is the opposite of iNtuition (N). Thinking (T) contrasts with Feeling (F), and Judging (J) with Perceiving (P). In combination with one another these eight polarities constitute sixteen distinct preference types, each of which has been shown to react quite differently to life. Oswald and Kroeger describe these eight polarities:

Extraverts relate more to the outer world of things, people, and environment. They ask the question, How do I relate to what is going on out there? Their primary source of interest and energy comes from the outer world. Extraverts feel a loss of energy if they engage in too much introspection.

Introverts prefer to relate more to the inner world of ideas, concepts, and feelings. They ask the question, How does what is going on out there relate to me? Energy expended relating to the outer world returns when Introverts are alone and can look inside themselves.

Those with a preference for Sensing allow the world to touch them deeply through their five senses. They want to be grounded in the practical, concrete aspects of life.

Those with a preference for iNtuition want to perceive meanings, possibilities, and relationships in reality. They tend to be future oriented and prefer to rely on their imagination.

Those with a preference for Thinking are more comfortable with logical decisions. If possible they prefer to stand outside a situation and analyze its cause and effect.

The preference for Feeling is marked by comfort with value-centered decisions. Those who prefer Feeling over Thinking prefer to stand inside situations to decide what they like and dislike.

The Judging preference identifies persons who want their lives ordered, structured, and planned. They like to plan their lives and live their plan.

Those with a preference for Perceiving want to respond to life rather than plan it. At all times they work to keep their options open so that they are free to respond to situations in a variety of ways.

As you can see, the opposite ends of the four continua above represent very different ways of looking at life. Though we have a capacity to operate on both sides of the line, we prefer one way over the other, just as we prefer writing with one hand over the other. These basic, inbred preferences can sometimes bring us into conflict—with ourselves and with others. So when we say, I just don't understand that person. He must not be my type, we may be hitting the nail right on the head.[3]

It is difficult for those who are not well acquainted with the MBTI, to keep sixteen types in mind as they try to understand others with whom they live and work. Fortunately, the research of David Keirsey and Marilyn Bates has discovered that four *temperaments* can summarize some of the most important dimensions of type preference. Two temperaments are related to those who prefer iNtuition (N). The other two relate to those who prefer Sensing (S).

This is not the place to describe in detail the sixteen types or the four temperaments. Oswald and Kroeger in *Personality Type and Religious Leadership* have done a thorough job of showing how they affect a pastor's style of ministry. They describe the pastoral strengths and potential difficulties of ministers with each of the four different temperaments. One who prefers Sensing and Perceiving (SP) they call an "Action-Oriented Pastor." There are very few SP pastors. One who prefers Sensing and Judging (SJ) is a "Conserving, Serving Pastor." An "Intellectual, Competence-Seeking Pastor" is one who prefers Intuition and Thinking (NT), and an "Authenticity-Seeking, Relationship-Oriented Pastor" is one who prefers Intuition and Feeling (NF). Oswald and Kroeger deal with the effect of personality type on religious leadership, pastoral role and function, prayer, and spirituality, and warn of pitfalls for pastors with various type preferences.

In our study, we found no statistically significant difference between Empowering Pastors and Other Pastors in the Myers-Briggs types or the Keirsey/Bates temperaments. We did find differences on some of the questions we used in our study. Most of these were what one might expect from a knowledge of Keirsey temperaments. For example, SJ pastors are more likely than those with other temperaments to rate themselves as very effective or effective in calling on the sick and shut-ins, and in taking time for family. But they are less likely to take time for recreation. They are more likely to rate themselves as very skillful or skillful in organizing. NF pastors are more likely to rate high in empathizing, and in taking time for prayer and meditation. NT pastors rate themselves high in strategizing. They also rate highest in visioning, followed closely by NFs.

NF pastors are more likely than those with other temperaments to favor an activist approach to social issues, to favor an educational approach to individual salvation, and to want their congregations to have a high tolerance for theological diversity. SJ pastors are more likely than those with other temperaments to favor an educational approach to social issues, and least likely to favor an educational approach to individual salvation or a high tolerance for theological diversity. Women pastors in our study were more likely than men to be introverts and to be NFs.

These examples are given in the hope that they will encourage readers to go more deeply into their understanding of the Myers-Briggs Type Indicator as a tool for understanding themselves and others. Assuming that you know your Myers-Briggs type and understand the characteristics of your particular temperament, turn again to reflection.

REFLECT on how your style of ministry is influenced by your temperament preferences. What strengths does your temperament bring to ministry? What pitfalls common to your temperament do you need to guard against? How might you do this? To what extent have you developed your least-favored preferences so as to achieve a healthy balance in your ministry? For suggestions, study Oswald and Kroeger, *Personality Type and Religious Leadership*.

RECORD ways in which you might want to develop your less-favored style preferences in order to achieve a healthy balance in your ministry.

STEP 4
Assess Your Level of Self-esteem

In chapter 5 we saw how essential it is to have a relatively high level of self-esteem. To stimulate your thinking about your level of self-esteem use Exercise 12.D.

REFLECT on what the basic sources are of your self-esteem. What sustains or renews your self-esteem? What might you do to increase the level of your self-esteem or to recover it when you are threatened? Review chapter 10 for suggestions.

RECORD any ways you might want to maintain a higher level of self-esteem.

Exercise 12.D

To what extent do the following statements describe your feelings about yourself and your ministry? Use this code:
1 = not at all; 2 = to a very limited extent; 3 = to some extent;
4 = to a great extent; 5 = to a very great extent.

I feel very good about myself and my ministry.	1	2	3	4	5
Leaders of the congregation where I serve are very responsive to my ideas.	1	2	3	4	5
I feel I am accomplishing more in my ministry than I did five or ten years ago.	1	2	3	4	5
My gifts and style of ministry meet the needs and expectations of my present congregation.	1	2	3	4	5
I have a high level of self-esteem.	1	2	3	4	5

STEP 5
Evaluate Your Sources of Stress and Your Ways of Responding to Crises

Take a brief stress inventory by completing Exercises 12.E, 12.F, and 12.G. REFLECT on which sources of stress in your life occur most frequently. How severe is the stress that they create? What might you do to relieve that stress?

Exercise 12.E

How often do the following situations create stress in your life? Answer using the following code:
1 = not at all; 2 = rarely; 3 = occasionally; 4 = often; 5 = very often.

Too many demands on my time	1	2	3	4	5
Feeling of powerlessness in my work	1	2	3	4	5
Conflicting or ambiguous expectations for my work	1	2	3	4	5
Inadequate compensation or finances	1	2	3	4	5
Personal or family situations	1	2	3	4	5

Exercise 12.F

When you face a crisis, what is your typical response?

( ) I find my energy increases and I become more effective.
( ) I keep calm and deal with it as best I can.
( ) I find it difficult to act as quickly or as skillfully as I would like.

Exercise 12.G

Have you ever suffered burnout? If so, how did you deal with it?
Check those that apply.

( ) Revised priorities (rest, exercise, recreation, family/friends, outside activities)

( ) Spiritual renewal (prayer, retreats, spiritual director, Bible reading, fasting)

( ) Time away (time off, time out of town, vacation, sabbatical, extended leave)

( ) Counseling, psychotherapy, career counseling

( ) Left position (retired, took another parish, interim work, nonpastoral position)

( ) Found support (colleagues, family, friends, congregation, support group)

( ) Study activities (continuing education, study leave, academic program, reading)

( ) Kept keeping on (time passed, did not deal with it, still suffering)

( ) Worked with personnel committee and/or judicatory staff

( ) Other

How might you improve your ability to deal with stress or crises? Chapter 10 offers suggestions.

For those who have recovered from a period of burnout: In the light of your experience, what would you do differently if you burn out again? How do you manage your life and ministry now, to minimize the possibility of burning out again? See chapter 10 for suggestions.

RECORD any steps you might want to take to reduce the levels of stress in your life and ministry and avoid burnout.

STEP 6
Decide about Counseling or Therapy

REFLECT on whether some form of counseling or psychotherapy would be helpful to you right now. Use Exercise 12.H to help you consider this option. If you are unsure of your needs, you may wish to consult with someone whose judgment and discretion you trust.

RECORD any conclusions you reach on the potential value of counseling at this stage of your life and ministry.

STEP 7
Assess Your Style of Ministry and Your Effectiveness

Use Exercise 12.I to guide you in assessing your style of ministry. You may find it helpful to have your personnel committee or pastor-parish committee join you in this assessment by asking them to answer the same questions.

Exercise 12.H

Which of the following forms of counseling, therapy, or support (if any) might be most helpful to you right now?

Career counseling: To clarify at a career center the next steps in my career as a minister. (Are my gifts best suited to what I am presently doing or would they be better suited to some other form of ministry or some other occupation?)

Pastoral counseling: To work on some personal or spiritual issues that are important to me right now.

Spiritual director: To reflect with me on my spiritual life and help me grow there.

Family counseling: To work on problems with my marriage or with my children.

Psychotherapy: To work on deep-seated personal issues such as dealing with past trauma or developing a healthier level of self-esteem.

Organizational consulting: To work with church officers on problems in the life of our congregation.

Exercise 12.I

To what extent do each of the following statements accurately describe how you carry out your ministry? Answer using the following code:
1 = not at all; 2 = to a very limited extent; 3 = to some extent;
4 = to a great extent; 5 = to a very great extent.

Makes creative use of diversity	1	2	3	4	5
Lives with consistency, integrity, and spiritual authenticity	1	2	3	4	5
Relates the gospel to issues people face in their personal lives and in society	1	2	3	4	5
Helps people find meaning for living through worship, preaching, teaching, and so forth	1	2	3	4	5
Inspires members to reach out beyond the congregation in sharing the good news	1	2	3	4	5
Inspires members to reach out beyond the congregation in service to others	1	2	3	4	5
Helps people discover, develop, and channel their gifts into appropriate service	1	2	3	4	5
Inspires the congregation to grow into a caring community	1	2	3	4	5
Actively shares power with church officers and staff	1	2	3	4	5

REFLECT on the various styles of ministry. Which of these styles do you feel are most important? Which, if any, are relatively unimportant? Which style in your ministry would you most like to adopt and emphasize? How might you do that?

RECORD any of these styles you would like to develop further. Describe how you might develop them.

STEP 8
Evaluate Your Effectiveness in Various Ministerial Roles

There are several ways to evaluate your effectiveness in different roles. You might use Exercise 12.J for a self-evaluation and ask members of your personnel committee to do the same. Then you can compare your responses. Or you could ask a minister colleague to join you and a trusted member of your church to meet and discuss your answers. Of course, you can do this without involving anyone else. But you will get better results if a caring, objective person helps you. Remember that lay persons often rate ministers higher than ministers rate themselves. Their evaluations might encourage you.

REFLECT on which areas of your ministry and life you would like to increase your effectiveness. How might you do this? Think of as many ways as possible. Then select not more than three of your answers.

RECORD the three functions of ministry in which you would most like to increase your effectiveness.

Exercise 12.J

Rate your effectiveness in each of the following areas of your ministry and life. Use the following code:
1 = ineffective; 2 = somewhat ineffective; 3 = somewhat effective; 4 = effective; 5 = very effective.

Preaching and preparing sermons	1	2	3	4	5
Leading in worship	1	2	3	4	5
Teaching	1	2	3	4	5
Leading in Christian education	1	2	3	4	5
Making crisis pastoral calls	1	2	3	4	5
Calling on regular members	1	2	3	4	5
Counseling	1	2	3	4	5
Planning, organizing, supervising, evaluating, committees	1	2	3	4	5
Taking time for family	1	2	3	4	5
Taking time for exercise and recreation	1	2	3	4	5
Taking time for prayer and/or meditation	1	2	3	4	5

STEP 9
Review Important Formative Experiences in Pastoral Ministry

Our congregations shape us, just as we shape them. From a list of twenty-seven formative experiences that have contributed to their effectiveness, pastors in our study most frequently select "lessons learned from churches they have served." Eighty-five percent of them say this has been very important or important to the development of their effectiveness.

REFLECT on the experiences in churches you have served that have made a major contribution to the development of your effectiveness in ministry. List the three most important experiences. Do you continue to be open to learning from your congregation? Has your openness grown or declined? What has been the biggest challenge in your ministry in the past five years? How have you dealt with this challenge? What, if anything, do the things you have learned from past or present congregations suggest for ways in which you might grow in your effectiveness?

RECORD any ways you might wish to grow in light of the insights your reflection has given you.

STEP 10
Evaluate the Skills You Possess

There are several ways to rate your levels of skill. You might rate yourself on each of the skills in Exercise 12.K and ask members of your personnel committee to do the same. Then you can compare your responses. Or you could ask a minister colleague to join you and a trusted member of your church to meet and discuss your answers. Remember that most church officers tend to rate their pastors higher than pastors rate themselves.

REFLECT on your own skills. In which five skills have you rated yourself the highest? Mark them with a plus sign. In which five have you rated yourself the lowest? Mark them with a minus sign. Of your highest-rated skills, which would you like to develop further? How might you do that? Of your lowest-rated skills, which are critical to your increased effectiveness in your present congregation? What might you do to develop those skills?

If you wish to evaluate the relative strength of your skills related to Factor A: leadership in mission achievement, Factor B: responsiveness to others, and your energizing facilitating skills, complete Exercise 12.L as well.

REFLECT also on how well balanced your skill development is, based on Factors A and B. In which group of skills do you need to concentrate additional skill development? How might you do that?

How close to an ideal servant-leadership relationship is your relationship with your congregation? What resistance, if any, have you encountered to that style of leadership? Which skills might you develop to enhance your servant-leadership style in your present congregation?

RECORD not more than three skills you would like to develop further.

Rate your ability in each of the following skills. Use the following code:
1 = no skill; 2 = very little skill; 3 = moderately skillful;
4 = skillful; 5 = very skillful.

Empathizing: The ability to place oneself in the shoes of
others, feeling what they feel, without manipulating
or judging them   1   2   3   4   5

Strategizing: The ability to plan activities that lead
toward accomplishment of objectives and tasks related
to the congregation's mission   1   2   3   4   5

Empowering: The ability to establish a climate in which
people feel free to grow, learn, explore, and use their
gifts in Christian ministry without fear of retribution   1   2   3   4   5

Listening: The ability to hear other people fully, with
understanding of thoughts and feelings and with
unconditional respect for their opinions   1   2   3   4   5

Resolving conflict: The ability to help others in a conflict
situation to make use of differing ideas and opinions
without losing their self-esteem   1   2   3   4   5

Guiding: The ability to guide and manage the work of
board and key committees for maximum productivity   1   2   3   4   5

Collaborating: The ability to work cooperatively with
others without need to dominate or take credit for
accomplishments   1   2   3   4   5

Visioning: The ability to see new possibilities for the
future and to express the vision to others   1   2   3   4   5

Communicating: The ability to express thoughts clearly
and understandably to a broad range of individuals
and groups   1   2   3   4   5

Serving: The ability to place the needs of one's
congregation above the need for self-fulfillment
and advancement   1   2   3   4   5

Persuading: The ability to convince people of one's
position and convictions and to motivate them to
take specific courses of action   1   2   3   4   5

Assessing situations: The ability to understand what is
happening in work and social situations and relate
appropriately to them   1   2   3   4   5

Delegating: The ability to assign tasks to others with
clear instructions and with confidence in their ability
to accomplish the tasks   1   2   3   4   5

Identifying gifts: The ability to identify and assess one's
own talents and the talents of others   1   2   3   4   5

Organizing: The ability to plan and manage the life and
work of the congregation so that all elements fit
together in an ordered whole   1   2   3   4   5

Exercise 12.L

In the blank opposite each skill word, enter the number of the skill rating you have given yourself in Exercise 12.K. Then add the total in each column and divide by the number indicated below that total. The result is your average skill rating for each factor.

	FACTOR A	*FACTOR B*	*ENERGIZING*
EMPATHIZING		_____	
STRATEGIZING	_____		
EMPOWERING			_____
LISTENING		_____	
RESOLVING CONFLICT			_____
GUIDING	_____		
COLLABORATING		_____	
VISIONING	_____		
COMMUNICATING			_____
SERVING		_____	
PERSUADING	_____		
ASSESSING SITUATIONS			_____
DELEGATING	_____		
IDENTIFYING GIFTS	_____		
ORGANIZING	_____		
ENTER COLUMN TOTAL	_____	_____	_____
DIVIDE BY THIS NUMBER	7	4	4
AVERAGE SCORE	_____	_____	_____
	FACTOR A	FACTOR B	OTHER

Interpret your average skill for each factor using the following: 4.5 to 5.0 = very skillful; 3.5 to 4.5 = skillful; 2.5 to 3.5 = moderately skillful; 1 .5 to 2.5 = very little skill; 0 to 1.5 = no skill.

STEP 11
Understand Your Conflict-Management Style

Read or review *A Lay Person's Guide to Conflict Management,* by Speed B. Leas. Then answer the forty-five forced-choice questions in Leas's *Discover Your Conflict Management Style* and determine the conflict-management styles you are most likely to use in different situations.

REFLECT on whether your favored conflict-management styles are effective in most of the pastoral situations you encounter. If not, which styles might be more productive in helping you discover creative solutions to conflicts? How might you learn to develop those styles? How might you increase your range of conflict skills? A seminar or workshop might be the place to start.

RECORD the conflict-management styles you might want to develop and ways you might develop them.

STEP 12
Review Your Spiritual and Professional Disciplines

Use Exercise 12.M to help you assess the relative value of disciplines you use to develop your spiritual life.

REFLECT on your pattern of spiritual development. Has it been consistent or sporadic? What might you do to make it more effective?

RECORD one or two spiritual disciplines you would like to develop further. Include ways in which you might develop them.

STEP 13
Review Your Pattern of Continuing Education

Use Exercise 12.N to review the extent of your involvement in continuing education since graduation from seminary.

REFLECT on your pattern of continuing education. Has it been proactive or reactive? Do you have a long-range plan for your professional development? How have you selected the subjects you study and events you attend? Have you tended to concentrate too much on certain areas and to neglect other areas? Right now, what areas of continuing education might be most helpful to your own growth and development? What areas would be most helpful to your congregation?

RECORD two long-range goals for your continuing education for each of the following: (1) for your own development, and (2) for the benefit of your present congregation.

Exercise 12.M

How valuable have the disciplines listed below been in your personal and professional development? Use the following code:

1 = of no value; 2 = of little value; 3 = somewhat valuable;
4 = valuable; 5 = very valuable.

Prayer and meditation	1	2	3	4	5
Journaling	1	2	3	4	5
Fasting	1	2	3	4	5
Spiritual direction	1	2	3	4	5
Bible study and exegesis	1	2	3	4	5
Lectionary study with other ministers	1	2	3	4	5
Lectionary study with church members	1	2	3	4	5
Preparation for preaching, teaching, or worship	1	2	3	4	5

Exercise 12.N

Since graduation from seminary, in each area listed below, to what extent have you undertaken formal continuing education in a workshop, seminary, or other academic institution? Use the following code:

1 = none; 2 = very little; 3 = little; 4 = moderate;
5 = extensive; 6 = very extensive.

Biblical studies, church history, theology, homiletics, or worship	1	2	3	4	5	6
Pastoral care, clinical pastoral education, and/or counseling	1	2	3	4	5	6
Stewardship	1	2	3	4	5	6
Evangelism	1	2	3	4	5	6
Group process, education, community organization, administration	1	2	3	4	5	6
Other (specify) _____	1	2	3	4	5	6
_____	1	2	3	4	5	6

STEP 14
Assess Your Sources of Support

Exercise 12.O may help you assess the areas of support that you are finding most helpful at this time in your life. You may use it for evaluating sources of overall support or support in specific areas of your life and ministry.

REFLECT on the sources of support that have been most helpful to you. What have been least useful and why? Select not more than two areas of support you would like to improve or develop. What might you do to improve or develop it?

RECORD the areas of support you would like most to improve or develop. Include ideas on how you might develop such support.

TASK THREE
DEVELOP YOUR GROWTH PLAN

The time has come for you to develop your own growth plan, with specific objectives for study, skill development, and spiritual development. It will be best if that plan can have both long-range and immediate goals. When you have formulated your plan, you may wish to test it with someone whom you trust such as the personnel committee of your church, a ministerial colleague, or someone else whose advice you respect.

STEP 1
Summarize What You Have Learned

Review your responses to the exercises you have completed under Task One and Task Two. In the light of that review: (1) List your special strengths. (2) List

Exercise 12.O

How helpful to you in your ministry, spiritual life, family life, and personal life are the following sources of support? Use the following code:
1 = of no help; 2 = of little help; 3 = of some help;
4 = helpful; 5 = very helpful.

Member or group of your congregation	1	2	3	4	5
Member of board or personnel committee	1	2	3	4	5
Ministerial colleague or support group	1	2	3	4	5
Spouse	1	2	3	4	5
Executive or committee of governing body	1	2	3	4	5
Mentor	1	2	3	4	5
Spiritual director	1	2	3	4	5
Friend outside the congregation	1	2	3	4	5
Pastoral or marital counselor or therapist	1	2	3	4	5
Other	1	2	3	4	5

any limitations you have identified. (3) Place a check in front of any strengths or limitations in which you might like to grow. (4) List as many possible growth goals as you now feel might be important for your future effectiveness. At this stage do not try to evaluate them. Feel free to add any new potential goals that occur to you. Lay this work aside until step 3.

STEP 2
Decide on Growth Priorities

What are your long-range and immediate priorities for growth? Do you want to give priority to developing your strengths or to overcoming some crucial weaknesses? Do you need to give priority to family in relation to church responsibilities? Or does some form of self-development need to take priority? If you are seeking a balance, what needs specific attention in order to achieve that balance? What difference in priorities might there be, if any, between those for the next year and those for the next five years?

Write a brief statement of your priorities for the next year and another statement of your priorities for the next five years.

STEP 3
Set Long-range, Achievable Growth Goals

Now look again at the list of possible goals that you made under step 1. In light of the priorities you have established for yourself, select five to seven goals you judge to be most important. Place a "1" opposite the most important, a "2" opposite the next most important, and so forth. Decide which of these goals should be long-term (five-year) goals and which should be immediate (one-year) goals.

Are the goals you have selected achievable? If not, either modify them so you feel you can reach them, or eliminate them from your list.

Choose two or three long-range growth goals and two or three immediate growth goals. If you select too many growth goals you are not likely to keep them in sharp focus.

STEP 4
Design a Strategy to Reach Your Growth Goals

For each growth goal ask yourself what you need to do in order to achieve your goal. Are there continuing-education programs or graduate education programs that deal with the areas of growth you have selected? How much of your progress can be achieved by home study within the normal time constraints of your work? Can you change your time priorities and delegate responsibilities to others in order to find the time you need? Is your study leave time adequate for your goals or will you need a sabbatical? Does your growth depend upon changing something you are now doing within the congregation you serve?

STEP 5
Identify Resources You Need to Implement Your Strategy

Will you have the financial resources required, or will you need to secure supplementary funding? What other resources will you need? Books? Consultants? Counseling or therapy? Who in your congregation can help you secure any necessary approval for the plans you are developing? You will think of many other questions in designing your own strategy and related action plans.

STEP 6
Plan Action Steps for the Next Year and Beyond

Once you have decided on a strategy, make specific plans for work you will do in any of the following categories that apply to your growth goals:

Continuing education plans
Home study plans
Spiritual disciplines
Family relationships
Personal needs (e.g., enhancing your self-esteem)
Church priorities

Here is a sample strategy for one growth goal, together with action steps and a timeline:

GOAL: I will develop my ability to share leadership with church officers. I will have accomplished this if I am less at the center of everything that happens in the church, and if more of the responsibility and implementation of ministry is actually being carried by lay leaders of the congregation.

STRATEGY: I will work closely with church officers to help them understand the vitality that can be set loose in a congregation that shares leadership and implements partnership in ministry. Then I will seek to secure their commitment to sharing ministry. Finally I will seek to gain a wider level of support for shared ministry among members of the congregation.

ACTION STEPS:

1. Study books that will help me understand the possibilities and pitfalls of shared leadership.
2. Get counseling to help me grow in my self-esteem so I will not have such a strong need to keep control of everything. I will also seek to grow in my ability to gain satisfaction from the achievements of others.
3. Attend a workshop on servant leadership to deepen my understanding of what will be involved. Then concentrate on developing my skills for assessing gifts of others and for delegating to them.
4. Select several contagious multipliers (key members of the board who can make a difference in the congregation if they catch the vision). Share my vision for this new dynamic with them. Secure their commitment to help others accept the idea.
5. Engage in dialogue with church officers on the meaning of ministry, considering biblical images of ministry of the whole people of God and discussing what shared ministry between pastor and church officers might be like.
6. Through these discussions seek a common understanding of a pastor's servant leadership and what this means for participation in leadership by church officers.
7. Covenant together with church officers to share ministry with one another and with members of the congregation.
8. With the board, develop specific procedures for participative planning.
9. Develop policies and procedures that will enable the board to delegate authority to groups to take action within commonly agreed-upon policy guidelines.
10. Enlarge the circle of those who are committed to shared ministry:
    Keep working with the contagious multipliers and chairpersons of committees.
    Focus on helping new members to recognize their responsibility for ministry.
    Widen the circles of influence until enough members of the congregation are committed to shared ministry so we reach a "tipping point," a large enough group so that the idea is generally accepted as a norm in our congregation.

TIMELINE: The first year I will focus on steps 1 and 2. The second year I will continue with step 2 and work on 3 through 6. In the third year I will work on steps 7, 8, and 9. Step 10 will be a gradual process throughout the five years, with intensive work to be completed in years four and five.

TASK FOUR
GET GOING AND KEEP GROWING

A growth plan will be no better than what you actually do with it. So once you have it, get going! Establish a schedule with specific dates for completion of your different action steps. Invite key people and groups to help you on your journey. Enroll in academic programs or continuing-education events. Gather books or other materials. Develop your support network. Go to work and keep growing. Then monitor your progress every three to six months and revise your growth plan in the light of changing needs in your congregation or in your own life.

In closing, I wish God's rich blessing on you, your family, and your congregation as you continue to grow in effectiveness.

God wants us to grow up, to know the whole truth and tell it in love—like Christ in everything. We take our lead from Christ, who is the source of everything we do. He keeps us in step with each other. His very breath and blood flow through us, nourishing us so that we will grow up healthy in God, robust in love. (Eph. 4:15–16, TM)

And I am sure that God who began the good work within you will keep right on helping you grow in his grace until his task within you is finally finished on that day when Jesus Christ returns. (Phil. 1:6, *The Living Bible*)

NOTES

Introduction

1. Donald P. Smith, *Congregations Alive: Practical Suggestions for Bringing Your Church to Life through Partnership Ministry* (Philadelphia: Westminster Press, 1981).

2. Donald P. Smith, *How to Attract and Keep Active Church Members* (Louisville, Ky.: Westminster/John Knox Press, 1992).

Chapter 1: Empowering Transforms Ministry

1. Marvin Johnson et al., *Growth in Ministry: The Relationship between Pastors' Effectiveness and Satisfaction and Other Psychological and Sociological Variables* (Philadelphia: Lutheran Church in America, 1975), 154–55.

2. Samuel W. Blizzard, "The Protestant Parish Minister's Integrating Roles," *Religious Education* 53, no.4 (July–Aug. 1958): 374–80.

3. Lyle Schaller, *The Senior Minister* (Nashville: Abingdon Press, 1988), 26.

Chapter 2: Meaning Empowers

1. Smith, *How to Attract and Keep*, 47.

2. Wade Clark Roof, *A Generation of Seekers: The Spiritual Journeys of the Baby Boom Generation* (San Francisco: HarperCollins, 1993), 2.

3. Ibid., 158.

4. John Stott, as quoted by Donald Mc Cullough, "Enlarging the Mind to Expand the Ministry," in *Mastering Personal Growth*, ed. Maxie Dunham et al., 96 (Sisters, Ore.: Multnomah Press, 1992).

5. McCullough, "Enlarging the Mind," 103–04.

6. Part of this difference may be explained by the fact that a slightly higher proportion of small congregations are served by Other Pastors. Small congregations may tend to be more oriented toward history and tradition. However, we found that 61 percent of Empowering Solo Pastors (who tend to serve smaller churches) compared with 38 percent of Other Solo Pastors also describe their congregation as influenced more by contemporary ideas and trends or by an equal mix with history and tradition. And 63 percent of Other Solo Pastors describe their congregations as influenced more by history and tradition.

7. We found no statistically significant differences in the proportion of small, medium, and large congregations in the Empowering and Other groups of pastors.

8. The differences between Empowering Solo Pastors and Other Solo Pastors on these two questions are significant at the .06 and .10 levels. This may be due to the size of the samples.

9. Roof, *A Generation of Seekers*, 252. See M. Scott Peck, *The Different Drum: Community-Making and Peace* (New York: Simon & Schuster, 1987), 59.

10. Roof, *A Generation of Seekers*, 260.

11. Peter M. Hobbie, review of *A Generation of Seekers*, by Wade Clark Roof, *The Presbyterian Outlook* (Oct. 4, 1993): 9.

12. Roy M. Oswald, *How to Build a Support System for Your Ministry* (Washington, D.C.: Alban Institute, 1991), 98.

13. Smith, *Congregations Alive*, 87–88.

14. This statement is my oversimplified summary of the rather complex Grubb Theory of Oscillation as Oswald describes it in *How to Build a Support System*, 41–44.

15. Oswald, *How to Build a Support System*, 98–101.

16. Smith, *How to Attract and Keep*, 57.

Chapter 3: Free to Grow

1. Stephen Covey, *The Seven Habits of Highly Effective People* (New York: Simon & Schuster, 1989), 237.

2. Ibid., 240.

3. Ibid., 245.

4. Smith, *Congregations Alive*, 50.

5. Glen E. Robinson, "Effective Schools Research: A Guide to School Improvement," *Concerns in Education*, Educational Research Service (Feb. 1985): 5 –6.

6. For a description of the Logos program, see Smith, *How to Attract and Keep*, 117–18.

7. Kurt Lewin, as quoted in Chris Argyris, *Integrating the Individual and the Organization* (New York: John Wiley & Sons, 1964).

Chapter 4: Leading Powerfully as Servants

1. Robert K. Greenleaf, *Servant Leadership: A Journey into the Nature of Legitimate Power and Greatness* (Ramsey, N.Y.: Paulist Press, 1977), 7.

2. Ibid., 13–14.

3. Robinson, "Effective Schools," 7.

4. Greenleaf, *Servant Leadership*, 15–16.

5. For more information on this congregation, see Smith, *Congregations Alive*, 27.

6. Jackson W. Carroll, "Understanding Church Growth and Decline," *Theology Today* 35 (1978): 78–80.

7. Robinson, "Effective Schools," 7–10.

8. Johnson, *Growth in Ministry*, 155–56.

9. Ibid., 158.

Chapter 5: Empowered to Be Real

1. Covey, *Seven Habits*, 238.

2. Ibid., 21–22.

3. David S. Schuller et al., *Ministry in America: A Report and Analysis, Based on an In-Depth Survey of Forty-Seven Denominations in the United States and Canada, with Interpretation by Eighteen Experts* (San Francisco: Harper & Row, 1980), 19.

4. Nathaniel Branden, *How to Raise Your Self-Esteem* (Deerfield Beach, Fla.: Health Communications, 1992), 123.

5. Ben Patterson, "Performance Factor: Being a Pastor and Being Yourself Don't Always Go Together," *Leadership* (Summer 1992): 24–30.

6. Ibid., 28.

7. The Presbyterian Panel is a scientifically designed poll of Presbyterian ministers, elders, and church members that is used regularly to learn what they think and feel about various subjects.

8. Differences in ratings by lay leaders on risk-taking and approaches to change tended in the same direction as those of their pastors. However, differences were not large enough to be statistically significant.

9. Edward A. White, "What Kind of Pastor Will Most Likely Empower Laity?" in *Congregations*, ed. Celia A. Hahn (Washington, D.C.: Alban Institute, 1994).

10. Covey, *Seven Habits*, 49.

11. Ibid., 51.

12. Branden, *Raise Your Self-Esteem*, 7–8.

13. James Battle, *Culture-Free Self-Esteem Inventories*, 2d ed. (Austin, Tex.: Pro-ed, 1992), 3.

14. Branden, *Raise Your Self-Esteem*, 28.

15. Ibid., 6.

16. Nathaniel Branden, *The Power of Self-Esteem* (Deerfield Beach, Fla.: Health Communications, 1992), vii.

17. Branden, *Raise Your Self-Esteem*, 7–8.

18. James Battle, *Self-Esteem: The New Revolution* (Edmonton, Ala.: James Battle & Associates, 1990).

19. Branden, *Raise Your Self-Esteem*, 29.

20. This list is my summary of chapters 3–8 in Branden, *Raise Your Self-Esteem*.

Chapter 6: The Power in Becoming

1. Thomas E. Kadel, ed., *Growth in Ministry* (Philadelphia: Lutheran Church in America and the Lutheran Church, Missouri Synod, 1980), viii.

2. Connolly Gamble, *The Continuing Education of Parish Clergy: Report of a Survey* (Collegeville, Penn.: Society for the Advancement of Continuing Education for Ministry, 1984), 18–19.

3. Research Unit of the Support Agency, Presbyterian Panel, *The November 1983 Questionnaire: Continuing Education for Ministers of the Word* (New York: Presbyterian Church [U.S.A.], 1983), 2.

4. Gamble, *Continuing Education*, 55.

5. Kadel, *Growth in Ministry*, 120.

6. Mark Rouch, "Getting Smart about Continuing Education," in Kadel, *Growth in Ministry*, 124.

7. Keith M. Wulff, "Continuing Education for Pastors," *Monday Morning* (May 6, 1991):12.

8. Rouch, "Getting Smart," 131.

9. Chester P. Michael and Marie C. Norrisey, *Prayer and Temperament* (Charlottesville, Va.: The Open Door, 1991).

10. Roy M. Oswald and Otto Kroeger, *Personality Type and Religious Leadership* (Washington, D.C.: Alban Institute, 1992), 90–123.

11. This definition is from a brochure about the Certificate in the Art of Spiritual Direction offered by the San Francisco Theological Seminary.

12. Eugene H. Peterson, *Working the Angles* (Grand Rapids: Wm. B. Eerdmans Publishing Co., 1987), 5.

13. Ibid., 3–4.

Chapter 7: The Power in Your Hands

1. Our computer analysis does not make clear whether the differences in these choices are statistically significant. However, differences between Empowering Pastors and Other Pastors on their choice of the five most important abilities seem to be substantial. Therefore the patterns are at least strongly suggestive.

Chapter 8: The Power in Mission Achievement

1. Robinson, "Effective Schools," 7.

Chapter 9: The Power in People Skills

1. This illustration comes from John C. Peterson, quoting Joe McMillan, a football coach at San Jose State University.

2. Greenleaf, *Servant Leadership*, 17.

3. Ideas for this series of questions come from various sources, including Kermit Moore, "Learning to Listen," *American Way* (March 1984): 40–43; "The Act of Listening," from the Royal Bank of Canada, "Monthly Letter" 60, no.1 (January 1979); and advice on listening collected by Joan DeJean.

4. From Frederick W. Faber, *Spiritual Conferences*, vol. 6 (Baltimore: John Murphy & Co., 1858), 59, as quoted by Aubrey Brown, "Koinonia," *The Presbyterian Outlook* (Feb. 22, 1993): 6.

5. The original, which was contributed by Joan DeJean, was in the form of a poem without punctuation. I have adapted it to a prose form.

6. Covey, *Seven Habits*, 185.

7. Ibid., 186.

8. Ibid., 188ff.

9. Ibid., 207ff.

10. Ibid., 262 ff.

11. Ibid., 264–65.

12. Smith, *How to Attract and Keep*, 99.

13. Speed B. Leas, *A Lay Person's Guide to Conflict Management* (Washington, D.C.: Alban Institute, 1979), 3–4.

14. For more information on pinch-hearers, see John S. Savage, "Role Negotiation Model" (Reynoldsburg, Ohio: L.E.A.D. Consultants, 1987), videotape. Also see Smith, *How to Attract and Keep*, 77, 101.

15. Leas, *Lay Person's Guide to Conflict*.

16. Ibid., 6.
17. "The Conflict Intensity Chart," Presbyterian Church (U.S.A.).
18. Smith, *How to Attract and Keep*, 99–100
19. Leas, *Lay Person's Guide to Conflict*, 9.
20. Ibid., 10–14.

Chapter 10: Power to Live with Stress

1. Edgar W. Mills and John P. Koval, *Stress in the Ministry* (Washington, D.C.: Ministry Studies Board, 1971), 9–11, 54–55.
2. Charles L. Rassieur, *Stress Management for Ministers* (Philadelphia: Westminster Press, 1982), 20–21.
3. Ibid., 19.
4. These points are largely derived and adapted from John A. Sanford, *Ministry Burnout* (Louisville, Ky.: Westminster/John Knox Press, 1982), 5–16; and Rassieur, *Stress Management*, 20–33.
5. The report from the Menninger Foundation is quoted in Rassieur, *Stress Management*, 22, from Donald C. Houts, "Pastoral Care for Pastors: Toward a Church Strategy," *Pastoral Psychology* 25, no.3 (Spring 1977): 190.
6. Sanford, *Ministry Burnout*, 6.
7. Ibid., 7.
8. Ibid., 9.
9. Ibid., 11–12.
10. Ibid., 14.
11. Rassieur, *Stress Management*, 23.
12. Houts, "Pastoral Care for Pastors," 190.
13. Jürgen Moltmann, *The Crucified God*, trans. R. A. Wilson and John Bowden (London: SCM Press, 1974), 7.
14. Moltmann, *Crucified God*, 22.
15. Ibid., 24–25.
16. Rassieur, *Stress Management*, 23–26.
17. Barbara G. Gilbert, *Who Ministers to Ministers? A Study of Support Systems for Clergy and Spouses* (Washington, D.C.: Alban Institute, 1987), 9–14.
18. W. Benjamin Pratt, "Burnout: A Spiritual Pilgrimage," in *Surviving in Ministry: Navigating the Pitfalls, Experiencing the Renewals*, ed. Robert R. Lutz and Bruce Taylor, 117 (New York: Paulist Press, 1990).
19. Rassieur, *Stress Management*, 43.
20. Ibid., 36.
21. This paragraph is a summary of Rassieur, *Stress Management*, 37–51.
22. Rassieur, *Stress Management*, 43.
23. Covey, *Seven Habits*, 149ff.
24. Ibid., 151.
25. Ibid., 154.
26. The following two paragraphs present some highlights I have selected from the chapter on Habit 2 in Covey, *Seven Habits*, 96–144.
27. Donald McCullough, "Time for Things That Matter," in Dunham, *Mastering Personal Growth* (Sisters, Ore.: Multnomah Press, 1992) 144.
28. Ibid., 140–41.

29. Ibid., 145.
30. Ibid., 147.
31. Ibid., 148.

Chapter 11: Three Secrets of Sustaining Power

1. The conviction of a call over the years seems to have been consistently higher for Empowering Pastors than for Other Pastors, but only at a .07 to .09 level of significance. The only significant differences at a .05 level or better have been in two measures of calling: (1) For some reason, five years ago, Empowering Pastors felt a significantly stronger sense of calling than Other Pastors felt. (2) Between then and now, Other Pastors have felt a significantly greater increase in the strength of their calling. The significant difference in their present sense of calling is only at the .08 level.

2. Interpretation of Richard Niebuhr's categories of the call draws on Roy W. Fairchild, *Discerning Your Call and Your Gifts for Ministry* (New York: United Presbyterian Church, 1979).

3. McCullough, "Time for Things That Matter," 138–39.

4. Jackson W. Carroll and David A. Roozen, "Congregational Identities in the Presbyterian Church," *Review of Religious Research* 31, no. 4 (June 1990): 351ff.

5. Carroll and Roozen's original questionnaire also contained the following seven-point scales. These may also be useful in exploring congregational identity:

   1. Our church is primarily oriented toward serving the members. . . . Our church is primarily oriented toward serving the world beyond its membership.

   2. Our congregation feels like one large family. . . . Our congregation feels like a loosely knit association of individuals and groups.

   3. Our church is known as a prestigious church in the area. . . . Our strengths notwithstanding, our church is not considered one of the "status churches in the area."

   4. The congregation has a strong sense of its Presbyterian identity. . . . Visitors would find it difficult to know that this is a Presbyterian congregation.

6. By means of extensive statistical analysis Carroll and Roozen developed six clusters based on different combinations of responses on the nine scales. These describe six different congregational identities that help to explain congregational culture: Sojourner, Activist, Evangelical, Civic, Old First, and Family.

7. The following two illustrations are from Roy M. Oswald, *How to Build a Support System for Your Ministry* (Washington, D.C.: Alban Institute, 1991), 20–21.

8. Ibid., 22.

9. Ibid., 25.

10. Ibid., 26.

11. John G. Koehler, "The Minister as a Family Man," in *The Minister's Own Mental Health*, ed. Wayne E. Oates, 160 (Great Neck, N.Y.: Channel Press, 1961).

12. Koehler, "Family Man," 162.

13. Oswald, *Support System*, 24.

14. McCullough, "Friends for the One at the Top," in Dunham, *Mastering Personal Growth*, 42–43.

15. Ibid., 47.

16. Ibid., 49, 51.

17. Oswald, *Support System*, 31–65.

18. The inventories used in the Carlisle Project are given in Roy M. Oswald, *Clergy Self-Care: Finding a Balance for Effective Ministry* (Washington, D.C.: Alban Institute, 1991).

19. Oswald, *Support System*, 41–46.

20. Mills and Koval, *Stress in the Ministry*, 11.

21. The differences between Empowering Pastors and Other Pastors on the influence of role models is significant at the .10 level.

22. The Shalem Institute for Spiritual Formation can be reached at Mount St. Alban, Washington, D.C. 20016. It offers workshops in spiritual direction and extension programs.

23. The Certificate in the Art of Spiritual Direction is given by the Program in Christian Spirituality at San Francisco Theological Seminary, San Anselmo, Calif. 94960.

24. Mills and Koval, *Stress in the Ministry*, 26.

Chapter 12: The Disciplined Path to Growing Power

1. David Keirsey and Marilyn Bates, *Please Understand Me* (Del Mar, Calif.: Prometheus Nemesis Books, 1978).

2. Roy M. Oswald and Otto Kroeger, *Personality Type and Religious Leadership* (Washington, D.C.: Alban Institute, 1988).

3. Ibid., 2–3.

RESOURCES
FOR FURTHER STUDY

Allen, Diogenes. *Christian Belief in a Postmodern World: The Full Wealth of Conviction.* Philadelphia: Westminster/John Knox Press, 1989.

Augsburger, David W. *Conflict Mediation across Cultures: Pathways and Patterns.* Louisville, Ky.: Westminster/John Knox Press, 1992.

Battle, James. *Culture-Free Self-Esteem Inventories.* 2d ed. Austin, Tex.: Pro-ed, 1992.

Biersdorf, John F. *How Prayer Shapes Ministry.* Washington, D.C.: Alban Institute, 1992.

Bos, A. David. *A Practical Guide to Community Ministry.* Louisville, Ky.: Westminster/John Knox Press, 1993.

Branden, Nathaniel. *How to Raise Your Self-Esteem.* New York: Bantam Books, 1988.

———. *The Power of Self-Esteem.* Deerfield Beach, Fla.: Health Communications, 1992.

Brekke, Milo L., et al. *Ten Faces of Ministry.* Minneapolis: Augsburg, 1979.

Brown, Robert McAfee. *Reclaiming the Bible: Words for the Nineties.* Louisville, Ky.: Westminster John Knox Press, 1994.

Bullock, A. Richard. *Sabbatical Planning: For Clergy and Congregations.* Washington, D.C.: Alban Institute, 1987.

Buttrick, David. *A Captive Voice: The Liberation of Preaching.* Louisville, Ky.: Westminster John Knox Press, 1994.

Carroll, Jackson W. *As One with Authority: Reflective Leadership in Ministry.* Louisville, Ky.: Westminster/John Knox Press, 1991.

———. *Ministry as Reflective Practice: A New Look at the Professional Model.* Washington, D.C.: Alban Institute, 1986.

Carroll, Jackson W., and Wade Clark Roof, eds. *Beyond Establishment: Protestant Identity in a Post-Protestant Age.* Louisville, Ky.: Westminster John Knox Press, 1993.

Carroll, Jackson W., and David A. Roozen. "Congregational Identity in the Presbyterian Church." *Religious Research* 31, no. 4 (June 1990): 351–69.

Chapman, Thomas W., ed. *A Practical Handbook for Ministry: From the Writings of Wayne E. Oates.* Louisville, Ky.: Westminster/John Knox Press, 1992.

Chilstrom, Herbert W., and Lowell G. Almen. *The Many Faces of Pastoral Ministry.* Minneapolis: Augsburg, 1989.

Coate, Mary Anne. *Clergy Stress: The Hidden Conflicts in Ministry.* London: SPCK, 1989.

Coger, Marian. *Women in Parish Ministry: Stress and Support.* Washington, D.C.: Alban Institute, 1985.

Covey, Stephen R. *Principle-Centered Leadership.* New York: Simon & Schuster, 1992.

————. *The Seven Habits of Highly Effective People: Restoring the Character Ethic.* New York: Simon & Schuster, 1989.

Craig, Robert H., and R. C. Worley. *Dry Bones Live: Helping Congregations Discover New Life.* Louisville, Ky.: Westminster/John Knox Press, 1993.

Cueni, R. Robert, and Herb Miller, eds. *The Vital Church Leader.* Nashville: Abingdon Press, 1991.

Dale, Robert D. *Pastoral Leadership: A Handbook of Resources for Effective Congregational Leadership.* Nashville: Abingdon Press, 1986.

Dudley, Carl S., ed. *Building Effective Ministry: Theory and Practice in the Local Church.* San Francisco: Harper & Row, 1983.

Dudley, Carl S., and Sally A. Johnson. *Energizing the Congregation: Images That Shape Your Church's Ministry.* Louisville, Ky.: Westminster/John Knox Press, 1993.

Dunham, Maxie, et al. *Mastering Personal Growth.* Sisters, Oreg.: Multnomah Press, 1992.

Fletcher, John C. *Religious Authenticity in the Clergy.* Washington, D.C.: Alban Institute, 1975.

Freeman, Forster. *Readiness for Ministry through Spiritual Direction.* Washington, D.C.: Alban Institute, 1986.

Gardner, John W. *On Leadership.* New York: Free Press, 1990.

Gilbert, Barbara G. *Who Ministers to Ministers? A Study of Support Systems for Clergy and Spouses.* Washington, D.C.: Alban Institute, 1987.

Greenleaf, Robert K. *Servant Leadership: A Journey into the Nature of Legitimate Power and Greatness.* New York: Paulist Press, 1977.

Halverstadt, Hugh. *Managing Church Conflict.* Louisville, Ky.: Westminster/John Knox Press, 1991.

Hands, Donald R., and Wayne L. Fehr. *Spiritual Wholeness for Clergy.* Washington, D.C.: Alban Institute, 1993.

Harbaugh, Gary L. *Caring for the Caregiver: Growth Models for Professional Leaders and Congregations.* Washington, D.C.: Alban Institute, 1992.

Harbaugh, Gary L., et al. *Beyond the Boundary: Meeting the Challenge of the First Years of Ministry.* Washington, D.C.: Alban Institute, 1986.

Harris, John C. *Stress, Power, and Ministry.* Washington, D.C.: Alban Institute, 1977.

Hoge, Dean R., B. Johnson, and D. A. Luidens. *Vanishing Boundaries: The Religion of Mainline Protestant Baby Boomers.* Louisville, Ky.: Westminster John Knox Press, 1994.

Johnson, Ben Campbell. *Pastoral Spirituality: A Focus for Ministry.* Philadelphia: Westminster Press, 1988.

————. *Speaking of God: Evangelism as Initial Spiritual Guidance.* Louisville, Ky.: Westminster/John Knox Press, 1991.

Johnson, Marvin, et al. *Growth in Ministry: The Relationship between Pastors' Effectiveness and Satisfaction and Other Psychological and Sociological Variables.* The Growth in Ministry Project Research. Philadelphia: Division for Professional Leadership, Lutheran Church in America, 1975.

Kadel, Thomas E., ed. *Growth in Ministry.* Philadelphia: Fortress Press, 1980.

Keirsey, David, and Marilyn Bates. *Please Understand Me.* Del Mar, Calif.: Prometheus Nemesis Books, 1978.

Kliewer, Stephen. *How to Live with Diversity in the Local Church.* Washington, D.C.: Alban Institute, 1987.

Lakein, Alan. *How to Get Control of Your Time and Your Life.* New York: New American Library, 1973.

Leas, Speed B. *A Lay Person's Guide to Conflict Management.* Washington, D.C.: Alban Institute, 1979.

———. *Leadership and Conflict.* Nashville: Abingdon Press, 1982.

Lee, Harris W. *Effective Church Leadership: A Practical Source Book.* Minneapolis: Augsburg, 1989.

Leith, John H. *From Generation to Generation: The Renewal of the Church according to Its Own Theology and Practice.* Louisville, Ky.: Westminster/John Knox Press, 1990.

Lindbeck, George A. *The Nature of Doctrine: Religion and Theology in a Postliberal Age.* Philadelphia: Westminster Press, 1984.

McCullough, Donald. "Enlarging the Mind to Expand the Ministry." In *Mastering Personal Growth,* ed. Maxie Dunham et al. Sisters, Oreg.: Multnomah Press, 1992.

———. "Friends for the One at the Top." In *Mastering Personal Growth,* ed. Maxie Dunham et al.

———. "Time for Things That Matter." In *Mastering Personal Growth,* ed. Maxie Dunham et al.

Meyers, Eleanor Scott, ed. *Envisioning the New City: A Reader on Urban Ministry.* Louisville, Ky.: Westminster/John Knox Press, 1992.

Michael, Chester P., and Marie C. Norrisey. *Prayer and Temperament: Different Prayer Forms for Different Personality Types.* Charlottesville, Va.: Open Door, 1991.

Mills, Edgar W., and John P. Koval. *Stress in the Ministry.* Washington, D.C.: Ministry Studies Board, 1971.

Mitchell, Kenneth R. *Multiple Staff Ministries.* Philadelphia: Westminster Press, 1988.

Moltmann, Jürgen. *The Crucified God.* Trans. R. A. Wilson and John Bowden. London: SCM Press, 1974.

Moreman, William M. *Developing Spiritually and Professionally.* Philadelphia: Westminster Press, 1984.

Mount, Eric, Jr. *Professional Ethics in Context: Institutions, Images, and Empathy.* Louisville, Ky.: Westminster/John Knox Press, 1990.

Myers, Isabel Briggs. *Introduction to Type.* Palo Alto, Calif.: Consulting Psychologists Press, 1981.

Nelson, C. Ellis, ed. *Congregations: Their Power to Form and Transform.* Philadelphia: Westminster Press, 1988.

Nuechterlein, Anne Marie. *Improving Your Multiple Staff Ministry.* Minneapolis: Augsburg, 1989.

Oates, Wayne E., ed. *The Minister's Own Mental Health.* Great Neck, N.Y.: Channel Press, 1961.

Oswald, Roy M. *Clergy Self-Care: Finding a Balance for Effective Ministry.* Washington, D.C.: Alban Institute, 1991.

———. *How to Build a Support System for Your Ministry.* Washington, D.C.: Alban Institute, 1991.

Oswald, Roy M., and Otto Kroeger. *Personality Type and Religious Leadership.* Washington, D.C.: Alban Institute, 1988.

Pastoral Activities Index. New York: Vocation Agency Presyberian Church (U.S.A.), 1984.

Pastoral Performance Profile. New York: Vocation Agency Presyberian Church (U.S.A.), 1984.

Peterson, Eugene H. *The Message: The New Testament in Contemporary English.* Colorado Springs: Navpress, 1993.

————. *Working the Angles.* Grand Rapids, Mich.: Wm. B. Eerdmans Publishing Co., 1987.

Pneuman, Roy W., and Margaret E. Bruehl. *Managing Conflict: A Complete Process-Centered Handbook.* Englewood Cliffs, N.J.: Prentice-Hall, 1982.

Rassieur, Charles L. *Stress Management for Ministers.* Philadelphia: Westminster Press, 1982.

Rice, Howard L. *Reformed Spirituality: An Introduction for Believers.* Louisville, Ky.: Westminster/John Knox Press, 1991.

Roof, Wade Clark. *A Generation of Seekers: The Spiritual Journeys of the Baby Boom Generation.* San Francisco: HarperCollins, 1993.

Rouch, Mark A. *Competent Ministry: A Guide to Effective Continuing Education.* Nashville: Abingdon Press, 1974.

Sanford, John A. *Ministry Burnout.* Louisville, Ky.: Westminster/John Knox Press, 1982.

Schnase, Robert. *Ambition in Ministry: Our Spiritual Struggle with Success, Achievement, and Competition.* Nashville: Abingdon Press, 1993.

Schuller, David S., et al. *Ministry in America: A Report and Analysis, Based on an In-Depth Survey of Forty-Seven Denominations in the United States and Canada, with Interpretation by Eighteen Experts.* San Francisco: Harper & Row, 1980.

Smith, Donald P. *Clergy in the Cross Fire.* Philadelphia: Westminster Press, 1973.

————. *Congregations Alive.* Philadelphia: Westminster Press, 1981.

————. *How to Attract and Keep Active Church Members.* Louisville, Ky.: Westminster/John Knox Press, 1992.

Stevens, Paul R., and Phil Collins. *The Equipping Pastor.* Washington, D.C.: Alban Institute, 1993.

Walrath, Douglas Alan. *Leading Churches through Change.* Nashville: Abingdon Press, 1987.

Westerhoff, John. *Spiritual Life: The Foundation for Preaching and Teaching.* Louisville, Ky.: Westminster John Knox Press, 1994.

Williamson, Clark, and Ronald J. Allen. *The Teaching Minister.* Louisville, Ky.: Westminster/John Knox Press, 1991.

Willimon, William H. *Preaching about Conflict in the Local Church.* Philadelphia: Westminster Press, 1987.

————. *Preaching and Leading Worship.* Philadelphia: Westminster Press, 1984.

Willimon, William H., and Stanley Hauerwas. *Preaching to Strangers: Evangelism in Today's World.* Louisville, Ky.: Westminster/John Knox Press, 1992.

Wilson, Marlene. *How to Mobilize Church Volunteers.* Minneapolis: Augsburg, 1983.

Wind, James P., et al., eds. *Clergy Ethics in a Changing Society: Mapping the Terrain.* Louisville, Ky.: Westminster/John Knox Press, 1991.

ACKNOWLEDGMENTS

Grateful acknowledgment is made for permission to reprint material from the following works:

How to Build a Support System for Your Ministry by Roy M. Oswald, copyright © 1991; *Personality Type and Religious Leadership* by Roy M. Oswald and Otto Kroeger, copyright © 1992; and *A Lay Person's Guide to Conflict Management* by Speed B. Leas, copyright © 1979, with permission from The Alban Institute, Inc., Suite 433 North, 4550 Montgomery Avenue, Bethesda, Maryland 20814. All rights reserved.

How to Raise Your Self-Esteem by Nathaniel Branden. Copyright © 1987 by Nathaniel Branden. Used by permission of Bantam Books, a division of Bantam Doubleday Dell Publishing Group, Inc.

"Congregational Identities in the Presbyterian Church" by Jackson W. Carroll and David A. Roozen, in *Review of Religious Research* 31, no. 4 (June 1990). Used by permission of Jackson W. Carroll.

Effective Schools Research: A Guide to School Improvement by Glen E. Robinson, in *Concerns in Education,* Educational Research Service (Feb. 1985: 5–6). Used by permission of Educational Research Service, 2000 Clarendon Boulevard, Arlington, Virginia 22201.

Selected excerpts from pages 2, 158, 252, 260 from *A Generation of Seekers* by Wade Clark Roof. Copyright © 1993 by Wade Clark Roof. Reprinted by permission of HarperCollins Publishers, Inc.

Portions from *The Message: The New Testament in Contemporary English* by Eugene H. Peterson. Copyright © 1993 by NavPress. Used by permission.

Servant Leadership by Robert K. Greenleaf. Copyright © 1977 by Robert K. Greenleaf; copyright © 1991 by The Robert K. Greenleaf Center. Reprinted by permission of Paulist Press.

Excerpts from the book *Mastering Personal Growth* by Maxie Dunham, Gordon MacDonald, and Donald W. McCullough; Multnomah Books, Questar Publishers. Copyright © 1992 by Christianity Today, Inc.

The Seven Habits of Highly Effective People by Stephen R. Covey. Copyright © 1989 by Stephen R. Covey. Reprinted with the permission of Simon & Schuster Inc.

Stress Management for Ministers by Charles L. Rassieur. Copyright © 1982 by The Westminster Press. Used by permission of Westminster John Knox Press.

Ministry Burnout by John A. Sanford. Copyright © 1982 by John A. Sanford. Used by permission of Westminster John Knox Press.

SUBJECT INDEX